THE 82ND AIRBORNE DIVISION

A PHOTOGRAPHIC HISTORY
VOLUME 1
TRAINING SICILY SALERNO ANZIO

Phil Nordyke

First published in 2015 by Historic Ventures, LLC.
Copyright © 2015 by Phil Nordyke

All rights reserved. With the exception of quoting brief passages for the purposes of review, no part of this publication may be reproduced without prior written permission from the Publisher.

ISBN 978-0-9847151-4-5

CONTENTS

MAPS 8

ACKNOWLEDGMENTS 9

INTRODUCTION 11

TRAINING 13
    CAMP CLAIBORNE, LOUISIANA 15
    FORT BENNING, GEORGIA 41
    FORT BRAGG, NORTH CAROLINA 71
    FRENCH MOROCCO 83
    TUNISIA 121

SICILY 147
    THE 505TH REGIMENTAL COMBAT TEAM 10-11 JULY 1943 149
    THE 504TH REGIMENTAL COMBAT TEAM 11-12 JULY 1943 171
    THE SICILY CAMPAIGN 15-23 JULY 1943 183
    OCCUPATION DUTY 24 JULY - 18 AUGUST 1943 201
    PREPARING FOR THE NEXT OPERATION 211

SALERNO 229
    SAVING THE BEACHHEAD 13 - 18 SEPTEMBER 1943 231
    THE LIBERATION OF NAPLES 28 SEPTEMBER - 1 OCTOBER 1943 249
    THE 504TH INTO THE MOUNTAINS 27 OCTOBER - 27 DECEMBER 1943 271

ANZIO 297
    THE 504TH BEACH LANDING 22 JANUARY 1944 299
    THE BATTLE FOR THE MUSSOLINI CANAL 23-30 JANUARY 1944 303
    THE BATTLE FOR CARROCETO AND APRILIA 3-8 FEBRUARY 1944 .. 319
    STALEMATE 8 FEBRUARY - 23 MARCH 1944 321

BIBLIOGRAPHY 327

INDEX 331

MAPS

NORTH AFRICA 87

PLANNED AIR ROUTE OF THE 505TH RCT KAIROUAN TO SICILY 9–10 JULY 1943 148

DROP PATTERN OF THE 505TH RCT – SICILY 10 JULY 1943 151

DROP PATTERN OF THE 504TH RCT – SICILY 10 AND 12 JULY 1943 182

SICILY CAMPAIGN 184

SALERNO 13–14 SEPTEMBER 1943 228

ALTAVILLA AND HILL 424 16–18 SEPTEMBER 1943 236

THE ITALIAN CAMPAIGN 12 OCTOBER – 11 DECEMBER 1943 272

THE ANZIO LANDINGS 22 JANUARY 1944 298

ANZIO 23–24 JANUARY 1944 305

ANZIO 25 JANUARY 1944 311

ANZIO 29–30 JANUARY 1944 313

3RD BATTALION 504TH 7–8 FEBRUARY 1944 318

ACKNOWLEDGMENTS

This book is the first of a multivolume photographic history of the legendary 82nd Airborne Division during World War II. My previous photographic history of the division consisted of 365 images, with most of the photos grouped in three or four to a page, thereby precluding the detail which larger images provide. With this book and those which follow, I am including far more photographs, with most of them being of larger half and full page formats. This book has 450 photographs covering the division's reactivation, training in the United States and North Africa, the invasion of Sicily, Salerno, through fighting in the mountains of Italy, and finally Anzio.

I am indebted to a great many people who graciously shared their collections or provided invaluable assistance during searches in various repositories. Two individuals in particular, Steve Mandle and Chris Russell provided treasure troves of images. Steve's father, Lieutenant William S. Mandle, was an officer with the Demolition Platoon, Headquarters Company, 504th Parachute Infantry and wrote the original 504 history, *The Devils in Baggy Pants*. Steve generously shared his father's huge collection of photos, without which the book would not be a comprehensive work, especially of the fighting in Italy. Chris Russell's father, Major Clyde Russell, commanded Company E, 505th Parachute Infantry, and later at the battalion staff level during the war. His father's collection included a great number of images of the training at the Parachute School and Fort Benning, Georgia. Chris was so kind to share those photos, without which the book could not as effectively provide a visual journey through those four weeks of grueling training.

Tommy Taylor provided rare images of the 80th Airborne Antiaircraft (Antitank) Battalion, John Patton shared a rare photo of three 82nd Infantry Division soldiers at Camp Claiborne, and Annie Zaya supplied photos from the collection of her father, Dr. Daniel McIlvoy, all for which I am appreciative.

John Sparry shared a photo of his grandfather, Lieutenant Colonel Mark Alexander, and other 505th officers, for which I am thankful.

Mike St. George and Robert W. Lowery, a veteran of the 504th Parachute Infantry and an early pathfinder, gave me a rare image of his pathfinder team, taken at the pathfinder school at the Comiso airfield in Sicily for which I am grateful.

The National Archives at College Park, Maryland provided a great many photographs taken by the United States Army Signal Corps during the war. The people in the Still Pictures Reference department were extremely helpful and I want to thank them.

A good many images were taken from the Air Force photographs which are available free of charge at www.fold2.com. It is a valuable source for photos related to the Army Air Corps and airborne troops.

My good friend in the Netherlands, Jan Bos, graciously shared his photographs. Gilles Guignard, another friend in Europe provided a rare never before published photo of 505th paratroopers inspecting a captured Tiger tank shortly after the battle of Biazzo Ridge.

Doug Rhodes gave me access to a wealth of photos from his outstanding website dedicated to Camp Claiborne for which I am thankful. Historian Rickey Robertson shared priceless photos of Camp Claiborne from his collection which I greatly appreciate.

Veterans like Thomas Kent, Albert Slivitz, Jerry Huth, and Les Cruise provided snapshots taken during their service with the 82nd, which are priceless and some of which have never previously been published.

Michelle Riggs provided previously unpublished photos from the Camp Claiborne Picture Book, by Barbara Ann Grass, part of the Central Louisiana Collection of the James C. Bolton Library at Louisiana State University at Alexandria. I wish to thank her for her efforts.

The renowned historian and author, Martin K. A. Morgan kindly gave me several superb images of the Italian pillboxes and defensive positions located at a key crossroad northeast of Gela that was the initial objective in Sicily of the 505th Regimental Combat Team.

I want to particularly thank my wife, Nancy, for her undying support of my writing and for the outstanding proofreading to find errors in the text. I am most indebted to her.

I am sure there are other people, who I have inadvertently omitted from acknowledging, and for that, please accept my apologies and know that I am nevertheless appreciative of your help with making this book possible.

INTRODUCTION

The 82nd Airborne Division was one of the elite combat units of the Second World War. It had earned a great combat record as an infantry division during World War I, but had been deactivated when America demobilized after the war. The division was reactivated in March 1942, where it began training as an infantry division at Camp Claiborne Louisiana, then was selected to become the United States Army's first airborne division in August 1942. At the same time, the division was split in two to provide the officers and men to create the 101st Airborne Division. The 504th and later the 505th Parachute Infantry Regiments and other parachute engineer and artillery units became a part of the division. After advanced training at Fort Bragg, North Carolina, it sailed for North Africa, where it trained in brutal conditions in French Morocco to toughen and prepare the troopers for the first combat operation.

On July 10, 1943, the 505th Regimental Combat Team, reinforced by the 3rd Battalion, 504th, spearheaded the invasion of Sicily by conducting the first mass parachute assault operation of the war by the United States Army's airborne forces. Just two months later, it was called upon to save the beachhead at Salerno, Italy when a powerful counterattack by German armor and infantry threatened to drive the 36th and 45th Infantry Divisions back into the sea. The division then led the drive to Naples, where it liberated the first large European city by Allied forces. The 82nd Airborne next drove German troops across the Volturno River at the town of Arnone, north of Naples. The 504th Regimental Combat Team was then detached from the division and on October 27, 1943, began operations in the Apennine Mountains, where it fought in very tough conditions until late December, securing key hills overlooking San Pietro, forcing the withdrawal of German troops from the town. The division, without the 504th RCT, left Naples on November 18, 1943 destined first for Northern Ireland and ultimately England to train for the coming invasion of Normandy. After less than a month of rest, the 504th RCT made an amphibious landing with Fifth Army forces near Anzio on January 22, 1944, to draw German reinforcements away from the stalemated Monte Cassino line. There, the 504th secured the right flank of the American forces along the Mussolini Canal and conducted several assaults along the canal to divert German troops away from major attacks conducted by the 3rd Infantry Division to capture the key town of Cisterna. In early February 1944, 3rd Battalion of the 504th was attached to the British Army on the northern side of the beachhead, where it earned a Presidential Unit Citation for stopping a major German breakthrough which threatened the beachhead.

This book was written to give readers a visual journey not a narrative history. It begins with the division's training in the United States and in French Morocco, through preparations in Tunisia for the invasion of Sicily. It next takes the reader through the combat jump in Sicily, the subsequent battle of Biazzo Ridge against tanks and infantry of Fallschirm-Panzer Division 1 Hermann Göring, the friendly fire tragedy of the 504th jump, and finally the division's drive of some 150 miles in just six days to clear the western coast of Sicily. The book then covers training for the next operation after the island was secured, to the emergency jumps of September 13 and 14 to bolster the beach landed forces at Salerno, Italy to the battle for Altavilla and Hill 424, the drive to and liberation of Naples, and the tough fighting in the Italian mountains by the 504th Regimental Combat Team. It concludes with the 504th RCT at the Anzio beachhead, one of the bloodiest campaigns of the war. The book makes no attempt to provide a narrative history of the division during this period as it is better told in books such as my division history, *All American All The Way*, the regimental histories of the 505th, *Four Stars of Valor*, and 504th, *More Than Courage*, as well as books others have written about the division. Readers would be well served to have a basic knowledge of the division's history during this period to fully enjoy this book. It can also serve as a great companion book to the narrative histories. The captions provide much of the detail regarding the content of the images, as well as other facts related to them. In addition to the captions which accompany the images, short quotes from veterans on the same or adjacent pages as individual photos bring the images alive by adding context, depth, and perspective.

The 450 photographs in the book come from a wide variety of sources such as snapshots supplied by veterans, photos from extensive collections such as those of the Mandle and Russell families, digital repositories such as the www.fold3.com United States Air Force images, the huge collection of the United States Army Signal Corps photos at the National Archives, still images taken from newsreel films and combat camera footage, and rare previously unpublished images provided by veterans, family members of veterans, and others. While most books of this type maximize the image count and minimize the page count, this book provides readers with the greatest visual detail by maximizing the sizes of the photos. There are 228 half page or larger and 43 full page images contained in this book. And finally, there are fourteen large maps for reference.

This book is dedicated to the courageous young men of the 82nd Airborne Division who fought Nazi and Fascist tyranny so many years ago and whose service and sacrifice should never be forgotten. This book is meant to preserve their memory.

TRAINING

The reborn 82nd was to be a new experiment in mobilization. Heretofore, draftees had been sent directly to existing regular army or National Guard divisions, trained and integrated into the units. The 82nd would spring to life full-blown, almost overnight, composed of an experienced ten percent cadre (700 officers and 1,200 enlisted men), mostly from the 9th Infantry Division at Fort Bragg, North Carolina and about 16,000 draftees who would come to us directly from the reception centers. The challenge was large; the danger of failure, or even disaster, lay everywhere. —Major General Omar N. Bradley, Headquarters, 82nd Infantry Division

CAMP CLAIBORNE LOUISIANA

AFTER ACHIEVING A STELLAR COMBAT RECORD during the First World War, in which it participated in every major battle fought by the United States Army in France and had more days in combat than any other American division, the 82nd Infantry Division was deactivated after the war. During World War I, it was known as the All American Division because it had been formed with officers and enlisted men from every state in the union. With America's entry into World War II, a massive mobilization resulted in the reactivation of some of the divisions which had fought in the First World War. The division was reactivated on March 25, 1942 at Camp Claiborne, Louisiana, where it would undertake basic training.

During a ceremony at Camp Claiborne, Louisiana on March 25, 1942, Major General Omar N. Bradley (second from left) receives the orders reactivating the 82nd Infantry Division, which had a proud history from World War I. General Bradley commanded a division composed of troops from every state in the union, unlike National Guard units, which were comprised of troops from individual states. Brigadier General Matthew B. Ridgway was assigned as the executive officer and assistant division commander. Colonel Maxwell D. Taylor was assigned as the division's chief of staff. *United States Army Signal Corps photograph.*

This is an oblique angle photo of part of Camp Claiborne, Louisiana, which was located southwest of Alexandria. *Photograph courtesy of the Camp Claiborne Historical Research Center.*

It was a proud division, but it was a name, a legend, a memory only, in February of 1942, when General Bradley and I reported to Camp Claiborne, Louisiana. It had been deactivated in 1918, and had gone out of existence. Now the German was on the march again, and it was our job to recreate it, from a cadre of professionals picked from the best units of the Regular Army. We had nothing on which to build, except this fine nucleus of trained regulars and the bright legend of the old 82nd. To both General Bradley and me it seemed vitally important to indoctrinate each new recruit with the proud spirit of the old division—to plant in each man's mind that valor endured from generation to generation; that the great deeds their fathers had performed could be repeated by the sons. —Brigadier General Matthew B. Ridgway, Headquarters, 82nd Infantry Division

In January [of 1942] I left the 36th Division to join a cadre at Fort Benning, Georgia. After a month of refresher training and demonstration of new methods of fighting, we split up into three new divisions and I was assigned to the 325th Infantry, which was part of the old World War I famous All American 82nd Division. We started at Camp Claiborne, Louisiana on 20 February 1942 and began receiving the enlisted personnel in March. The division was commanded by Major General Omar Bradley, who later became one of the best that the army had. We trained long and hard and by summer of 1942 had a well rounded and efficient unit. The days were long and hot and the leaders ambitious. —Captain Bennie A. Zinn, Company F, 325th Infantry Regiment

I conceived the notion—radical at the time—that we would do everything within our ability to make the draftees feel they were coming to a "home" where people really cared about their welfare. This is not to say we intended to coddle the recruits. In fact, we intended to be tough as hell on them, but in an intelligent, humane, understanding way. At the same time, we would evoke and build upon the 82nd's illustrious history, giving our conscripts the impression they were not only coming to a home, but a famous, even elitist, one. Most of our draftees came from Southern states—Georgia, Alabama, Mississippi, Tennessee. When the time came, Doc Eaton sent teams of men from G-1 ahead to the reception centers to greet, interview, classify and assign each draftee to a specific paper unit and duty, according to his civilian background (cook, truck driver, clerk, lineman, carpenter, plumber, etc.). When the trains backed into Camp Claiborne, we greeted each with a brass band, formed the men into their preassigned units and marched them to preassigned tents, where they found their equipment on a cot with bedding. A hot meal waited in the mess tent. We even instituted rush cleaning and laundry so that the draftees could refurbish travel stained uniforms. This system worked so well, I'm proud to say, that General McNair gave us a hearty pat on the back and recommended that all new divisions adopt it. —Major General Omar N. Bradley, Headquarters, 82nd Infantry Division

This two story building at Camp Claiborne housed the 82nd Infantry Division headquarters. *Photographs courtesy of Thomas W. Kent and Doug Rhodes.*

This is the view of the division headquarters building looking south. *Photograph courtesy of Thomas W. Kent and Doug Rhodes.*

This is the main gate at Camp Claiborne with the guard post at right center. *Photograph courtesy of Thomas W. Kent and Doug Rhodes.*

This is the post chapel at Camp Claiborne. *Photograph courtesy of Thomas W. Kent and Doug Rhodes.*

This is the sports arena, which was located near the main gate at Camp Claiborne. *Photograph courtesy of Thomas W. Kent and Doug Rhodes.*

This is one of eight Camp Claiborne theaters where soldiers could watch movies and newsreels during their off duty hours. Five of the theaters were wooden buildings, two were tent theaters, and one was an open air amphitheater. *Photograph courtesy of Thomas W. Kent and Doug Rhodes.*

This is one of two outdoor tent theaters set up at Camp Claiborne. *Photograph courtesy of Thomas W. Kent and Doug Rhodes.*

The service club at Camp Claiborne provided recreation and food for the enlisted men and non-commissioned officers. *Photograph courtesy of Doug Rhodes.*

This is one of the mess halls at Camp Claiborne, which typically could serve a company of soldiers in a single setting. *Photograph courtesy of Thomas W. Kent and Doug Rhodes.*

This building served as headquarters for the 325th Infantry during its time at Camp Claiborne. *Photograph courtesy of Thomas W. Kent and Doug Rhodes.*

This is a squad tent where Private Thomas W. Kent with Service Company, 325th Infantry Regiment, was quartered during part of his training at Camp Claiborne. *Photograph courtesy of Thomas W. Kent and Doug Rhodes.*

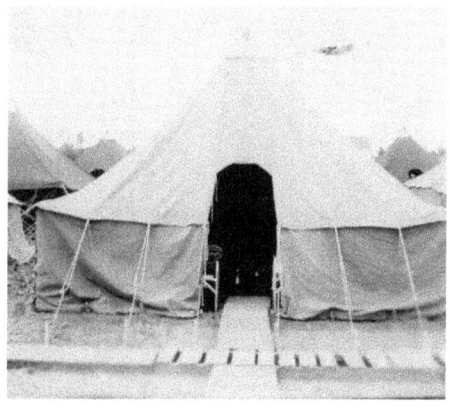

I was inducted into the army at Camp Beauregard, just north of Alexandria, Louisiana. From there, I was sent to Camp Claiborne, this was just south of Alexandria. At the time I arrived, the only ones there was the cadre that had been sent down from up north to activate the 82nd Division. They asked for volunteer truck drivers, so I responded. They needed trucks to haul baggage into the camp area from the railroad spur. Troops were beginning to come in at that time. I was placed in Service Company, 325th. —Private Thomas W. Kent, Service Company, 325th Infantry Regiment

I arrived at division headquarters and reported in and was greeted by the G1 [division assistant chief of staff, personnel], an affable colonel. He had my assignment to [Company] M, 325th Infantry. It was a tent city—pyramidal tents and mess hall on one end and the latrine at the other. —Lieutenant James E. Baugh, Company M, 325th Infantry Regiment

This is a typical company street of wooden floored tents at Camp Claiborne, where soldiers with the 326th Infantry (left center) are lined up for an apparent inspection or instruction, while others (right center) review what appears to be a map tacked to the wooden side wall of the first tent on the right. *Photograph courtesy of Rickey D. Robertson, Jr.*

Soldiers with the 326th Infantry listen to a lecture during training at Camp Claiborne. *Photograph courtesy of Rickey D. Robertson, Jr.*

The 2 ½-ton trucks and jeeps in this photograph belonged to the 325th Infantry Regiment's motor pool at Camp Claiborne. Truck and jeep drivers as well as mechanics were trained to operate and maintain these vehicles. *Photograph courtesy of Thomas W. Kent and Doug Rhodes.*

This building was used by personnel from Service Company, 325th Infantry for the maintenance of the regiment's motor pool vehicles. *Photograph courtesy of Thomas W. Kent and Doug Rhodes.*

This 2 ½-ton truck, known as a "deuce and a half" was a 6x6 drive vehicle that would be the workhorse of the United States military to transport troops and supplies and pull artillery and equipment during World War II. *Photograph courtesy of Thomas W. Kent and Doug Rhodes.*

The jeep was the primary light utility vehicle used by the United States military during World War II. It was originally developed as a four wheel drive reconnaissance car. Private Thomas W. Kent is shown in the jeep he drove for the 325th Infantry's S-2 (intelligence) officer, Lieutenant Michael Berkut. *Photograph courtesy of Thomas W. Kent and Doug Rhodes.*

Soldiers practice marksmanship at the rifle range at Camp Claiborne as they begin the process of becoming proficient in the use of their rifles. *Photograph from A Camera Trip Through Camp Claiborne.*

The rifle range targets can be seen on the horizon in the center of the photo. This is where instruction for various infantry small arms was applied as soldiers learned to fire their assigned weapons. *Photograph courtesy of Thomas W. Kent and Doug Rhodes.*

This view of the rifle range shows the raised area (left center) used for observation. *Photograph courtesy of Thomas W. Kent and Doug Rhodes.*

We did close order drill, manual of arms, marching in small and larger formations, and received instruction in the care and cleaning of the M1 rifle. The latter meant that we spent an inordinate amount of time pushing oiled rags through the bores of our rifles and also learned how to assemble and disassemble said rifle blindfolded. To our amazement, we all learned... We practiced aiming our rifles through the process called triangulation, and one of the high points of the training was our visit to the rifle range. There, we all took turns operating and marking targets for the other guys and had our turns at two hundred and three hundred yards, using the four firing positions we had learned: standing, prone, kneeling, and sitting.
—Private Leonard Lebenson, Headquarters Company, 82nd Infantry Division

In every possible way, we evoked the history of the division to build morale and fighting spirit. In this connection, it occurred to me that we ought to invite Sergeant York down to talk to the men. He readily agreed. We laid out the red carpet and staged a division review—the whole division on parade—for him. There was intense media interest in his visit. He addressed the troops and his simple, unpretentious yet inspiring words were carried live on a nationwide radio hookup. Sergeant York was my house guest during the visit and I served as his personal escort a large part of the time. During the interludes between official events, I queried him closely on his experiences in France. One important fact emerged from these talks: most of his effective shooting had been done at very short range—twenty-five to fifty yards. As a result of these talks, I had the staff set up a short range firing course in the woods with partially concealed cans for targets. The men had to traverse this wooded course, spot the cans and shoot quickly. It was a radical departure from the standard static long distance firing range.
—Major General Omar N. Bradley, Headquarters, 82nd Infantry Division

The most famous soldier of World War I, Sergeant Alvin C. York, who served with Company G, 328th Infantry Regiment of the 82nd Infantry Division, addresses the assembled division at Camp Claiborne, Louisiana on May 7, 1942. Major General Bradley (fourth from the left) listens as Sergeant York gives a stirring speech to the division. *United States Army photograph.*

This is a panoramic view of the entire 82nd Infantry Division which was assembled for the first time since reactivation for Sergeant York's speech. *Photograph by Spencer and Wyckoff, Detroit, Michigan.*

Private Albert E. Slivitz (right) and a buddy are holding Springfield rifles, which was the United States military's primary infantry weapon during World War I. These rifles were still in use in the early stages after the United States' entry into World War II. The enlisted trainees were quartered in squad tents with wooden floors (left). *Photograph courtesy of Albert E. Slivitz.*

Private Slivitz (center) flanked by two buddies poses behind a .30-caliber air cooled machine gun during training at Camp Claiborne. *Photograph courtesy of Albert E. Slivitz.*

Soldiers with the 82nd Infantry Division smoke meat over an improvised rotisserie. *Photograph courtesy of Albert E. Slivitz.*

Major General Omar N. Bradley did such a thorough and effective job of training the 82nd Infantry Division that he was selected to assume command of the 28th Infantry Division, a National Guard unit that was not progressing satisfactorily through training. His last day as commanding officer of the 82nd Infantry Division was June 25, 1942. Bradley would rise to four star general and would command the 12th Army Group during the European campaigns. *United States Army photograph.*

Brigadier General Matthew B. Ridgway succeeded Bradley as the commanding officer of the 82nd Infantry Division on June 26, 1942. He was promoted to the rank of major general on August 7, 1942. Ridgway would later be promoted to lieutenant general after the Normandy campaign and would command the newly formed XVIII Airborne Corps. *United States Army photograph.*

Brigadier General William M. Miley became the assistant division commander on August 18, 1942, replacing Colonel Don F. Pratt, who became the assistant division commander of the newly formed 101st Airborne Division. General Miley would later command the 17th Airborne Division. *United States Army photograph.*

Colonel Maxwell D. Taylor succeeded Colonel George Pope as Chief of Staff on July 6, 1942. Taylor would later command the 101st Airborne Division from Normandy through the end of the war. *United States Army photograph.*

Colonel Harry L. Lewis replaced Colonel Claudius M. Easley as the commanding officer of the 325th Glider Infantry Regiment, when Easley was promoted and transferred to the 96th Infantry Division as its assistant division commander. Lewis commanded the 325th until the Normandy campaign, during which he was evacuated because of an illness, which later was diagnosed as stomach cancer. Lewis died on April 16, 1945. *United States Army Signal Corps photograph.*

Three soldiers with the 82nd Infantry Division pose with a .50 caliber machine gun which could be used to provide either antiaircraft or ground fire. This mount was far too heavy for use when the division was later redesignated as an airborne unit. *Photograph courtesy of the collection of John Patton.*

The training regimen of the 82nd Infantry Division included long marches to toughen the young soldiers in preparation for the rigors of combat. *Photograph courtesy of Rickey D. Robertson, Jr.*

The rigorous program of physical conditioning we put the men through also had a great deal to do with the development of their fighting spirit, too. Though neither General Bradley nor myself had ever been in battle, we both knew that to survive the weariness, the long marches, the loss of sleep, the tremendous exertion that men in combat must undergo, each of them had to be as finely trained as a champion boxer. Many a battle has been lost merely because the fighting men have burned themselves out physically, have come up to the last attack too tired to fight. An extremely difficult obstacle course, made up of deep ditches, log barriers, high walls, and culverts, was one excellent device we used for hardening the men physically. It was both mine and General Bradley's idea that every officer in the division, no matter whether he had a staff job or a field command, should be required to go through the same toughening process as the men. That applied to us as well as to the others, and I will never forget the great roar of laughter that went up when Brad and I demonstrated our own skill at traversing the course. The last obstacle was a fairly wide creek, which, unfortunately, served as the drainage ditch from the reservation's sewage plant. This was traversed by running full tilt to the bank, grabbing a knotted rope, and swinging across in the manner of Tarzan of the apes. General Bradley and I ran the course together, with me, as the younger man and his junior in rank, keeping about a half stride behind him as we leaped ditches, scrambled over walls, and crawled through culverts. We reached the last obstacle still going strong, but in mid-air General Bradley's hands slipped off the rope and he fell with a tremendous splash into that malodorous stream. The sight of a two-star general in such a predicament seemed to be a source of vast delight to all ranks, and the incident became one of the memorable high lights of the training period. My first impulse, of course, on seeing my senior in such a fix, was to turn loose and fall in with him, but my decision, made in mid-swing, was that this would be carrying military courtesy too far. —Brigadier General Matthew B. Ridgway, Headquarters, 82nd Infantry Division

An officer observes soldiers with the 326th Infantry navigate the obstacle course. They have cleared the low obstacle in the foreground by jumping over it and are now climbing over and down the other side of the log wall. *Photograph courtesy of Rickey D. Robertson, Jr.*

Soldiers with the 326th Infantry climb over a solid wall (center) as officers on the other side observe their progress. A long culvert (right) through which trainees had to crawl was another of the course's obstacles as was the low log barrier (left). *Photograph courtesy of Rickey D. Robertson, Jr.*

This section of the obstacle course consisted of earth embankments and a trench followed by barbed wire strung between low wooden stakes over which soldiers had to cross by high stepping over and through it. *Photograph courtesy of Rickey D. Robertson, Jr.*

This series of obstacles consisted of wooden posts that soldiers first had to duck under, then climb over a low log wall, then duck under another two lines of posts, and then over another low log wall. *Photograph courtesy of Rickey D. Robertson, Jr.*

This obstacle consisting of beams extending across a wide trench was designed to test the balance of the soldiers running the obstacle course. *Photograph courtesy of Rickey D. Robertson, Jr.*

This rope swing across the drainage ditch was the last obstacle on the course used by the 82nd Infantry Division during its training at Camp Claiborne. *Photograph courtesy of Rickey D. Robertson, Jr.*

Generals Bradley and Ridgway swing across the drainage ditch as they finish the obstacle course. *United States Army photograph.*

30   TRAINING

The Browning M1917 heavy machine gun was water cooled and used during World War I, but still saw extensive use by the United States military, including glider infantry heavy weapons companies of all of the airborne divisions throughout World War II. The troops in this photo are firing the machine gun at Camp Claiborne. *United States Army Signal Corps photograph, National Archives.*

Floyd Parks, a two-star general from the Training Division of GHQ, came down to visit me, wearing an air of mystery. He came into my office, shut the door, looked about him cautiously, and then in a voice that was almost a whisper asked me how I'd like to command an airborne division. I told him I didn't know what an airborne division was. He said that nobody else knew much about it either. But as we all knew the Germans had used paratroopers and glider men with great success against the British garrisons on Crete. Obviously, a new form of warfare was coming into being and the 82nd, as the best of the divisions then in training, had been chosen to develop its tactics. My knowledge of airborne operations at that moment was exactly nil. I didn't have the faintest idea what the table of organization of an airborne unit would be, how it would be armed, or what its tactical employment would be. —Major General Matthew B. Ridgway, Headquarters, 82nd Airborne Division

Major General Ridgway and three other officers wait to be driven to the parade ground at Camp Claiborne for a division review on August 15, 1942. *Photograph courtesy of Rickey D. Robertson, Jr.*

The 82nd Band marches along the road leading to the parade ground prior to the division review. *Photograph courtesy of Rickey D. Robertson, Jr.*

The 82nd Infantry Division band begins the division review as it marches across the parade ground toward the reviewing stand. *Photograph from Camp Claiborne Picture Book, by Barbara Ann Grass, courtesy of Central Louisiana Collections, James C. Bolton Library, Louisiana State University at Alexandria (Alexandria, Louisiana).*

The band plays patriotic marches as it passes the reviewing stand. Note the 82nd Infantry Division emblem on the bass drum head. *Photograph from Camp Claiborne Picture Book, by Barbara Ann Grass, courtesy of Central Louisiana Collections, James C. Bolton Library, Louisiana State University at Alexandria (Alexandria, Louisiana).*

The division band marches past the reviewing stand before marching to its designated position where it will provide music as the rest of the division passes in review. *Photograph from Camp Claiborne Picture Book, by Barbara Ann Grass, courtesy of Central Louisiana Collections, James C. Bolton Library, Louisiana State University at Alexandria (Alexandria, Louisiana).*

The division staff watches as units of the division pass the reviewing stand. General Ridgway is in the center of the line of five officers on the left. *Photograph from Camp Claiborne Picture Book, by Barbara Ann Grass, courtesy of Central Louisiana Collections, James C. Bolton Library, Louisiana State University at Alexandria (Alexandria, Louisiana).*

The 2nd Battalion, 326th Infantry Regiment lowers its guidons and salutes as the battalion approaches the reviewing stand. *Photograph from Camp Claiborne Picture Book, by Barbara Ann Grass, courtesy of Central Louisiana Collections, James C. Bolton Library, Louisiana State University at Alexandria (Alexandria, Louisiana).*

The 2nd Battalion, 326th Infantry Regiment troops march past the reviewing stand. Note the fixed bayonets on the rifles slung over the shoulders of the soldiers. *Photograph from Camp Claiborne Picture Book, by Barbara Ann Grass, courtesy of Central Louisiana Collections, James C. Bolton Library, Louisiana State University at Alexandria (Alexandria, Louisiana).*

The 319th Field Artillery Battalion, under the command of Lieutenant Colonel William H. Bertsch, passes in review at Camp Claiborne on August 15, 1942. Unknown to all but the division staff, General Leslie McNair, the commanding officer of Army Ground Forces, had decided to create the army's first two airborne divisions. The plan called for the 82nd Infantry Division to be converted to an airborne division and a new division, the 101st, would be formed using a cadre drawn from the 82nd Division. Major General William C. Lee, who would command the 101st Airborne Division, met with Ridgway in secret to plan for the personnel changes. *Photograph by Spencer and Wyckoff, Detroit, Michigan.*

We got orders to split the 82nd in two, so that another airborne division, the 101st, could be built around the cadre from the 82nd. This created a problem in morale, for already there was a great unit spirit in the 82nd, and nobody wanted to go into the new division, even under such a magnificent soldier as General William C. Lee, who was to command the 101st. Usually in a situation such as this, when you are ordered to furnish a cadre, you pick all your goof-offs and screwballs and send them along to the new command. I wouldn't even consider doing this to my old friend Bill Lee. So I proposed that we take all the ranks and skills in the division and divide them up into as nearly two equal halves as we could. Then we'd flip a coin, and the man who won could pick the half he wanted. Bill said nothing could be fairer and we did it that way. I don't remember now who won, but I do know that the 82nd lost some fine soldiers to its offspring, the 101st. After this split, the 82nd was given another parachute regiment, the 504th, which turned out to be one of the finest fighting outfits in the airborne.
—Major General Matthew B. Ridgway, Headquarters, 82nd Infantry Division

Tomorrow our destinies divide. That which was one division becomes two. That which was one team must be rebuilt into two. —Major General Matthew B. Ridgway, commanding officer, 82nd Airborne Division

The 320th Field Artillery Battalion, under the command of Lieutenant Colonel Francis A. March, passes in review at Camp Claiborne, Louisiana on August 15, 1942. At the conclusion of the full dress review, Major General Ridgway announced over a public address system to the assembled division that it would be split to form two airborne divisions, the 82nd and 101st Airborne Divisions. The three infantry regiments would be split into three glider infantry regiments—each with only two battalions—instead of the army's standard three infantry battalion configuration. The 325th and 326th Infantry Regiments would remain with the 82nd Airborne Division, but each would transfer a battalion to the 101st Airborne to form the 401st Glider Infantry Regiment. The 327th Infantry Regiment was transferred to the 101st Airborne. *Photograph by Spencer and Wyckoff, Detroit Michigan.*

The next morning we had 4,500 men AWOL. Ridgway called me in. He was baffled. He said, 'What in the world made them do that?' I said, 'You scared the pants off 'em.' He couldn't understand why everyone wasn't as fired up as he was—wasn't as patriotic and gung-ho. He couldn't see that they didn't want to go to the 101st. Above all, they didn't want to be gliderists! I knew how they felt. I wasn't happy either—I'm not that brave. I told him not to worry, they'd all be back in three or four days, except the ones who'd have deserted anyway. And they did come back. —Anonymous member of the division staff

I had my car at Camp Claiborne and needed to get it home before the transfer to Fort Bragg. I went to Captain Zinn, who said I needed to get higher permission; to battalion, same answer; to regiment, same; and they told me that only division could help me and I being an ignorant first lieutenant, got permission to speak to division. It turned out to be General Ridgway and I think that it surprised him, so that I got my leave. From then on, General Ridgway called me by name when we met. —Lieutenant Joe B. Gault, Company F, 325th Glider Infantry Regiment

I had never been up in an airplane. Shortly after, they asked for volunteers to go to parachute school. I reasoned that I'd rather be in a plane with a parachute than in a glider without one. After seeing the gliders after landing, I had made the right choice. The extra money and the shiny boots helped. I joined the 376th Parachute Field Artillery Battalion after graduating from jump school. The four weeks at Fort Benning were the hardest weeks I have ever experienced: push-ups and double time were rough. —Private Wesley Pass, Company B, 325th Glider Infantry Regiment

The 307th Engineer Battalion passes the reviewing stand, August 15, 1942. The battalion was initially under the command of Lieutenant Colonel Peter E. Bermel. Major Robert S. Palmer assumed command of the battalion on July 14, 1942. It was later reorganized, with Headquarters, Headquarters and Service Company, and Company A remaining glider borne, while Companies B and C were composed of parachutists. *Photograph by Spencer and Wyckoff, Detroit, Michigan.*

Troopers with Service Company, 325th Glider Infantry load duffle bags into one of the regiment's 2 ½-ton trucks for the trip from Camp Claiborne to Fort Bragg, North Carolina. *Photograph courtesy of Thomas W. Kent and Doug Rhodes.*

Colonel Stuart Cutler (center), the commanding officer of the 326th Infantry, speaks to the regiment (below) shortly after the division review on August 15, 1942, about the conversion of the regiment to a glider infantry unit. The 325th and 326th would be reorganized into the division's two glider infantry regiments. On February 10, 1943, the 326th would transfer out of the division when the table of organization changed to one glider infantry regiment per airborne division due to a shortage of gliders. The 326th would subsequently be assigned to the newly forming 13th Airborne Division. *Photographs courtesy of Rickey D. Robertson, Jr.*

A tough regimen of calisthenics and Judo was a key part of "A" Stage, which was designed to force weak trainees out of the Parachute School. *United States Army Signal Corps photograph, courtesy of Christopher Russell.*

FORT BENNING GEORGIA

THE UNITED STATES ARMY PARACHUTE SCHOOL was located at Fort Benning, Georgia. All of the trainees were volunteers and enlisted men above the rank of private had to take a reduction in grade to private in order to attend the school. The training was rigorous and designed to rid the weak and those unwilling or unable to endure it. Officers who volunteered to become paratroopers were treated the same as the enlisted men during the four week program. Trainees had to double time everywhere they went while at the school. Calisthenics, long runs, and endless pushups for the slightest infractions were part of the training in addition to how to parachute from an airplane.

New trainees at the Parachute School at Fort Benning, Georgia practice parachute landing falls (PLFs) on gym mats during the first week of training, designated as "A" Stage. *United States Army Signal Corps photograph, courtesy of Christopher Russell.*

Trainees climb ropes during "A" Stage to build strength in their triceps that they will need in order to collapse their parachutes upon landing. *United States Army Signal Corps photograph, courtesy of Christopher Russell.*

Immediately after reveille formation, we'd do a two mile run. And then we'd come back for the breakfast meal and immediately following that, we'd go through a period of calisthenics. Then we would pair off for judo training. During this stage, there was extensive physical fitness testing that we had to undergo. You had to do a required number of pull-ups, push-ups, sit-ups, knee-bends, and quite a broad spectrum of physical events to qualify. If you failed to measure up in any of these events, you were disqualified—your school training was terminated. —Private Elmo E. Bell

"A" Stage was an all out effort to washout all but the most determined. The regimen was constant physical exercise, calisthenics and double time. While in ranks you were at Attention, Parade Rest or Double Timing in place. Pushups were given as punishment at the slightest provocation. You had the added pressure of knowing an instructor could wash you out at any time, and for any reason. Rope climbing and tumbling exercises were repeated over, and over again. This was to build upper body strength and taught body control on landing. During this week when you sat for instructions, which was rare, you sat upright as near as possible to Attention. When standing there were only two acceptable positions, at Attention or Parade Rest, you dared not lean on anything. Your hands were at your side or locked behind your back at all times. You did not wipe your brow or scratch your butt, without being instructed to do more pushups. In retrospect, I realize the instructors had their orders to make it tough on us, but some seemed to take a sadistic joy in taking it out on the few guys that were having the most trouble. Our one pleasure in life was daydreaming about catching that bastard in town and teaching him some manners. It was July in Georgia and very hot, we had men pass out in ranks from heat exhaustion. If you made an effort to help the fallen man, you were instructed to "Leave him lay soldier, he ain't dead." The men in my class that were washed out or quit for whatever reason were transferred immediately. When we returned to barracks they and their belongings were gone. —Private William T. Dunfee

The "Trainasium" was a series of scaffolds, platforms with wooden planks, steep ramps, and climbing ropes designed to build strength and agility during "B" Stage. *United States Army Signal Corps photograph, courtesy of Christopher Russell.*

The training was directed by specially trained sergeants. They all seemed to be glad for the chance to give orders to officers. "A" Stage was designed to weed out the weaklings, those lacking stamina and character. The weeding out process was in pushing us physically beyond what we were capable of. The sergeants running this stage were in superb physical condition; much better condition than any of the trainees. For one week they pushed us beyond our physical capability, primarily with long runs. You could pass out from fatigue. But, if you quit, you were washed out. Only about fifty percent of the class that started "A" Stage got their jump wings. —Lieutenant William H. Hayes

The first week, every time my left foot hit the ground I said, 'What in the hell am I doing here?' Because you ran everywhere you went, you didn't walk. They told you that you were going to forget how to walk; and you did. The first week was strictly physical training, eight, nine hours a day. Everywhere you went, you ran. You climbed ropes. You had to be able at the end of the week to climb a rope thirty-five feet high; climb up and then to hold it until they told you, and then come down. You had to be able to do a minimum of thirty pushups and a five-mile run. There were certain things you had to do. If you didn't, you were out. We had sawdust in the building where you climbed the ropes. This one guy spit in the sawdust. The instructors made him get down with his mouth and pick it up, and go outside and spit it out. —Private W. A. Jones

Full gear or stripped for a shower, you ran and if you were caught walking, you were ordered down on your belly and gave the all mighty deity who was looking out for you, one hundred pushups. Never smart-mouth the man and ask which arm you were supposed to do this or that with, or you could end up doing one arm pushups. —Private Howard C. Anderson

After trainees learn the basic PLFs, they are next executed from platforms to acclimate them to the impact of landing. This training is part of the week long "B" Stage. *United States Army Signal Corps photograph, courtesy of Christopher Russell.*

"B" Stage was a continuation of all the exercises, calisthenics and double time of "A" Stage. The tumbling exercises were elevated onto two-foot, three-foot and four-foot platforms. On these platforms you took the position of "tumblers at ease." On command, you jumped to the ground, simulating a downward pull on the risers and tumbled forward, or to one side or the other, per instructions. After we became proficient at landing forward, we jumped off backward and simulated a landing coming in backward. In parachute school you learn by doing. We were taught hand-to-hand combat and judo, the goal was to kill a man silently. Bayonet and knife training was emphasized and the silent kill was constantly impressed on us. The area we trained in was a sawdust covered field, with about an inch of sawdust covering the baked Georgia clay. We were ordered on numerous occasions not to spit in the sawdust. Those dumb enough to ask what to do with the sawdust they got in their mouth were told to swallow it. The officers in our class received no special favors. There was a lieutenant colonel in my group who was caught spitting sawdust out, after being dumped in a Judo class. The instructor had him dance around on one leg reciting 'I will not spit in the sawdust' over and over again for some period of time. Rank has no privilege at parachute school. We were suspended in a parachute harness that was attached to a circular pipe ring that was four or five foot in diameter. This taught us to guide the parachute while descending by pulling down on the risers. By pulling down on the right hand or left hand risers, you could slip the chute to the right or left. By pulling down on the front or rear risers, you could slip forward or backward. By pulling down on one riser only, the parachute would turn slowly. If you were landing backward, you could put your right arm behind your head and grasp the left riser, and with your left hand grasp the right riser and pull with both hands. This action would turn you and the harness one hundred eighty degrees and you would land moving forward. —Private William T. Dunfee

We had a gadget where you would climb up and hang on a bar and slide down this cable. While you were sliding down this cable, he'll holler and tell you to do a right body turn or a left body turn. When you got to the end and hit the dirt, you jumped up and stood at exaggerated Attention. —Private Louis E. Orvin, Jr.

During the second week of parachute school, "B" Stage, trainees were familiarized with the parachute harness and taught how to use the risers to guide their parachutes. *United States Army Signal Corps photograph, courtesy of Christopher Russell.*

An instructor controls the speed of the trainee's descent as the mechanism to which the parachute harness is attached slides down a diagonal rail. The instructor orders the trainee to perform various movements using the parachute harness. *United States Army Signal Corps photograph, courtesy of Christopher Russell.*

In the photo above, trainees use a mockup of a transport aircraft to master the proper technique of exiting an aircraft during a parachute jump. *United States Army Signal Corps photograph, National Archives.*

The mockup was employed after the completion of parachute training as a tool for a stick of paratroopers to practice exiting a plane quickly as a group using the correct procedures. *United States Army Signal Corps photograph, National Archives.*

The men who jump together and who follow each other out the door as fast as possible were called a "stick". We needed to get the stick out of the plane at the rate of about two per second. The faster we got out of the plane, the closer together we would be when we hit the ground, and the quicker we could assemble and the sooner we'd be ready to fight as a cohesive unit. Again and again we practiced on a wooden mockup plane getting the stick out of the door as fast as possible. —Lieutenant William H. Hayes

The thirty-four foot tower was used during "C" Stage to instruct trainees in the proper techniques for exiting the door of an aircraft. *United States Army Signal Corps photograph, courtesy of Christopher Russell.*

A pulley with the parachute harness attached slides along a steel cable from the thirty-four foot tower to a pile of sawdust, where trainees perform a parachute landing fall. *United States Army Signal Corps photograph, courtesy of Christopher Russell.*

"C" Stage—here we continued our physical training and our ground training of how to exit the plane, how to control our chute, and how to land. It was the thirty-four foot towers that washed so many guys out of the course. They had us climb to the top of the tower where there was a mockup of the door of the C-47 airplane. There was a steel cable that went past the mock-up door and ended, one hundred feet away, just over a twenty foot pile of sawdust. We put on a parachute harness that was secured to fifteen foot straps with a snap hook at the other end. An instructor helped us into the harness and snapped the hook to a pulley on the cable. We had to jump out and take the proper exit position, which was head down, knees bent, and hands clasping the reserve chute on our chest. After we jumped, we would slide down the cable until we hit the sawdust pile. A lot of trainees could not force themselves to jump. I think it was because the ground was so close. Although they knew, theoretically, that the strap holding them to the cable would catch them just before they hit the ground, they just couldn't make themselves jump. Instead, they would have to get down by climbing down the ladder, which meant they were washed out of the course. —Lieutenant William H. Hayes

The worst beast of all—the ogre that washed out more would-be parachutists than any one of the monsters to which we were exposed—the thirty-four foot tower. This was a shed, in which the floor was raised to thirty-four feet above the ground and the inside built as closely as feasible to the inside of a C-47, the plane we'd be jumping out of. In it was a steel cable running end to end, and attached to it was a static line twelve feet long, comparable to the one attached to the apex of our chutes. The purpose of this unit was to train us in the proper exiting procedures—that we keep our heads down and our bodies upright. What made this training aid so intimidating, I guess, is that it was so close and yet so far from the ground. They may have arrived at the figure of thirty-four feet after a long period of research showed it to be the optimum height to inspire the greatest fear. Or, the height may have been simply an arbitrary decision. At any rate, most agreed that it was much harder to jump from that than from a plane at fifteen hundred to two thousand feet above the ground. —Private David V. Bowman

In the photos above, a wind machine was used during "C" Stage to inflate parachute canopies so that trainees could practice the proper technique for collapsing them. *United States Army Signal Corps photographs, courtesy of Christopher Russell.*

The trainee in this photo has been able to get to his feet and is running to overtake the parachute canopy so that he can collapse it. *United States Army Signal Corps photograph, courtesy of Christopher Russell.*

First, there was the wind machine, an airplane motor and propeller that created the air. We were put in a harness and would lie on the ground, face down. Two men would hold the parachute up to catch the air. When everything was ready, they would turn on the machine. It would drag one; we would roll over on our backs and come up on our feet, then run around and collapse the parachute. If you were not successful, it would drag you. —Private Lawrence C. Warthman

Four 250-feet high towers were designed to simulate various aspects of a static line parachute jump. *United States Army Signal Corps photograph, courtesy of Christopher Russell.*

Trainees watch as two of them sitting in a buddy seat are raised to the top of the 250-feet high "A" tower. *United States Army Signal Corps photograph, courtesy of Christopher Russell.*

"A" tower was a chair. Two guys went up in this chair all the way up to the top and all of a sudden they released you real quick and scared the heck out of you, but brought you back down. "B" tower was when they strapped you in an actual harness and you were alone and they took you up and released you and you fell and came back down. The third tower was really scary. That was the one where most of the guys [who quit] got out; they couldn't take it. The guys [who dropped out] wouldn't even go up; they fell out. The last tower was the best. An actual parachute was hooked up, and when you reached the top, it automatically released you. You were floating along like a regular parachute. The instructor was down below with a bullhorn and they taught you how to pull on your risers to guide you down. Then you had to land exactly right. They always taught you to land on the balls of your feet and either go over your left shoulder or right shoulder and make a roll. If it was really windy you had to try to get up and run around behind your chute and collapse it, or it would really drag you.
—Private Howard C. Goodson

For the "B" tower, trainees wore a parachute harness and were suspended from a parachute canopy, then raised to the top, then released on a guided descent using guide wires attached to the frame holding the canopy. *United States Army Signal Corps photograph, National Archives.*

The first ["B" tower] we were put on was a guided descent. You were standing in a parachute harness beneath an open parachute. You were then pulled to the top of the 250 feet tower and released. The parachute having guide wires around its perimeter brought you down where you started. This did teach you the downward pull, and to land properly. —Private William T. Dunfee

[The "C" tower] was a device with elastic straps; the harness was equipped with a ripcord release. We were strapped in a face down prone position. They would pull us to the top and then tell us to pull the [D-ring attached to a] ripcord. We would fall about 15–20 feet, then the elastic straps would give us a jerk similar to the opening shock of a parachute, then the cable would let us down at the speed of a falling parachute. Do not drop the [D-ring attached to the] ripcord, that is more push-ups. —Private Lawrence C. Warthman

On another tower ["C" tower], we are rigged up in a shock harness and pulled up to the top suspended by a cable and fastened to in a harness horizontal to the ground. You can imagine the feeling you receive being 250 feet off the ground and lying with your arms and legs horizontal to the ground. At the command from below, you pull the ripcord, which opens the harness and lets you fall about thirty feet before your fall is broken, then you bounce and swing all over like a jumping jack. This is supposed to simulate the initial shock received by the opening of your chute. –Lieutenant James Megellas

The second tower ["D" tower] was 250 feet with opened parachutes suspended below. The difference in this tower was when the parachutes were released at the 250 foot height, you were independent of guide lines and it was your responsibility to guide the chute down. You were cautioned to slip the chute away from the tower. If the chute and you went into the tower, it could collapse the chute and you would go into a free fall of a couple hundred feet. This tower gave you a realistic feeling of completing a parachute jump. —Private William T. Dunfee

We were harnessed into a chute, pulled to the top of the tower, and released. This gave us the experience of landing in a parachute, which is the most dangerous part of the jump. As we came down we had to turn our back to the wind, look at the horizon (never look at the ground), bend our knees, and as we land, do a right or left tumble to take up the shock of the landing. We were told that the landing shock was equivalent to jumping from the second story of a house. The 250 feet towers were a snap. —Lieutenant William H. Hays

Next Page: Three trainees descend from the "D" tower underneath their respective parachute canopies. Parachute canopies are attached to a mechanism that holds them in a deployed or open state. The canopies and the trainees are then raised to the top of the tower and released to freely descend to the ground below. *United States Army Signal Corps photograph, courtesy of Christopher Russell.*

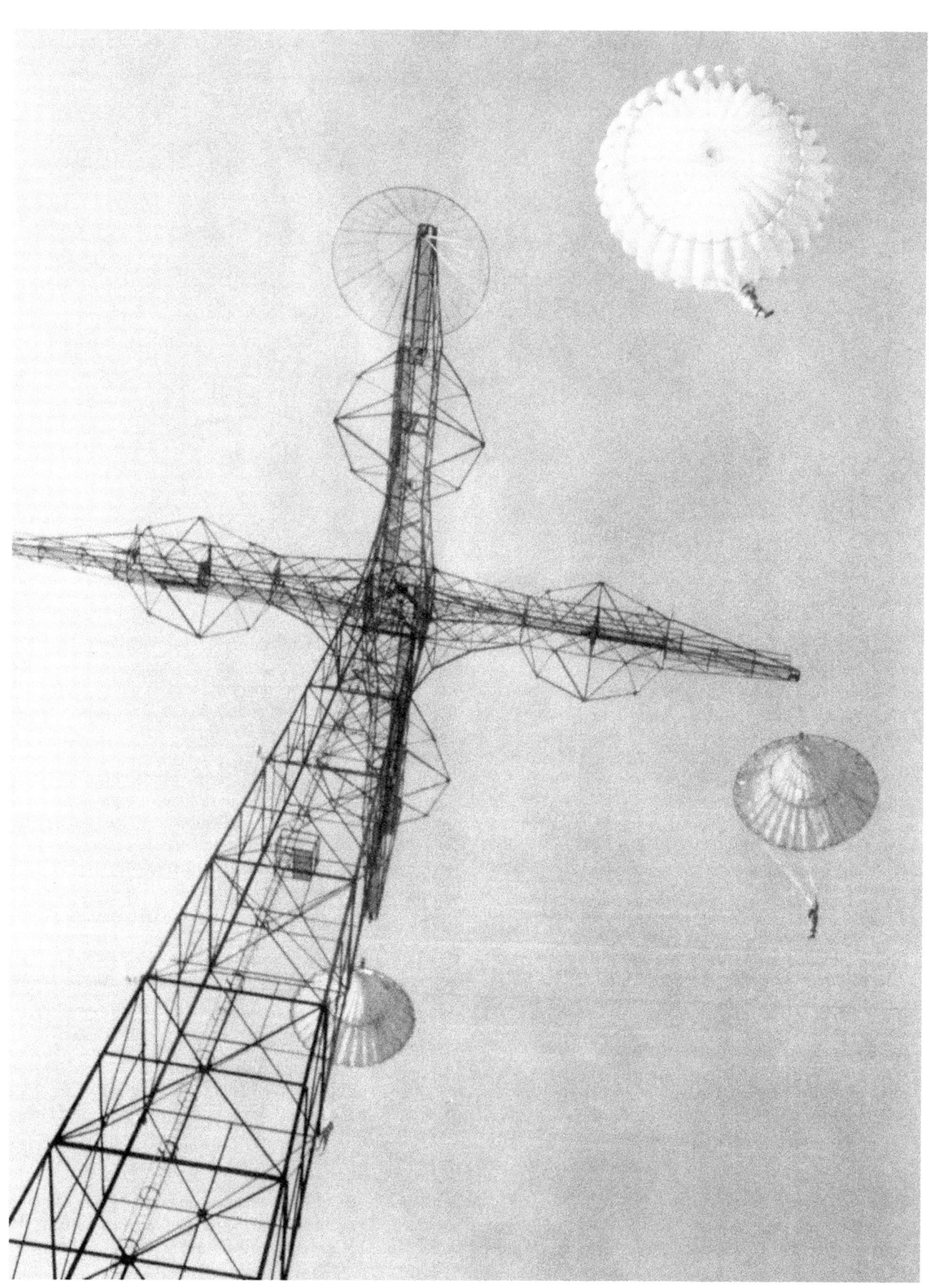

On Friday of "C" Stage, trainees learn how to properly pack their own parachutes that they will use for their first jump the following Monday during "D" Stage. *United States Army Signal Corps photograph, courtesy of Christopher Russell.*

We had been double timing around the airfield and out on the drop zone. Everyone was ready to drop. It had all been planned, but we did not know that. The instructor had us fall out for a break. At that time, a C-47 appeared over the drop zone. The instructor said, "I think we are going to see a jump." At that time the jumper came out, the parachute immediately tangled into a streamer and the jumper plunged to earth, hit the ground in a cloud of dust with a loud thud, bounced about ten feet and lay still. The instructor said, "What you have witnessed was a streamer. How many want to go look?" Some got sick. He said, "We will all go look." It was a dummy. We all had a laugh and double timed back. —Private Lawrence C. Warthman

"C" Stage—here we continued our physical training and our ground training of how to exit the plane, how to control our chute, and how to land. Now we began to learn to pack a parachute. Every trooper had to learn to pack a chute. As incentive to pay attention and learn, we would have to jump with the parachutes we had packed. Believe me, that's a real incentive.
—Lieutenant William H. Hays

I always thought that the reason they let us pack our own chutes was because if they failed to open, well, you had nobody to complain to. —Private Tomaso W. Porcella

The exercises, calisthenics and double time continued. However, morale was excellent, because we could see the light at the end of the tunnel. The most exciting part of this week was in making five jumps in five days. We had stars in our eyes looking forward to the ten day furloughs we were promised on completing our training. We usually jumped in the mornings and packed our chutes in the afternoon for the jump the following day. A critique was held daily by the instructors to point out any real or imagined goofs we had made. We enjoyed these ass chewings, because as each day went by we were that much closer to graduating. We could dream that special dream of getting a particular instructor in Columbus, Georgia, and teaching him some manners. —Private William T. Dunfee

An instructor performs an equipment check for each of these trainees prior to one of the five qualifying jumps required to graduate from the Parachute School. *United States Army photograph, courtesy of Christopher Russell.*

Monday morning of 'D' Stage we were marched to the packing sheds to draw the chutes that we had so carefully packed the Friday before. We were then trucked to the airfield, where the C-47s were waiting. We were formed in sticks of twelve, and climbed aboard a plane—one stick per plane, and sat down on the bucket seats along each side of the plane. The plane circled for a while, then headed for the drop zone (DZ). The instructor-jumpmaster took us through the jump sequence we had practiced so often. "Stand up and hook up...Check your equipment...Sound off for equipment check...Stand in the door." Finally, when we were over the DZ, the jumpmaster shouted to the first man, "Go" and out he went. As each man would come to the door the jumpmaster would shout, "Go...Go...Go..." until we all had jumped. But that was the last time we jumped as individuals. Thereafter, when the first man jumped, the rest of the stick followed him as fast as possible—which was the way we would expect to jump in combat. Monday night everyone went to the packing shed to pack a chute for Tuesday's jump—all but the officers, who had to pack two, one for Tuesday's jump and one for Wednesday's jump. On Tuesday night, the officers took jumpmaster training while the enlisted men were packing a chute for Wednesday's jump. The jumpmaster, usually an officer, was in charge of the paratroops during the flight into the DZ and would be the first to jump, leading the stick out the door. Finally, Friday and the fifth jump, which qualified us as paratroopers, qualified to wear jump wings and parachute boots. We had received our parachute boots at the beginning of 'B' Stage, and immediately stepped into a wash tub of water and walked the boots dry. This was the quickest way to break them in and adapt them to our feet. After that, we shined them everyday. We had worn the boots during jump training; but until we made our fifth qualifying jump, we could not wear them out of the training area. Now we could blouse our pants legs at the top of our boots and wear them anywhere so that everyone would know we were paratroopers. You might say that our jump boots were our greatest reward for being a paratrooper, and our proudest possession. And, boy did we ever keep them shined. —Lieutenant William H. Hays

Trainees descend on the drop zone at Fort Benning under white parachute canopies characteristic of qualification jumps. Parachute units employed camouflage main parachute canopies and white reserve canopies. *United States Army Signal Corps photograph, courtesy of Christopher Russell.*

I really felt exhilarated on the first jump and as I was coming down, I thought, "Oh gee, this was something I could do because this was such a wonderful experience. I'm ready to do this immediately." I would have gone back up in five minutes. But I think overnight, as you gave it more thought, you became more concerned about the second jump. And I think I was more anxious during the second jump than the first jump, much more so. The jump that I really, really recall was when I led the stick—that was my last qualifying jump. We had a jumpmaster who stood with us while we were waiting, who warned us for the green light. I remember he was singing these little songs that were all gruesome and telling me, 'Look down, find that ambulance, and keep it in your mind, because he's waiting for you.' I'll never forget that pleasant conversation we had before I led out. —Private Leo M. Hart

I will mention that anytime prior to your fifth jump, you may quit without prejudice. Once you make five jumps and are qualified, it's a court martial offense to refuse to jump. Refusing in combat is considered cowardice in the face of the enemy. A personal note, I had never been in an airplane prior to my joining the army. I made ten or twelve parachute jumps before landing in an airplane. At age nineteen, I was willing to try anything, the extra fifty dollars a month hazardous duty pay was an added incentive. —Private William T. Dunfee

I was so thrilled to walk up on that stage and get my wings; I've still got them. —Private Charles H. Miller

As trainees land on the drop zone, the individual at the lower left of the photograph looks skyward as the shadow from a parachute canopy appears over him. *United States Army Signal Corps photograph, courtesy of Christopher Russell.*

Officer trainees learn how to drop door bundles containing various equipment, weapons, and supplies as part of jumpmaster training during "D" Stage. *United States Army Signal Corps photograph, courtesy of Christopher Russell.*

Lieutenant Colonel Reuben H. Tucker, III, was one of ten officers and eighty-six enlisted men, primarily from the 504th Parachute Infantry Battalion, who were the cadre to form the 504th Parachute Infantry Regiment on May 1, 1942. Tucker became the regiment's executive officer and was promoted to the rank of lieutenant colonel and assumed command of the regiment on December 16, 1942 and led it throughout the war. *United States Army photograph.*

Colonel [Theodore L. "Ted"] Dunn was given command of the regiment and started to build the splendid outfit that was the regiment: Captain Cook, Captain Kouns, Captain Colville, Captain Beall, Major Freeman, Major Williams, and Major Tucker. The months of May and June were devoted to training the cadre. An intensive schedule was followed so that the cadre was well prepared to receive the newcomers during the first week of July. Our training was interrupted somewhat by the moving of one battalion at a time to the Alabama Area, but by the 19th of August, the entire regiment was in Alabama. August 15th, we were incorporated in the All-American 82nd Division. —Major Reuben H. Tucker, III, Headquarters, 504th Parachute Infantry Regiment

The 505th Parachute Infantry Regiment was activated on June 25, 1942. Lieutenant Colonel James M. Gavin took command of the regiment on July 6, 1942. The 505th joined the 82nd Airborne Division on February 10, 1943, replacing the 326th Glider Infantry Regiment.

Early in July 1942 the 505th Parachute Infantry Regiment was activated at Fort Benning, Georgia. I was assigned as its first commanding officer. Its training program was just about as tough and demanding as we could make it. The troopers responded well. However, despite the rigors of their training, they always seemed to have enough energy left to get into fights in Phenix City, Alabama, and its environs during time off... We sought to train the paratroopers to the highest peak of individual pride and skill. It was at this time that the use of nameplates [on uniforms] was adopted, the purpose being to emphasize the importance of an individual's personality and reputation. To the soldiers of another generation, it seemed to suggest too little discipline and too much initiative given to individual soldiers. We were willing to take a chance that this would not have a disrupting effect on larger formations. It did not. Aside from the impact of this type of training on the airborne formations themselves, it had tremendous significance to the army as a whole. The morale of the airborne units soared, especially after their first combat, when they could see for themselves the results of their training. —Lieutenant Colonel James M. Gavin, Headquarters, 505th Parachute Infantry Regiment

Jimmy, from the start put his imprint on the 505. He was a soldier's soldier, always on top of the training and in the field with the troops every day. Soldiers could empathize with him. I can remember walking down a company street behind a couple of young troopers and Jimmy was ahead of us. One of these young guys said to the other one, "I'd follow that guy through hell." What he didn't know was that was exactly where Jimmy was going to lead them! — Major David E. Thomas, Medical Detachment, 505th Parachute Infantry Regiment

These five troopers carry an equipment bundle which was used to drop crew served weapons, ammunition, medical supplies, extra rations, communications equipment, spare parts, and many other items required for a parachute unit to operate during combat after a jump. *United States Army Signal Corps photograph, National Archives.*

All of the enlisted men were double volunteers—not draftees. Called to arms by Pearl Harbor, they had volunteered for the army and again for the paratroops. Screened, tested, and jump qualified by the parachute school, they were the top of the line of America's citizen soldiers. Many would have been in college except for the war. The goal of the regimental cadre was to train them into as tough and intelligent a group of fighting men as ever pulled on jump boots. —Captain Benjamin H. Vandervoort, Company F, 505th Parachute Infantry Regiment

We had come a long way from the beginning, for one example, we used to push the equipment bundles out the door and then jump after them. Later, they were released from the bomb bays [racks] under the fuselage of the C-47s by the pressing of a button. —Sergeant Otis L. Sampson, Company E, 505th Parachute Infantry

Practice jumps were conducted for units of the 504th and 505th Parachute Infantry Regiments during training at Camp Billy Mitchell, known to most troopers as the Alabama Area. Equipment bundles are released from six racks below the wings and from the open door seconds before the stick begins its jump. *United States Army Signal Corps photograph, courtesy of Christopher Russell.*

Six loads were hung on the bottom of the C-47 in regular bomb shackles, two of the loads being ammunition. The other three howitzer parts, daisy-chained together would be pushed out the door ahead of the troopers. Early on we learned that you could not jettison the six loads under the plane simultaneously. The air turbulence would cause their parachutes to become entangled, and a number or all of the loads would come crashing down in one huge mass. A small electrical panel was installed just inside the door of the plane which contained a red light, a green light, and six toggle switches which individually controlled the release of each of the six loads under the plane. The senior person on board acted as the jumpmaster and kneeled down by the toggle panel when the red light went on and everyone was hooking up. When the green light went on, the lead trooper kicked the three loads out of the door and the others went out as fast as possible. At the same time, the jumpmaster individually toggled off the six loads from the bottom of the plane. It was amazing how just a split second between each load prevented tangling of the chutes. —Lieutenant Raymond M. Crossman, Battery C, 456th Parachute Field Artillery Battalion

Next Page: A stick of paratroopers jumped as closely together as possible to reduce the distance they had to walk in order to assemble on the ground. The three parachute canopies in various stages of deployment seen in this photo illustrate how closely the troopers have jumped. *United States Army Signal Corps photograph, courtesy of Christopher Russell.*

Canopies descend over a drop zone in this practice jump. The line of parachute canopies extending from behind the aircraft at the upper left to the edge of the photo reflect a stick minimizing the distance between its troopers. The standard nine plane V-of-V formation may be seen at the bottom center and right. *United States Army Signal Corps photograph, courtesy of Christopher Russell.*

We made a lot of practice jumps, and they were somewhat different from our first training jumps at 1,200 feet. Now, we were jumping at six hundred feet. When we jumped into a combat area, we wanted to be in the air as short a time as possible so we wouldn't present easy targets for the enemy on the ground. At six hundred feet, we were in the air only about twenty-five to thirty seconds. In combat, even that short amount of time can seem like an eternity...By then, we were learning to jump in sticks—leaving the plane in intervals of less than a second between jumps. —Lieutenant T. Moffatt Burriss, Headquarters Company, 3rd Battalion, 504th Parachute Infantry

Next Page: The T7 main parachute canopy used by paratroopers had a green camouflage pattern to reduce visibility to the enemy. *United States Army Signal Corps photograph, courtesy of Christopher Russell.*

Upon landing, paratroopers collapse their chutes and roll them up. *United States Army Signal Corps photograph, courtesy of Christopher Russell.*

Troopers construct an improvised rope bridge across the Chattahoochee River during training in the Alabama Area. *United States Army Signal Corps photograph, courtesy of Christopher Russell.*

After we finished the fourth week [of parachute training] a few of us were transferred to the 505, which was stationed in Alabama, next to the Chattahoochee River, across from Fort Benning. We went through rigorous training; five mile runs every morning, calisthenics, and field problems. Also, [we conducted] two more practice jumps. One of our field problems consisted of a twenty-four hour forced march, which covered fifty-four miles. Quite a few people dropped out. What brought this on was the 505 and other units had passes to Columbus, Georgia and got into fights. Twenty-seven people got thrown into jail. After the forced march, some people got on their class A uniforms and were heading back into town and Colonel Gavin made the remark that those able to do this must be some tough son-of-a-guns. —Private Norbert P. Beach, Company H, 505th Parachute Infantry Regiment

The training was rugged and intense. Some marches were twenty miles or more in a single day. We were given a lot of weapons training. We were taught how to operate our weapons in the dark. There were some times that I really thought I had made a mistake by joining the paratroopers and then I would see some scrawny guys who wouldn't quit, and I thought to myself, "If they can make it, so can I." At the end of the training I was beginning to appreciate it more and more. —Private Ross Pippin, Company C, 504th Parachute Infantry Regiment

We were trained in all phases of infantry combat and were developing swiftly, if not always too happily, into combat soldiers. Before we sailed, our unit could start on a forced march early in the morning, walk all day and late into the night, then bivouac along the road, for enough time for everyone to get to sleep. Then, if we were ordered to move out under combat conditions, each man would wake when touched, wake the man behind him, assemble his equipment, and be ready to move out with no noise or light. After such a unit has had combat experience, the ones who are left can be called a combat unit. —Lieutenant Frank P. Woosley, Company E, 505th Parachute Infantry Regiment

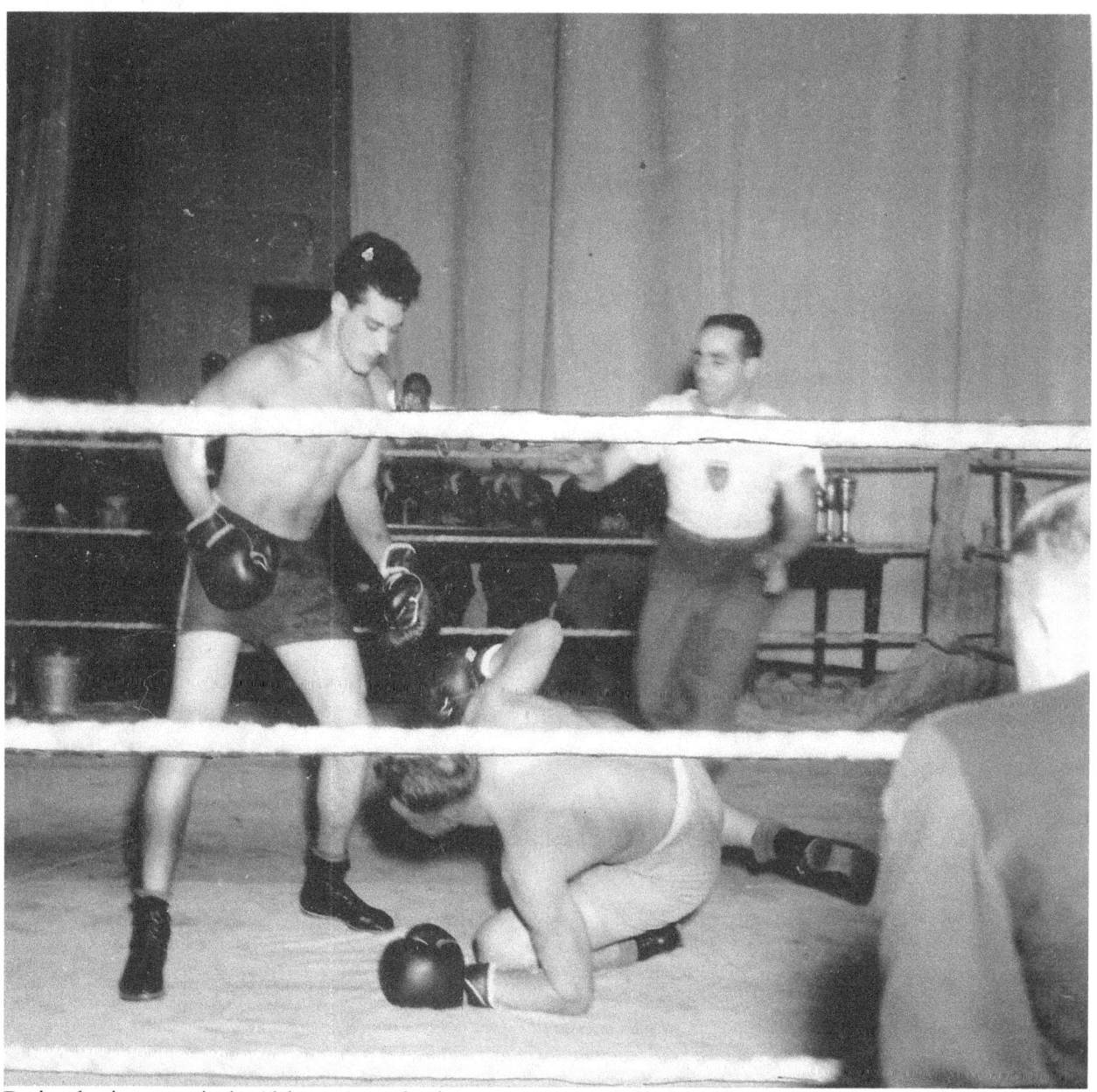

During the time spent in the Alabama Area a boxing tournament was held pitting the 504th Parachute Infantry's team versus the 505th team. The competition built respect among the troopers of each regiment for those of the other regiment. *Photograph courtesy of William S. Mandle.*

I did sign up for the boxing tournament in the Alabama Area. I wanted to win the championship belt for my son before leaving for overseas duty. After knocking out Sailor Robertson, the pride of the 504th Parachute [Infantry] and then see my name come up on the billboard to fight him again on the next card, I withdrew my name from the fight roster. I didn't think I had to lick any man more than once in a tournament; I was thirty-one years old and not quite as fast as I once was, experience and hard hitting had won the match. —Private Otis L. Sampson, Company E, 505th Parachute Infantry

Phenix City, Alabama and Columbus, Georgia were two towns frequented by the two regiments. Phenix City was the most notorious, and you didn't go to this town alone, except at great risk. Often fights would occur between [troopers of] the two regiments. Boxing was promoted between the two regiments, and Company G and the 3rd Battalion produced two champions, one being [Private Raymond H.] Tommy Thompson. —Private William L. Blank, Company G, 505th Parachute Infantry

Company H, 505th Parachute Infantry troopers relax in their barracks hut in the Alabama Area after a tough day of training. Three M1 rifles and a Thompson submachine gun are mounted on a storage cabinet and a jug of *Coca-Cola* sits on the table. *Photograph courtesy of Leslie P. Cruise.*

At the Alabama Area, we were put in more tarpaper barracks with a tarpaper mess hall, complete with a jukebox...One night in the barracks, we got to talking and found out several of the guys were happily married men. We'd always been told the paratroops were for single men only. There was some deep thinking and talking about that for a while. The rest of us didn't know if we wanted to jump behind enemy lines with guys who were worried about getting home to "Mama" or not. The married men turned out just as good as the others, but why would they want in a so-called suicide outfit in wartime is still beyond me...As the winter of 1942-1943 wore on, we'd get a skiff of snow once in a while. In our tarpaper barracks, we had army issue Scheilby stoves shaped like a teepee, setup at each end of the building. It was tough to get wood for them sometimes. I, being the back woodsman, would rustle a lot of wood and try to keep kindling ready for a quick fire each morning. A few of the guys who were married had their wives living close by and were allowed to go home some nights. They'd come in early for reveille and start fires in the stoves for us usually, provided I had the wood and kindling ready. —Private Dennis G. O'Loughlin, Company E, 505th Parachute Infantry

Christmas 1942 was in the barracks. Most of us were broke, had no money, because it was the end of the month. We got paid at the beginning of the month, so we pooled our money and had someone go into town and buy whiskey for our Christmas celebration. —Private Norbert P. Beach, Company H, 505th Parachute Infantry Regiment

Christmas came to us in the Alabama Area and as luck would have it, I was confined with my squad as "Fire Guard." It just happened to come our turn. Every time I hear the song "White Christmas" I like to close my eyes and let my mind drift back to that day as I lay on my cot listening to the radio. Bing Crosby did justice to that song. The Christmas dinner that [Private Dennis G.] O'Loughlin and I had been invited to, had an empty chair; the plans I had made for that day just didn't materialize. —Private Otis L. Sampson, Company E, 505th Parachute Infantry

Paratroopers conduct assault training at Fort Bragg, North Carolina. *United States Army Signal Corps photograph.*

FORT BRAGG NORTH CAROLINA

THE NEW AIRBORNE DIVISION began to take shape as the glider units began moving from Camp Claiborne to Fort Bragg on October 1, 1942 and the 504th Parachute Infantry Regiment arrived at Fort Bragg on October 14, 1942. The 82nd Airborne Division was composed of two glider infantry regiments, the 325th and 326th and one parachute regiment, the 504th. Due to a shortage of gliders to train pilots and glider-borne troops, a change was made in the composition of the United States Army's airborne divisions, with the new table of organization calling for one glider and two parachute regiments. On February 12, 1943, the 326th Glider Infantry Regiment was transferred to the newly forming 13th Airborne Division and the 505th Parachute Infantry Regiment joined the division. In addition, artillery battalions, the 376th and 456th Parachute Field Artillery Battalions were added to the 319th and 320th Glider Field Artillery Battalions, which had been formed at Camp Claiborne. While at Fort Bragg, the division conducted advanced training, with glider qualification training done at the Laurinburg–Maxton Army Airfield in southern North Carolina, and antiaircraft gun training for three batteries of the 80th Airborne Antiaircraft (Antitank) Battalions at Fort Fisher, on the coast of North Carolina. The division also conducted large scale exercises designed to facilitate teamwork among infantry, artillery, engineer, and antitank units to weld them into effective combined arms regimental combat teams.

The Waco CG-4A glider was the standard glider used by the United States Army glider-borne units during World War II. This glider could carry thirteen infantrymen fully equipped, or a 75mm pack howitzer, or ¼-ton jeep, or ¼-ton trailer, making it very useful for glider infantry and artillery units. Almost 14,000 of these versatile gliders were built during World War II. *United States Air Force photograph, www.www.fold3.com.*

Troopers emerge from their glider as white phosphorous ordnance explodes behind them during a training exercise. *United States Army Signal Corps photograph.*

Glider infantrymen exit their Waco glider during a training exercise. *United States Army Signal Corps photograph, National Archives.*

The airfields around Fort Bragg were numerous and adaptable to airborne activities. The training rides in the glider were first with personnel and later with a load of weaponry. The first couple of rides I took I was not fearful of the contraption. It left the ground ahead of the C-47, being towed by at least a hundred feet of rope. The rope would stretch, the glider would roll along, and become airborne without much fanfare. After going about the countryside at about 5,000 feet, we decided to pull the detach lever. The release was with a thud and a jerk; the pilot would veer the glider into a slight bank and begin circling for a landing. —Lieutenant James E. Baugh, Headquarters, 80th Airborne Antiaircraft (Antitank) Battalion

Glider artillerymen unload a 75mm pack howitzer during glider flight training conducted at the glider pilot training base located at Laurinburg–Maxton Army Airfield, North Carolina, near the border with South Carolina. *United States Army Signal Corps photograph, National Archives.*

Most of the training was old army infantry tactics, and every so often we marked off an 8x12 area and designated a door. We glider men loaded through this door and squatted opposite each other, then unloaded and fanned out into simulated combat. But no worry, we had seen stick bayonets and wooden machine guns. The men took it with a dry grin and went on training. We did see a glider flight at Pope Field and later did get a glider ride. —Lieutenant Joe B. Gault, Company F, 325th Glider Infantry

On 3 February, the regiment moved to Laurinburg–Maxton Army airbase, located about fifty miles south of Fort Bragg. Here, training was conducted seven days a week, twenty-four hours a day. The twenty-four hours were divided into three eight hour shifts; some companies were training on loading and lashing at night, while others were on the day shift. Orientation glider rides lasting about twenty minutes were given to everyone in the regiment. Some found this to be an exhilarating experience; others were not so sure. Most of these rides were smooth with little turbulence which raised morale and confidence...A few days after the orientation flights, an airlift of battalion strength and an attack problem brought a longer ride and some airsickness. On 26 February, the 2nd Battalion of the 325th helped make American airborne history. The entire battalion was airlifted from Laurinburg–Maxton airbase to Florence, South Carolina. Thirty-two C-47 tow planes and thirty-two CG-4A Waco gliders were used in this movement. The flight was in the air one hour and twenty-three minutes, but forty minutes of this was used to circle the takeoff field until all planes were airborne and in formation. —Lieutenant Wayne W. Pierce, Company E, 325th Glider Infantry

In February of 1943, we began taking a few glider rides. It wasn't all roses. When you jam thirteen men in full field packs, plus a pilot and copilot into one of those little CG-4A gliders you are crammed in tight. And gliding behind a tow plane wasn't quite like a seagull or eagle soaring gracefully through the air. Being towed in the prop wash behind a large airplane created a heavy vibration, almost like riding a truck at full speed down a rough gravel road. Add to that the glider swaying from side to side and dipping and rising and one-third to one-half of the men were airsick and throwing up into their helmets every flight. With all that I don't recall a single man ever wanting to get out of the outfit. —Lieutenant James B. Helmer, Headquarters Company, 1st Battalion, 325th Glider Infantry

Then we went off to Maxton, North Carolina, for a week of acclimation to these gliders, called the CG-4A. Instructions were given into how to load equipment into them, how to enter and leave the door, etc. The week was climaxed by taking a ride in the glider. None of us were impressed with them—they were made of metal tubing, plywood and canvas with the wires of the controls exposed throughout the cabin. I managed to avoid the glider ride because there weren't enough of them to carry everyone, and some of us rode in the tow planes, the famous C-47s, called the Dakota by the English and the DC-3 by the Douglas Company, which designed and produced them. It was my first airplane ride. —Technician Fourth Grade Leonard Lebenson, Headquarters Company, 82nd Airborne Division

Dust is still in the air from the glider landings as a trooper takes his place in a perimeter defense around it. *United States Army Signal Corps photograph.*

A parachute artillery crew fire a 75mm pack howitzer after it was air landed as part of an exercise at Camp Mackall. Other troopers lie prone around the simulated drop zone. *United States Army Signal Corps photograph.*

All three of the howitzer batteries (four guns each) and most of headquarters battery personnel were paratroopers. The antitank / antiaircraft battery and some of the service personnel motor pool, supply, etc) rode the CG-4A gliders. The AA-AT battery initially was equipped with a 37mm antitank gun that was not effective against anything more heavily armored than the lightest tanks. Later those guns were replaced with a high velocity 57mm gun. It could not penetrate heavy armor but could jam turrets and knock off tank tracks. The AA platoon was equipped with single-mount .50 caliber machine guns. They carried both the regular ground mounts and a light, unstable anti-aircraft mount that was little more than a tripod holding a vertical "gas pipe" with the gun at the top. It shook badly while being fired. —Captain Frank D. Boyd, Headquarters Battery, 376th Parachute Field Artillery Battalion

Batteries A, B, and C, 80th Airborne Antiaircraft (Antitank) Battalion and the two antitank platoons of Headquarters Company, 325th Glider Infantry initially trained and were armed with the 37mm antitank gun, which proved to be totally inadequate against German armored vehicles during combat by the United States Army in North Africa during 1943. An agreement was made with British forces in North Africa to trade the 37mm guns for British six-pounder (equivalent to 57mm) antitank guns, which had carriages that were narrow enough to fit inside the Waco CG-4A gliders. The division used the six-pounders through the end of the war. *United States Army Signal Corps photograph, National Archives.*

Company M [325th Infantry] was made into an antiaircraft battalion [the 80th Airborne Antiaircraft (Antitank) Battalion]. My understanding was that our weapons would be 40mm Bofers and .50 caliber machine guns. The 40mm guns were to be made so that they could ride in a glider. Actually they were never made, so instead the army gave us 37mm antitank guns. We ended up with three batteries of antitank guns and three batteries of .50 caliber machine guns...This weapon [37mm antitank gun] was manned by a gunner and an assistant gunner. The third man would ensure a ready supply of ammunition. The gun was towed by a jeep. The glider arrangement was the gun, jeep, or trailer with ammo. There would be a pilot, someone in the copilot's seat who knew little about the glider, and four men. —Lieutenant Charles A. Coleman, Headquarters, 80th Airborne Antiaircraft (Antitank) Battalion

Batteries D, E, and F, 80th Airborne Antiaircraft (Antitank) Battalion were sent to Fort Fisher, North Carolina for antiaircraft gunnery training. Three Battery D troopers pose with some of their weapons and ammunition. Sergeant Stokes M. Taylor (left) holds a .30-caliber water cooled machine gun with an ammunition belt extending from a box sitting to his left. Taylor would later transfer to Battery A and would be posthumously awarded the Distinguished Service Cross for extraordinary heroism during fighting east of the Salm River in Belgium on December 21, 1944. Corporal Michael Szopo (center) has a couple of .50-caliber machine gun bandoliers wrapped over his shoulders while holding a .30-caliber machine gun. Private First Class Lawrence S. Beaver is sitting at right. *Photograph courtesy of Tommy Taylor.*

Another experience was a tour of duty at Fort Fisher on the Carolina coast. There the three batteries of 50 caliber machine guns fired at sleeve targets towed by airplanes. It was rare when we made very many hits. We also fired at the seagulls that were always flying around, it was impossible to hit one of them. —Lieutenant Charles A. Coleman, Headquarters, 80th Airborne Antiaircraft (Antitank) Battalion

On March 23–24, 1943, General George C. Marshall, Army Chief of Staff; British Secretary of State for War, Sir Anthony Eden; and British Field Marshal Sir John Dill conducted an inspection tour of Fort Benning, Fort Keesler, Fort Maxwell, and Fort Bragg. In this photo, Sir Eden inspects the 505th Parachute Infantry at Pope Army Airfield adjacent to Fort Bragg after an airborne demonstration on March 24, 1943 as Colonel James Gavin follows him, with General Marshall behind them. *United States Army Signal Corps photograph, National Archives.*

General Ridgway watches his troopers march to the railroad station at Fort Bragg to board trains bound for Camp Edwards, Massachusetts on April 17, 1943. *United States Army Signal Corps photograph, National Archives.*

On April 17, the regiment and division started for Camp Edwards, Massachusetts. On April 20 at 5:05 boarded a troop train for the same destination, after first removing patches and all other identification from uniforms, hiding polished jump boots, using unordinary infantry leggings, much to everyone's disgust. —Private James Elmo Jones, Company B, 505th Parachute Infantry Regiment

We had covered our 82nd Airborne Division insignias and all other things that showed in any way that we were paratroopers. We did not know in any way where we were going or when we would arrive. —Private Henry D. Ussery, Jr., Headquarters Battery, 376th Parachute Field Artillery Battalion

As the afternoon passed into night, we settled down after eating out K-ration and other knick-knacks that we picked up at the PX [post exchange]. We attempted to sleep, but there was little rest during the night. The continuous thud and bumping of the wheels across the tracks disturbed our rest. By early the next morning, I was able to peep out around the shades, and it was evident we were approaching Washington D. C. We were served hot coffee with our ration, and the train finally came to a stop at the station in Washington. Everybody was all excited that by chance the President or a member of his staff would board the train for a few words of welcome and a send-off with gusto. This, of course, did not happen, and it was really understandable, with the large number of troops on the march and being transported through Washington. I wanted to leave the train to pick up a newspaper I saw on the newsstand, but I had to be satisfied with one passed around in the coach. As we stayed for a while, perhaps an hour there, I began to feel a sense of urgency to everybody in view. They were rushing about the train station and streets; the traffic was very heavy. This made us feel that we must be a part of an important undertaking. It was difficult to see the whole picture of the world from the vantage point of a railroad car. Going north to Philadelphia, then to New Jersey, I was impressed with the immensity of our country. I had never been north before. I was a southerner with roots back to the Civil War and beyond. My grandfather had fought in Northern Virginia and sustained a serious wound in the Battle of the Wilderness. The size of the buildings in this part of the country was impressionable. The train picked up speed in New Jersey, and as it was approaching New York, the speed was slowed. The tunnel under the Hudson (the Holland) was the signal that we had in fact crossed into the city of New York. The tall buildings were an impressive sight, surpassing anything seen in Washington. There was a pause at the station in New York City, and I could tell there were many rail lines, and they were all busy. Aboard the train there was a bustle of activity, with all sorts of instructions about the next leg of our journey that we would be going toward Boston. At no time, was I fully informed of our ultimate destination. We all thought we would be debarking in New York City, because from there, most embarkations took place for overseas service. As our train entered New England, I could fancy the stories about the early settlers in Massachusetts and Connecticut. From my point of vantage in the train, I saw weather that was comparable to winter weather in Georgia. It was misty, rainy, and cold. I would think that down home the farmer would be planting cotton. As we approached the coastline the fog was evident. The train slowed as we approached the Boston area. I wondered if we would stop here, but no—we were told we would proceed to a military base used for staging out on "Buzzard's Bay". The military base was Camp Edwards. Along the coast and out on Cape Cod, the train was very slow. We would be given assignments that we would only be at the area about seven days. I would remain with the headquarters detachment and supervise the vehicles, unless they were sent in ahead. My small group had already prepared to board ship. The train finally came to a stop, and we prepared to detrain. As our transportation arrived, we were driven to the billets on the small enclave, which was near a small town. The name of the waterfront was called "Buzzard's Bay". The whole area was unimpressive and not especially prosperous. There were stores, shops, and churches, and a cemetery not too far from where we stayed. Our daily meetings with the commanding officer consisted of fragments of projected schedules; we were to leave the staging area and proceed to our next stop, which would probably be New York City. There was nothing definite about this. I think the higher up officers did not want to be definite about anything for fear that this would be a tip-off that would endanger our crossing. —Lieutenant James A. Baugh, Headquarters Battery, 80th Airborne Antiaircraft (Antitank) Battalion

We had a very pleasant and interesting trip through the east to Massachusetts, arriving at Camp Edwards at 18:00 on 20 April. It was terribly cold but we had much to do and were restricted too. Supplies were taken on, CWS clothing was issued and shots were given for typhus. The division moved to the New York Port of Embarkation on 27–28 April and boarded the ships. We sailed before dawn on 29 April. We had seen the beauties of America and had seen the young and the old waving farewells to us as trains rolled by at thirty miles per hour. —Major Bennie A. Zinn, Headquarters, 325th Glider Infantry

At Camp Edwards I was selected to be on the advance party to the embarkation point at Staten Island representing division headquarters and also Headquarters Company. Each battalion, or possibly company, was represented by a man whose function was to familiarize himself with the area on the ship where his unit would be billeted and to meet his unit on their arrival at the Port of Embarkation and lead the men to their quarters. —Technician Fourth Grade Leonard Lebenson, Headquarters Company, 82nd Airborne Division

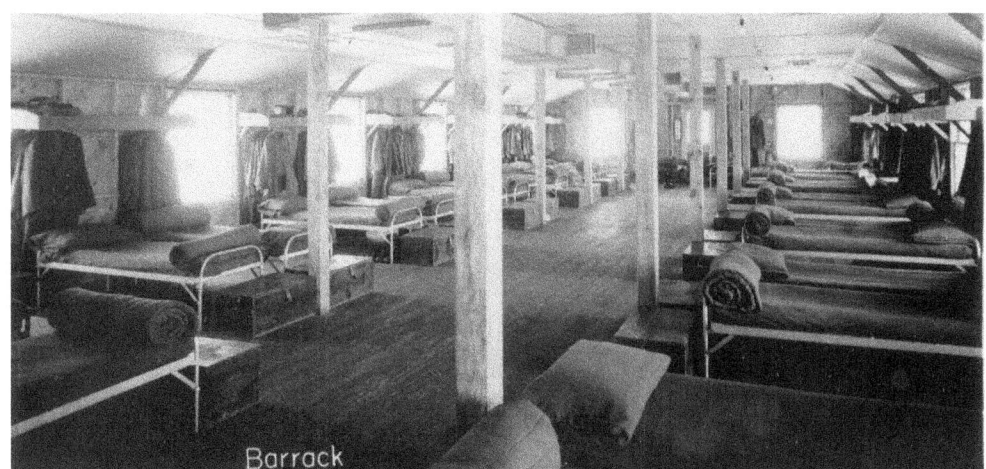
The barracks at Camp Edwards, Massachusetts were typical of those built during World War II. *Photograph courtesy of http://wwii-letters-to-wilma.blogspot.com.*

This mess hall, typical for Camp Edwards was setup to accommodate feeding a company sized group of 150–200 troops during a single setting. Note the potbelly stove at the far end of the mess hall (left center). *Photograph courtesy of http://wwii-letters-to-wilma.blogspot.com.*

On 26 April I received orders to entrain for POE [port of embarkation]. The following day the loading of the train was a riot. [Brigadier] General [Charles L. "Bull"] Keerans [Jr.] was in the way. He thought the men could put their full equipment and their barracks bags in their watch pockets and comfortably walk aboard. The G-1 fouled up the detail too by getting less cars for us than we were admittedly required. The train ride to New York was uneventful. —Major Robert H. Neptune, Headquarters, 376th Parachute Field Artillery Battalion

The train ride to New York was well planned, with even more security precautions than our trip from Fayetteville to Buzzard's Bay area. The time to depart was in the evening, which set our arrival time at least midnight or after. I had done all the preparing I personally could over the past week we had been in our staging area. April was about to become history, but due to the inclement weather we were all in a hurry to leave. The train was just an ordinary train with the windows [shades] pulled, and we entered and took our seats. The train pulled out of the Cape Cod area heading south, moving steadily with the too familiar clank of the wheels crossing the rails. I attempted to relax but could do little about that—there was much to think about and everybody was in a mood of great anticipation. —Lieutenant James E. Baugh, Headquarters, 80th Airborne Antiaircraft (Antitank) Battalion

The USS *Monterey* was built in 1931 as a passenger ship with the Matson Line and converted to an attack transport (USAT) during World War II and painted gray at that time. The ship transported the 505th Parachute Infantry Regiment and other units of the 82nd Airborne Division to Casablanca, arriving on May 10, 1943. *Photograph courtesy of www.arxipelagos.com.*

The USAT *George Washington* was a passenger liner built in Germany and launched in 1908. The ship was commissioned by the United States Army in April of 1943 as an attack transport. It transported the division headquarters, the 504th Parachute Infantry, the 376th Parachute Field Artillery Battalion, the 80th Airborne Antiaircraft (Antitank) Battalion, and a replacement battalion, EGB 448 to Casablanca. *Photograph courtesy of www.navsource.org.*

The USS *Santa Rosa* was built in 1932 and operated by the Grace Line on routes between the United States and South America. It was converted to an attack transport (USAT) during World War II. It transported the 325th Glider Infantry Regiment, the 319th Glider Field Artillery Battalion, and other units of the 82nd Airborne Division to Casablanca, arriving on May 10, 1943. *Photograph courtesy of www.swanseadocks.co.uk.*

It was plenty tough trying to carry two bags (A&B), plus all your field equipment and rifle. From here, we arrived in Staten Island, New York...a lonely trip...one a fellow can never forget. It seemed like hours before we arrived on the island, but actually it was only a few minutes. A million thoughts ran through my mind on that night. As we stepped off of the ferry, a fellow tried to help me off with the bags. I appreciated the hand but almost fell anyhow. The Red Cross was waiting on the pier with a pack of cigarettes and a doughnut. The doughnut tasted wonderful, especially after carrying those darn bags from the pier right on the boat and, what a boat: the George Washington—a German boat converted into a troop transport—one of the largest of its kind. —Private Henry D. Ussery, Jr., Headquarters Battery, 376th Parachute Field Artillery Battalion

I looked out the window [of the train passenger car] to find out we were at the wharf, and just alongside, was something that simply amazed me. It was a huge ship that was one of the largest afloat I was advised. It appeared to be multi-decked with a number of smoke stacks...Our unit lined up on the docks in columns of single file. The MPs were supervising activity. Each soldier had a tag on, and as we approached the gangplank, we would give our name and unit. From there, we would get an assignment. The process went smoothly. The officers were given rooms; the enlisted personnel were sent below deck to a spacious area with double deck bunks. I shared a room with about seven or eight individuals, so it could not really be considered a stateroom, but a little better than the GIs who were below. Soon came to know the ones who shared our little space. There was sufficient space to place personal items and available showers were adequate. There was only one very important item on each bunk—that was a life preserver or what was commonly referred to as a "Mae West". —Lieutenant James E. Baugh, Headquarters, 80th Airborne Antiaircraft (Antitank) Battalion

I got my first look of the Statue of Liberty. That is a beautiful and impressive monument. Our convoy was large. The battleship Texas was among our escort. A number of oil tankers were in the convoy. I wondered if my old fraternity brother who was a navy lieutenant "Hoot" Gibson might be aboard one of the vessels. The following day Champ and I were in charge of organizing troops and training them in boat drill for abandoning ship. This seemed very important to us and we took it quite seriously. The problem was to get the troops out of the below decks to topside (boat deck) as quickly as possible in event of a torpedo attack. Champ and I learned that ship's compartments for troops from stem to stern. We even found one compartment that the transport commander did not realize existed in the ship. We had some fun over that. The voyage across the ocean was the maiden trip for the refitted George Washington as a troop ship. The ship was huge, but only half big enough for the troops on board. Accommodations for the officers were poor, but for the men they were deplorable. The food the first day was good. B-1, where the junior officers were quartered was a "hole". —Major Robert H. Neptune, Headquarters, 376th Parachute Field Artillery Battalion

The ship we crammed onto was named the Washington and was a commandeered German merchant ship that had been seized by the U.S. and prepared for transporting troops. This was to be the ship's first use as such and it had been designed to accommodate as many men as could possibly be squeezed into it. Down to the lowest level of the ship, and there were probably eight levels as I recall, all the compartments were rigged out with three-level cots—very claustrophobic, particularly for those assigned to one of the lower levels as I soon found out we were. —Technician Fourth Grade Leonard Lebenson, Headquarters Company, 82nd Airborne Division

When Colonel [Harry L.] Lewis woke me up on the morning of 29 April, we were at sea and when I reached the deck, nothing was in sight except many ships. The 325th was aboard the Santa Rosa, which was a very capable ship. There were in the convoy, [the] battleship Texas, six transports, three liners, one carrier, three tankers, six freighters and nine destroyers. —Major Bennie A. Zinn, Headquarters, 325th Glider Infantry

Seeing destroyers and other naval craft, we felt strong, safe, and confident. The food was awful and mess lines seemed around the clock. Bunks were four high. Numerous inspections—boat drills—for exercise we climbed the rope ladders up the mast —Private Berge Avadanian, Headquarters Company, 2nd Battalion, 505th Parachute Infantry Regiment

There were about eighteen hundred in EGB 448—both officers and enlisted men—I guess we had three hundred officers. They had so many people that they would put half of them in the hold and half of them on the deck. In twenty-four hours, they would change over. We had about eight men to a compartment. It was so hot down there. —Lieutenant Reneau G. Breard, EGB 448

We were put in the G-1 compartment, a compartment that was pretty low down [in the ship]. In fact, we were so low down that we were under the water line and plenty stuffy too. We ate breakfast at 6 a.m. and again at 9 p.m. After dark, any man caught smoking on deck was put in irons. You were not allowed to smoke below, except in the latrine and the latrine was so crowded you could not get there, so no smokes. After about four days out to sea, a very bad disease broke out…diarrhea. The trip was plenty miserable from there out. The latrines were packed day and night. —Private Henry D. Ussery, Jr., Headquarters Battery, 376th Parachute Field Artillery Battalion

We had 'abandon ship' drills and began to learn the navy language and customs. I bunked with [Lieutenant Colonel John H.] Swede Swenson and had a very fine bunk. The weather was fine all except for one day when it became pretty rough. We stood at the rail and watched fish, the foam and the other ships. We read, talked and sang. We even had movies at night. We had classes to learn to speak to the natives of North Africa. The escort was on alert at all times and we had several sub scares. The last Sunday at sea we had retired and at about 01:00, a huge explosion rocked the ship and the captain called 'prepare to abandon ship.' Boy was I scared stiff. It was cold and I could not swim much. I do remember that we shook on the deck for an hour just waiting. But then the Texas signaled 'all clear. At 09:05 on 10 May 1943, the convoy was met by a large escort of British Corvettes and was split into two parts. It was indeed a pretty sight as the sun came up—ships as far as we could see. We continued on our course and the other part went through the Straits of Gibraltar to Oran. Our convoy sighted land at Casablanca at 05:30, 10 May 1943 and we pulled into the harbor at 13:00 the same day. —Major Bennie A. Zinn, Headquarters, 325th Glider Infantry

FRENCH MOROCCO

Carrying their weapons, duffle bags, and bed rolls, troopers disembark from the troop ships USAT *George Washington*, USAT *Monterey*, and the USAT *Santa Rosa* at the port of Casablanca, French Morocco on May 10, 1943. *United States Army Signal Corps photograph, courtesy of William S. Mandle.*

Our ship was unloaded by about 16:00 and we marched through the outskirts of Casablanca to Camp Don Passage, which was about five miles from town. My eyes really hurt with all the sights of the first foreign country. We saw soldiers of all nations and with all kinds of uniforms. We saw the people sleeping in the streets and on the walks. We saw the people tending to their toilet habits on the streets and in the roads. We saw the typical Arab dress, the sandals, the long baggy pants, the Harem Band working up a little business. We marveled at the tattoos of the Arabs and at the jewelry worn by them in ears and noses and on necks and wrists. The women were nearly all dressed in gaudy colored dresses with head cloths and no shoes. The men wore big seated pantaloons, sandals and head cloths of white or gaudy colors. The men rode small asses and the women walked. The men carried nothing and the women carried all sorts of boxes, baskets or bundles. —Major Bennie A. Zinn, Headquarters, 325th Glider Infantry

Troopers disembark from their troop ships at the port of Casablanca on May 10, 1943. *United States Army Signal Corps photograph, courtesy of William S. Mandle.*

With the cranes at the docks in the distance behind them, troopers carrying heavy loads make the long five mile march to Camp Don B. Passage. *United States Army Signal Corps photograph, courtesy of William S. Mandle.*

The troopers continue the march through Casablanca, where French architecture is seen in this photograph. *United States Army Signal Corps photograph, courtesy of William S. Mandle.*

The local population mingles with the troopers while they take a rest break during the trek to Camp Don B. Passage. *United States Army Signal Corps photograph, courtesy of William S. Mandle.*

Leaving Casablanca behind them, the long column of 82nd Airborne Division troopers continues on toward Camp Don B. Passage. *United States Army Signal Corps photograph, courtesy of William S. Mandle.*

We were all anxious to disembark, but that too was quite a problem, with full packs, arms and 'A' bags. It was dark by the time the battalion was completely unloaded. We marched on foot to Camp Don B. Passage. What a march. It was a five-mile torture with those heavy packs, especially after the twelve days of inactivity and rotten food on the ship. Camp Passage, we found, upon our eventual arrival was a field worked over by a bulldozer I guess to somewhat level the ground. We had made camp by midnight. The ground was rough and cold, but somehow we slept. —Major Robert H. Neptune, Headquarters, 376th Parachute Field Artillery Battalion

The Arabs swarmed all over us like roaches over food. They wanted to trade with us or, preferably, to steal. They were particularly interested in our sheets, mattress covers, cigarettes, and chocolate. For these things they offered trinkets and fresh food—dates, exotic bread, and meats of dubious origin. We were to post guards twenty-four hours a day in order to keep them from stealing everything we had. Theft was so common that we came to regard the Arabs with almost as much ill will as we did the Germans. When we shipped out, a sergeant exacted revenge for all of us. We had already boarded a train when an Arab came to the open window and offered to buy a mattress cover—anyone's mattress cover. A sergeant obliged. The Arab handed the money through the window and clutched the mattress cover, which was partially hanging out the window. At that moment, as the train started to move out, the Arab tried to pull out the cover. However, the sergeant had tied one end to the seat. When the train picked up speed, it dragged the Arab along with it. He turned a flip and let go of the cover. Scrambling to his feet, he chased the train for a few moments, shook his fist, and cursed in Arabic. Most of the soldiers laughed and jeered at him because Arabs had cheated or stolen from virtually all of them during their stay in Casablanca. —Lieutenant T. Moffatt Burriss, Headquarters Company, 3rd Battalion, 504th Parachute Infantry

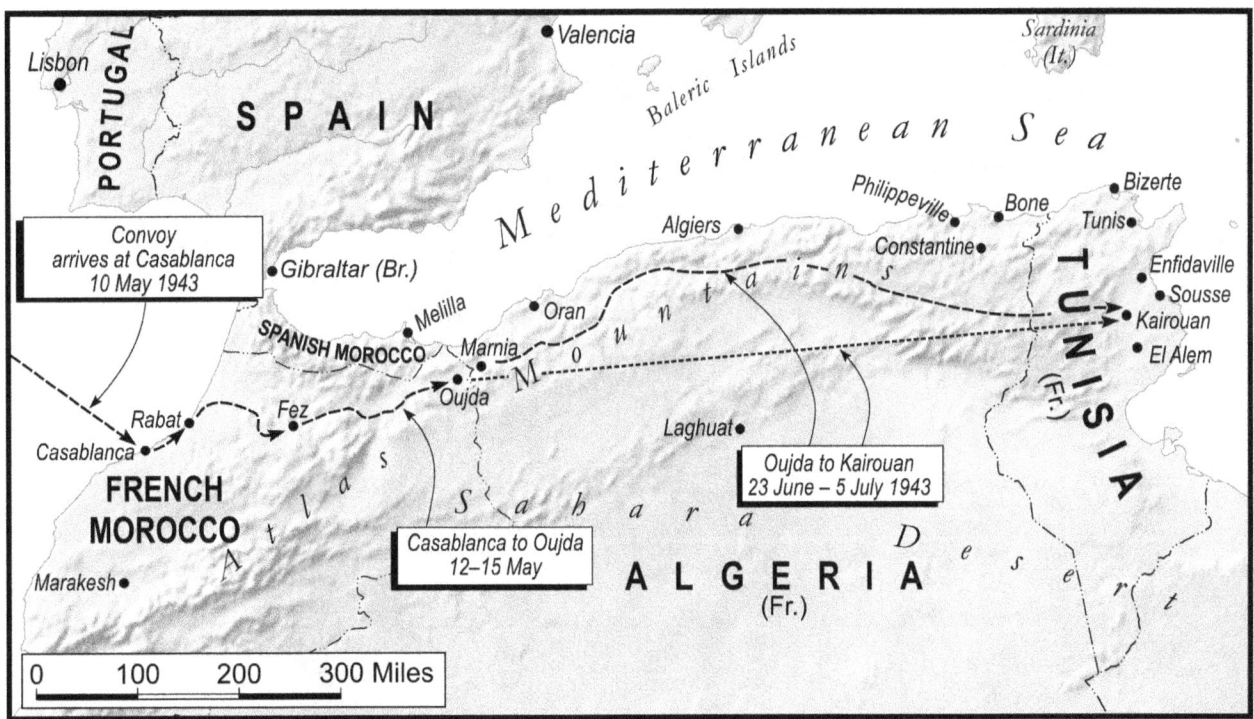

The division left Casablanca on May 12, 1943 in truck convoys and trains and traveled up the coast to Rabat, then eastward through Fez and on to Oujda, French Morocco, near the border with Spanish Morocco. The trains consisted of passenger cars, 40&8s, and open top freight cars. *Photograph courtesy of Jerome V. Huth.*

Back into Casablanca we went and loaded those famous (or should I say infamous) boxcars so prevalent in the French railroad system, the "Forty and Eights", inscribed on their sides is the capacity "40 Hommes – 8 Chevaux". We crammed only thirty-two men in each and ate cold C-rations for the three day trip. —Sergeant Patrick F. Norris, Company E, 325th Glider Infantry

We were loaded in old style WW I box cars. They were made to haul 40 men or 8 horses. Of course we had no horses so we put forty men in each car. No seats just the bare floor. I do not remember the type of rations that we had, probably C-rations cans of meat. The days were long and hot, but we slept pretty well at night. We were not always on the move. When we stopped the natives came begging for food or candy. —Lieutenant Charles A. Coleman, Headquarters, 80th Airborne Antiaircraft (Antitank) Battalion

This aerial view of a portion of the Fifth Army Airborne Training Center (Camp Kunkle) at Les Angades Aerodrome near Oujda, shows rows of tents organized by unit. *United States Army Signal Corps photograph, National Archives.*

This is another view of the Fifth Army Airborne Training Center near Oujda. The parachute units and headquarters of the 82nd Airborne Division were assigned here, while the glider units were at Camp Marnia to the north. The paratroopers lived in vast tent encampments and were subjected to intense heat and hot winds during their time at Camp Kunkle. *United States Army Signal Corps photograph, courtesy of William S. Mandle.*

We had picked, on purpose, land that was not in use for grazing or agricultural purposes. We trained in a fiery furnace, where the hot wind carried a fine dust that clogged the nostrils, burned the eyes, and cut into the throat like an abrasive. We trained at first by day, until the men became lean and gaunt from their hard work in the sun. Then we trained at night, when it was cooler, but the troopers found it impossible to sleep in the savage heat of the African day. The wind and the terrain were our worst enemies. Even on the rare calm days, jumping was a hazard, for the ground was hard, and covered with loose boulders, from the size of a man's fist to the size of his head. —Major General Matthew B. Ridgway, Headquarters, 82nd Airborne Division

Our company was assigned a particular area, which was further broken down into platoon and squad areas. The individual soldier had one-half of a pup tent, so we were paired, and two men lived in this pup tent. We were instructed to dig a trench around the tent to keep water out of the floor when it rained. Now, you can imagine how much good a trench would do on level ground when a torrential downpour came with an accompanying wind—and this occurred more than just a couple of times while we were there. —Private David V. Bowman, Company D, 505th Parachute Infantry

The camp site chosen was typical of sites for American training camps. On one side of the town there were the beautiful rolling plains, ankle high grass which looked like a soft green carpet flowing gently over the hills and blending into the beauties of the mountains on the left and the Mediterranean on the right. So the camp was located on the other side of the town, in the middle of the worst dust bowl on the continent of Africa. It was located in a desolate, sterile, rocky, dusty, heat seared valley, which seemed "no where in North Africa" than "somewhere in North Africa," found on the letterheads of these troops so recently from the States. Oujda brought the regiment the first taste of extended field conditions. Troops lived in long straight rows of pup tents, interspaced with slit trenches. They squatted on the ground and ate from mess kits at the field kitchens. They bathed, shaved, and washed in their helmets and learned the meaning of water discipline. They washed their clothing in wooden tubs or in halves of discarded oil drums. They gave each other haircuts. —Captain Adam A. Komosa, Headquarters Company, 504th Parachute Infantry

We established new camps in order that we might start training for Sicily. The 325th was stationed at Marnia [Algeria, just across the border about twelve miles to the northeast] and the rest of the division was at Oujda. —Major Bennie A. Zinn, Headquarters, 325th Glider Infantry

One of the division's bands entertains troopers as they eat a meal standing at improvised wooden tables. The band members are sitting on cans. *United States Army Signal Corps photograph, National Archives.*

Our kitchens were set up outdoors and the mess line was the same. Every day at meal time a dust storm would blow right down the mess line and the food would be full of dirt. —Private William L. Blank, Company G, 505th Parachute Infantry

The food was very bland, but at least nourishing—scrambled eggs made with powdered eggs, never fully mixed, so we ate powder. Powdered lemon juice—strong coffee with powdered milk. The bread was not bad, but the butter was substitute. We could see hamburgers grilling on the grills, but it was only an illusion—they were awful salmon patties. Spam was a regular fare; I hated it! It and the S.O.S. (shit on a shingle)—chipped beef on toast was often on the 'menu'. Powdered mashed potatoes and lousy beans would occasionally appear. Our cooks were called 'belly robbers.' —Private Berge Avadanian, Headquarters Company, 2nd Battalion, 505th Parachute Infantry

You take a bite of bread or anything, yellow jackets and hornets would land on it and you'd have to brush them off. They were almost in your mouth. It was absolute misery. —Private Russell D. McConnell, Company H, 505th Parachute Infantry

Life at Camp Marnia was very primitive. Our company consisted of two rows of pup tents, each ten yards apart, stretching back from the orderly room and kitchen tents. Since we pitched our pup tents by platoon, the mortar section wound up at the far end from the orderly room one day. It was about 475 yards. Considering our trips to the orderly room, to the kitchen, to the supply tents, and to the heads of the company street for every formation, some of us covered at least ten miles a day, exclusive of regular drill. The soil was strewn with rocks of all shapes and sizes, which made marching torturous. The slightest breeze or mass movement swirled up choking clouds of dust. Until we became accustomed to it, the sun seemed unmerciful. This then, was Camp Marnia, this open-air oven, where even our only respite, the cool evenings, was often taken from us and given over to torturous groping about on night problems. —Sergeant Patrick F. Norris, Company E, 325th Glider Infantry

General Ridgway called myself and Colonel Tucker up to orient us on our probable combat task. It had been directed by the GHQ, and was to be known as "Husky" and was to be executed July 10th. It contemplated the seizure of Sicily. The 505th CT was to spearhead the amphibious landing of the 1st or 45th Divisions. Our jump was to take place in moonlight the night of July 9th, 11:30 p.m. The exact mission was yet an issue. From an analysis of the probable missions it was clear that the effort would be a very risky one and a costly one. —Colonel James M. Gavin, Headquarters, 505th Parachute Infantry

When we started out in this desert or—I guess more precisely, semi-desert—in the morning, we had with us only one canteen of water and this was to last us through our whole day of exertion in the heat. 'Water discipline,' they called it. Occasionally, they would bring a Lister bag full of water, well heated in the desert sun, but this was rare. Equally painful to me was the skimpy amount of food we were allowed while there. But this may have been of minor importance to most, considering that many contracted malaria and yellow jaundice, and I think we all got dysentery at some time or another. —Private David V. Bowman, Company D, 505th Parachute Infantry

Troopers with Company E, 505th conduct calisthenics during the heat of the day at Oujda wearing shorts and their jump boots. *United States Army Signal Corps photograph, National Archives.*

The training, heat, food, dysentery, and malaria combined to toughen the division's troopers physically and mentally for the challenges of combat over the coming two years. *United States Army Signal Corps photograph, National Archives.*

The weather was so hot during the day it kept down the extensive training to night problems. We used the mornings for physical conditioning exercises. —Private William L. Blank, Company G, 505th Parachute Infantry

We continued the training, very much as before—physical exercises, night problems, assaults, defense, and other such military exercises and maneuvers. —Private David V. Bowman, Company D, 505th Parachute Infantry

Company E, 505th paratroopers pair off to practice judo. The exercise area appears to have been raked to remove most of the rocks. *United States Army Signal Corps photograph, National Archives.*

Troopers with Company E, 505th Parachute Infantry leap from platforms constructed for the purpose of practicing parachute landing falls (PLFs). *United States Army Signal Corps photograph, National Archives.*

We were training all day and due to the heat we were unable to sleep at night. Some mental pygmy got the bright idea to train at night and sleep in the daytime. We were in pup tents on the desert floor, which meant we were awake twenty-four hours a day, instead of only twenty or twenty-two. To further complicate our lives everyone had dysentery. While walking guard duty an entrenching shovel was a must. The sand blew constantly and the flies went from the mess tent to the latrines.
—Sergeant William T. Dunfee, Company I, 505th Parachute Infantry

Most of our training was over terrain as nearly like that to be found in Sicily as we could find and we had just about every type of training possible. We had attack problems, defense problems, meeting engagements, patrol, house to house fighting, withdrawals, CPXs and all kinds of supply and evacuation problems. We studied first aid and methods of escape from the enemy. We studied CIC activities, recognition of enemy planes and equipment. We worked on hand-to-hand fighting and in addition took much hardening work. —Major Bennie A. Zinn, Headquarters, 325th Glider Infantry

The training area consisted of a group of small prominent hills, about four miles away. We named the hills A, B, C, and D. The usual route to this area was past an Arab burial ground. Since it required blasting to dig a hole of any size, the Arabs buried their dead close to the top of the ground. Anyone passing through was likely to scuff off the top soil and expose earthly remains of some departed Arab. Just going past the place was an ordeal. —Sergeant Patrick F. Norris, Company E, 325th Glider Infantry

Troopers with Company E, 505th Parachute Infantry practice the same parachute landing falls that they were taught during parachute training in order to maintain the muscle memory of landing without being injured. A mockup of a C-47 fuselage (right) was used for practicing the rapid exit of a stick of paratroopers from an aircraft. *United States Army Signal Corps photograph, National Archives.*

Just about everything happened to us at Marnia and Oujda. We hit an Arab house with a mortar shell and killed the old man's wife, chicken and donkey. We paid him what he wanted which was $25 for the donkey, $2 for the chicken and $5 for his wife. He was happy for all except that he could not easily secure a new donkey. We caught thieves galore and even found our soldiers selling bed sacks at $20 each. We operated a 'cat house' in Oujda to fight venereal disease. We had parachute failures and had our first casualties from glider training, when two men were struck by an incoming glider and torn to bits. We found out what dysentery is like and how it hits a well man and pulls him down. We learned to barter with Arabs for eggs and a few fresh vegetables as we got tired of dehydrated foods. We learned how hot one hundred thirty degrees is and what it means to drop from one hundred thirty degrees at 17:00 to fifty degrees at 21:00. We learned how to keep water cool in the huge earthen jars that the Arab makes and sells. We learned how to make reconnaissance in a strange country. We saw our first bombings from a good comfortable distance and saw our bombers going out to Sicily and Italy. —Major Bennie A. Zinn, Headquarters, 325th Glider Infantry Regiment

If you were not suffocating from the heat and dust, the asps or snakes got you. You would burn up until around four in the afternoon, then the wind gave you a little relief, but dust came with it and what a dust! At night lizards and bugs run over you all night. This place was strictly no fun. —Private Henry D. Ussery, Jr., Headquarters Battery, 376th Parachute Field Artillery Battalion

Colonel James Gavin (left center), the commanding officer of the 505th Parachute Infantry Regiment, and Colonel Harry L. Lewis (right center), the commander of the 325th Glider Infantry Regiment, pin the insignia on the uniform of the newly promoted Colonel Reuben H. Tucker, III, the commanding officer of the 504th Parachute Infantry Regiment, as General Ridgway (far left), the division commander observes, May 29, 1943. *United States Army photograph, courtesy of William S. Mandle.*

General Ridgway (left) congratulates Colonel Tucker on his promotion, from lieutenant colonel to colonel, May 29, 1943. *United States Army photograph, courtesy of William S. Mandle.*

This trooper packs an equipment bundle containing primarily communication gear in preparation for an upcoming jump on June 3, 1943. *United States Army Signal Corps photograph, National Archives.*

Major Benjamin H. Vandervoort, the 505th regimental S-3 (plans and operations) staff officer, observes troopers with the 1st Battalion, 505th Parachute Infantry as they fasten the straps to secure an equipment bundle prior to a demonstration jump on June 3, 1943. *United States Army Signal Corps photograph, National Archives.*

Colonel James Gavin (center) inspects the 1st Battalion, 505th Parachute Infantry, prior to a demonstration jump on June 3, 1943 as Major Vandervoort (right) observes. *United States Army Signal Corps photograph, National Archives.*

Troopers load an equipment bundle into one of six racks underneath a C-47 prior to an upcoming demonstration jump on June 3, 1943. *United States Army Signal Corps photograph, National Archives.*

Lieutenant General Mark W. Clark (center), the commanding officer of the Fifth Army arrives at Oujda for a division review and demonstration jump, June 3, 1943. Major General Ridgway is at the right of the photo. *United States Army Signal Corps photograph, courtesy of William S. Mandle.*

Paratroopers with the 1st Battalion, 505th Parachute Infantry line up to board their C-47 aircraft prior to the demonstration jump as a part of the division review on June 3, 1943. *United States Army Signal Corps photograph, National Archives.*

Paratroopers with the 1st Battalion, 505th Parachute Infantry board their C-47 aircraft in the reverse order of their Form B load manifest prior to takeoff for the demonstration jump on June 3, 1943. The trooper about to enter the plane has a Griswold case holding his disassembled rifle strapped diagonally across his body underneath his reserve parachute. His musette bag is fastened to the left side of his body while his shovel is carried on his right hip and his main parachute on his back. *United States Air Force photograph, www.fold3.com.*

On the morning of June 3, 1943, dignitaries watch a demonstration jump by the 1st Battalion, 505th Parachute Infantry. In the front row of the reviewing stand from left to right are General Auguste Nogues of French Morocco; Lieutenant General Mark Clark, the commander of the United States Fifth Army; Lieutenant General Luis Orgaz, the high commissioner of Spanish Morocco; Lieutenant General George S. Patton, Jr., the commander of the United States Seventh Army; and Major General Ridgway. *United States Army Signal Corps photograph, courtesy of William S. Mandle.*

Parachute canopies fill the sky as the 1st Battalion, 505th Parachute Infantry conducts a demonstration jump on a drop zone near Oujda for visiting dignitaries on the morning of June 3, 1943. *United States Army Signal Corps photograph, National Archives.*

The oscillation of the parachute canopies of these two paratroopers during the demonstration jump by the 1st Battalion, 505th Parachute Infantry reflects the windy conditions under which the jump was made, resulting in a number of injuries. *United States Army Signal Corps photograph, National Archives.*

Another view of the descending troopers shows significant oscillation of the parachute canopies and a trooper on the ground working to collapse his canopy, both signs of windy conditions. *United States Army Signal Corps photograph, National Archives.*

Paratroopers with the 1st Battalion, 505th Parachute Infantry begin to assemble on the drop zone as three planes fly low overhead to simulate a resupply drop during the demonstration jump. *United States Army Signal Corps photograph, National Archives.*

Two troopers retrieve an equipment bundle from its white cargo chute before carrying it to their assembly point. *United States Army Signal Corps photograph, National Archives.*

At the conclusion of the demonstration jump, visiting dignitaries were driven to a covered stand to watch the 82nd Airborne Division pass in review, June 3, 1943. General Mark Clark is flanked in the jeep by General Auguste Nogues of French Morocco on his right and Lieutenant General Luis Orgaz, the high commissioner of Spanish Morocco, on his left. *United States Army Signal Corps photograph, courtesy of William S. Mandle.*

Despite the climatic conditions, the camp at Oujda was to become the greatest parade ground the regiment and division had graced to date. We were to be the proud recipient of virtually every dignitary in northwestern Africa. The proud 82nd paraded before fifteen allied generals in less than a month. The division colors were dipped for General Mark Clark, the commanding general of the Fifth Army; General [Carl A.] "Tohey" Spaatz, the colorful commander of our African Air Force; General Patton, commanding general of the Seventh Army; General Bradley, the division's first commanding general in World War II; Major General [Alfred M.] Gruenther; Fifth Army chief of staff, General Dwight D. Eisenhower, and an impressive row of French and Spanish dignitaries, including Lieutenant General Luis Orgaz, High Commissioner of Spanish Morocco, and many others. With all the visits we had been receiving from dignitaries, it was quite obvious that they had big things in store for us. —Captain Adam A. Komosa, Headquarters Company, 504th Parachute Infantry

One day we got orders to spit and polish everything, that we were going to parade for some dignitaries the next day. We were ordered to put gun oil on our steel helmets so that they would shine. The next day we were trucked a few miles into Oujda for the parade. On the reviewing stand was General George Patton, ivory handled revolvers and all; with him was the [High Commissioner] of Morocco. General Patton looked every bit the soldier that he was. —Private First Class Glendon C. Gilbert, Headquarters Company, 325th Glider Infantry

General Francisco Delgado Serrano of Spanish Morocco (wearing sunglasses) ascends the stairs at the covered reviewing stand prior to the division review. *United States Army Signal Corps photograph, courtesy of William S. Mandle.*

Standing at the front of the reviewing stand while waiting for the division review to begin are (left to right) Lieutenant General Mark Clark, General Auguste Nogues, Major General Matthew Ridgway, and an unidentified American major general. *United States Army Signal Corps photograph, courtesy of William S. Mandle.*

The dignitaries on the reviewing stand watch the 82nd Airborne Division pass in review. Those at the front of the stand are (left to right) Lieutenant General Luis Orgaz, the high commissioner of Spanish Morocco; Lieutenant General Mark Clark, the commander of the United States Fifth Army; General Auguste Nogues of French Morocco; Lieutenant General George S. Patton, Jr., the commander of the United States Seventh Army; and Major General Ridgway, an unidentified American major general; and Lieutenant General Omar N. Bradley, the commanding officer of the United States Army's II Corps. *United States Army Signal Corps photograph, courtesy of William S. Mandle.*

Colonel Gavin and his staff salute the dignitaries on the reviewing stand as they march at the head of the 505th Parachute Infantry Regiment. The entire 82nd Airborne Division, less the 1st Battalion, 505th, paraded past the reviewing stand over a two hour period. *United States Army Signal Corps photograph.*

A medical officer (the captain kneeling at the right), and another trooper (left) attend to a trooper who was injured during a practice jump conducted by the 3rd Battalion, 505th Parachute Infantry on June 5, 1943. *United States Army Signal Corps photograph, National Archives.*

There was terrible downdraft and almost everyone came in hard and actually bounced when they hit the ground. I know that I came in and bounced several times. After I hit, I lay there a few moments feeling spots on my body to be sure I had no broken bones. After my examination I decided I was okay. I got up and started to assemble with my company. The first person I came to was one of my company's lieutenants. He was lying on the ground; I'm sure as much from disappointment as from hurting. He lay there, moaning and saying, "I bent my collarbone. I bent my collarbone." I looked at him and could see that his shoulder was sticking straight up. I said, "Sir, it looks to me like you broke your collarbone." He said, "No, damn it. It's bent. I was in a car wreck in the States and had my right collarbone replaced with a silver one." He was disappointed because he knew he would have to return to the States and he wanted to stay with his outfit. —Private Richard E. Reid, Company H, 505th Parachute Infantry Regiment

As you got close to the ground, it was really windy. It took me, swung me up and slammed me down on the ground. I hit with those hand grenades in my pockets. I was purple and blue. —Private Howard C. Goodson, Company I, 505th Parachute Infantry

We made the jump and because of the wind that picked up around noon daily, sustained an above average number of jump injuries. One of the men in my company tangling with an equipment bundle had to be sent home (Huffman). —Sergeant William T. Dunfee, Company I, 505th Parachute Infantry Regiment

Even on the rare calm days, jumping was a hazard, for the ground was hard, and covered with loose boulders, from the size of a man's fist to the size of his head. Fatalities were few, but serious sprains, fractures and concussions were common. In one battalion jump, we had fifty-four severe injuries. Finally, we were losing so many key men, we had to cut down on the jumping. We trained the pilots to find the drop zones, and only the jumpmasters and one other jumper went out the door. —Major General Matthew B. Ridgway, Headquarters, 82nd Airborne Division

Beginning on the night of June 9–10, a number of night practice jumps were conducted by each of the three battalions of the 505th Parachute Infantry; the 3rd Battalion, 504th Parachute Infantry; and the 456th Parachute Field Artillery Battalion. The jumps involved only the jumpmasters (in the case of the 3rd Battalion, 504th a second jumper was also employed) and equipment bundles, while their respective units were positioned on the drop zones. After the jumps, attacks were executed on mockups of their objectives constructed on terrain similar to the actual targets in Sicily. *United States Army Signal Corps photograph, courtesy of William S. Mandle.*

A few days before leaving Oujda I was ordered to make a night jump as a training exercise for the troop carrier pilots. There was one non-com assigned to each C-47. The regiment was already dispersed on the ground at the selected DZ. We were to fly out over the Mediterranean, form up as a unit and then fly back to North Africa and hit the DZ where the regiment was waiting and on landing each of us representing a planeload, the ground problem would start. I had arrived at my plane and had loaded my gear aboard when Mike Fedora came over stating his plane had engine trouble and would not be going. I told him he was welcome to go with me if he wished, it was up to him. He decided to go along because we both knew it was a lot cooler in the air than where we were. We took off shortly, and knowing we had a couple of hours to kill, we promptly "sacked out." The next thing I knew the crew chief was yelling at me that it was about time to jump. This snapped me out of it and I noticed the red light was already on. With the crew chief's help we got our gear on and just in time when the green light came on. I was standing in the door looking down and all I could see were round rocks on the ground. Glowing in the moonlight, they reminded me of skulls. I said "Ready Mike" and jumped. We were close together on landing, but in looking around, we were all alone. Finally a detail of men that were on the ground found us and we joined our unit and moved out. On landing I came in backward, jamming my canteen into and cracking a couple of ribs. —Sergeant William T. Dunfee, Company I, 505th Parachute Infantry

An artillery crew with the 319th Glider Field Artillery Battalion prepares to load a 75mm pack howitzer into a CG-4A Waco glider at Les Angades Aerodrome at the Fifth Army Airborne Training Center (Camp Kunkle) as part of a training exercise on June 11, 1943. *United States Air Force photograph, www.fold3.com.*

In the next step of the process, troopers raise the nose of the glider to facilitate loading of their howitzer. *United States Army Signal Corps photograph, National Archives.*

After pulling the 75mm howitzer in through the opening created by raising the nose of the glider, the troopers with the 319th Glider Field Artillery Battalion secure the gun to prevent its movement. *United States Air Force photograph, www.fold3.com.*

After securing the gun, lowering the nose of the glider and fastening it to the fuselage, the five artillerymen take their seats inside the glider sitting behind the 75mm pack howitzer prior to takeoff. *United States Air Force photograph, www.fold3.com.*

Troopers with Battery A, 320th Glider Field Artillery Battalion watch as Private First Class Walter Kivisto lines up their jeep with the glider in preparation for loading it into a Waco CG-4A glider. *United States Air Force photograph, www.fold3.com.*

Glider troopers with Battery A, 320th Glider Field Artillery Battalion load a jeep into a Waco glider as part of a training exercise near Oujda, Morocco. *United States Air Force photograph, www.fold3.com.*

Private First Class Walter Kivisto, with Battery A, 320th Glider Field Artillery Battalion backs the jeep into the Waco glider. Afterward, the jeep is secured to the frame of the glider to prevent movement during flight. *United States Air Force photograph, www.fold3.com.*

After lowering the nose and securing it to the fuselage, a tow rope is attached in preparation for flight. *United States Air Force photograph, www.fold3.com.*

Troopers with Battery A, 320th Glider Field Artillery Battalion push their 105mm short barreled howitzer into a CG-4A glider in preparation for a training flight. *United States Air Force photograph, www.fold3.com.*

Troopers secure the howitzer to the tubular steel frame and plywood bases of the glider prior to lowering and closing the nose of the glider and attaching the tow rope. *United States Air Force photograph, www.fold3.com.*

Glider troopers board a Waco glider at the airfield near Oujda, Morocco in preparation for a flight as part of a training exercise. *United States Air Force photograph, www.fold3.com.*

General Dwight D. Eisenhower inspects the 504th Parachute Infantry's honor guard company during his visit to Oujda on June 19, 1943, accompanied by the honor guard commander, Captain Willard E. Harrison, and Generals Ridgway and Clark. *United States Army Signal Corps photograph, courtesy of William S. Mandle.*

A final division review was held for General Dwight D. Eisenhower on June 16, 1943. *United States Army Signal Corps photograph, courtesy of William S. Mandle.*

A closer view of the previous photograph reveals from among the officers in the front row reviewing the troopers as they march by are Brigadier General Maxwell Taylor, commanding officer of the division artillery, is fourth from left (wearing helmet) and General Ridgway, is fourth from right (wearing helmet). *United States Army Signal Corps photograph, courtesy of William S. Mandle.*

A C-47 tow plane or "tug" and the Waco CG-4A glider it is towing lifts off a dirt runway near Oujda on June 17, 1943. *United States Air Force photograph, www.fold3.com.*

On 17 June 1943, the 325 suffered its first fatal casualties overseas. A training mission using glider flights was being conducted from a dirt airstrip. Two men from 2nd Battalion Headquarters Company exited their glider on landing and ran into the path of another incoming glider. The wing struts hit the men while the glider was doing seventy miles an hour. Both men had been married shortly before departing for overseas. —Lieutenant Wayne W. Pierce, Headquarters Company, 2nd Battalion, 325th Glider Infantry

The preliminaries were over and we made plans to move to the Kairouan area. We flew most of our men and much of the equipment but had some carried by train and some by heavy truck. The trip was an experiment and turned out to be remarkable. Several gliders were forced down in the mountains but not a man was killed or badly injured on the mass movement over five hundred miles of mountains. I shall never forget that trip as the scenery was wonderful and the weather was fine, bad, and fine again. We made camps all around Kairouan; the 325th Combat Team going to El Alem (twenty-four miles from Kairouan). We located in a huge olive orchard and started the final stage of the Sicilian fight. The operation was to be known as "Horrified". We got all details set and ready to go. The training was indeed vigorous and thorough. —Major Bennie A. Zinn, Headquarters, 325th Glider Infantry

On 22 June an early morning flight over the fog shrouded Atlas Mountains crashed, killing fourteen men. Ten of them in the C-47 were from the 325. Flights were canceled for the balance of the day. With clear skies on 23 June, the regiment became airborne for the four hour flight to Tunisia. Rain squalls developed over the Atlas Mountains and in Tunisia, making flying hazardous. A number of C-47s and gliders did not make it to the designated landing strip in Tunisia, but landed at alternate fields. —Lieutenant Wayne W. Pierce, Headquarters Company, 2nd Battalion, 325th Glider Infantry

The 504th Regimental Combat Team, less the 3rd Battalion; the 2nd Battalion, 509th Parachute Infantry Regiment; the artillery, engineer, and antitank elements of the 325th Regimental Combat Team; the antitank elements of the 505th Regimental Combat Team; and the special troops of the 82nd Airborne Division moved by rail from Oujda aboard six trains to airfields in the Kairouan, Tunisia area. *Photograph courtesy of Jan Bos.*

A convoy carrying elements of the 82nd Airborne Division passes through a town on the way from Oujda to a staging area between Kairouan and Enfidaville, Tunisia. *United States Army Signal Corps photograph, courtesy of William S. Mandle.*

TUNISIA

This is a view of the city of Kairouan, Tunisia. *Photograph courtesy of William S. Mandle.*

The regimental combat teams were bivouacked in a huge arc around the city in scattered olive groves and cactus patches. This area was also very dusty and the scorching heat was unbearable. Within 275 short miles lay the enemy in Sicily, nervously waiting for the invasion which certainly would come soon. The troops began to sense the nearness of the battle. Situation huts were set up immediately and conferences were held concerning the pending attack on the iron-muscled underbelly of Festung Europa. Training was as usual 'continuous' with both day and night exercises. Troops got up at 04:30 and started at 06:00. They got madder and meaner. —Captain Adam A. Komosa, Headquarters Company, 504th Parachute Infantry

Kairouan was more of the same, like before, sand everywhere, in everything you ate, slept and it was still hot. Dysentery was a way of life. Morning reveille formations were never completed. There were more troops hurrying to the latrines than standing roll call formation. Best relief at Kairouan was the slight breeze we would get from the ocean, hot, but at least a partial relief. —Staff Sergeant Leonard D. Battles, Headquarters Battery, 376th Parachute Field Artillery Battalion

In the shade of the pear and almond trees, we took what refuge we could from the searing heat, but for those who had to work in the Quonset huts, there was no escape. It was like living and working inside a stove. There was always a wind, at times the hot sirocco, blowing off the desert like the breath of hell, and at midday the thermometer sometimes stood at 126 degrees. For the first time our supply system broke down and for one long stretch we lived almost exclusively on marmalade and Spam. —Major General Matthew B. Ridgway, commanding officer, 82nd Airborne Division

This Nissen hut housed the Red Cross at one of the airfields near Kairouan, Tunisia. *Photograph courtesy of William S. Mandle.*

A trooper with the 504th Parachute Infantry stands in front of his two man pup tent near a cactus hedge outside of the city of Kairouan. *Photograph courtesy of William S. Mandle.*

Three troopers with the 504th Parachute Infantry pitch bean bags in a game similar to horseshoes in Sousse, Tunisia near the regiment's encampment at an airfield outside of the town. *Photograph courtesy of William S. Mandle.*

A trooper walks along the road outside of Sousse, Tunisia to the encampment for the 504th Parachute Infantry. *Photograph courtesy of William S. Mandle.*

Under the shade of an olive tree at their bivouac near Kairouan, 504th troopers check their .30 caliber light machine guns before packing them in an equipment bundle. *United States Army Signal Corps photograph, National Archives.*

At the 82nd Airborne Division headquarters near Kairouan, Tunisia, Lieutenant General George S. Patton, Jr. (left), the commander of the Seventh Army, confers with Major General Ridgway (second from right) as Major General Omar N. Bradley (second from left), the commander of the II Corps, and Brigadier General Maxwell Taylor (right) listen. *United States Army Signal Corps photograph, National Archives.*

Paratroopers with the 505th Parachute Infantry carry their meals in their mess kits from the chow line at their bivouac in an orchard. *Photograph courtesy of Daniel B. McIlvoy.*

We were bivouacked in a huge olive grove and the small trees gave us some shade, it was a definite improvement over Oujda. The living was easy the next few days. On 6 July the regiment took time out for our first birthday party. For the big event, three fat steers were bought and barbecued by the battalion cooks. Some "angel of mercy" located enough kegs of beer that each man received a couple of canteen cups full. Colonel Gavin gathered his boys around for one of his talks. He reminisced about past campaigns such as Cotton's Fish Camp and the Town Pump and the tough training we had undergone. He noted we would be the first American paratroopers to face the Germans and he expected great things from us. "Slim Jim" Gavin was so admired and respected by those of us who had been with him since the Regiment was formed, that there wasn't a man that wouldn't go thru hell for him. —Sergeant William T. Dunfee, Company I, 505th Parachute Infantry

Colonel Gavin addresses his paratroopers on July 6, 1943 after they were treated to steaks and beer to celebrate the first anniversary of the regiment's formation. The following night, the 505th Parachute Infantry and the rest of the regimental combat team as well as the attached 3rd Battalion, 504th Parachute Infantry made the combat jump in Sicily.

Some old steer who had lived through much of the past history of early Africa finally found himself barbecued as a special treat for the 505th. It was special. Not counting the real steaks, we also had beer and if the cards were played right, one was able to slip back into line now and again, which some of them did. It was a good party. —Sergeant Otis L. Sampson, Company E, 505th Parachute Infantry Regiment

The USS *Monrovia* attack transport APA-31 served as the Western Naval Task Force's command vessel for Operation Husky. Lieutenant General George S. Patton, Jr. and his Seventh Army staff as well as General Ridgway and a small group of 82nd Airborne Division Headquarters and Headquarters Company personnel were aboard the ship when it departed from Algiers on July 6, 1943 for Sicily. *United States Navy photograph, courtesy of www.Navsource.org.*

And then I was called in and told that I was going to be included on the advance group to Sicily. General Ridgway was to be on the same ship as the army commander and he was taking a small group with him, including his aide, Captain [Don C.] Faith [Jr.]; his driver, [Staff] Sergeant [Frank G.] Farmer; the chief of staff, Colonel [Ralph P.] Eaton; the G-2, Colonel [George E.] Lynch; the intelligence sergeant [James E.] Spotswood; the G-3, Colonel [Richard K.] Boyd; and me, as the operations sergeant. Spotswood was a master sergeant and I was a T/4, equivalent to a three-striper...The rest of the section, officers and men, would follow up some days after the invasion and, would come about four or five days after D-Day, landing, to my best recollection, on a Sicilian airfield...So in early July we were driven to Algiers, the embarkation port. We found it to be exciting and bustling with troops and activity, and we loaded onto the USS Monrovia, which was fitted with all kinds of communications gear as the command ship of the Seventh Army and also of the fleet carrying us to battle. Admiral [Henry K.] Hewett, in charge of the fleet, was on board. It was the 3rd of July, 1943...The Monrovia, our ship, was a navy troop carrier, outfitted as a command ship, but operated with a full navy crew as compared with the Washington, which took us overseas from New York crewed by the merchant marine. The ship only had limited armament, some five inch cannon and a number 40mm and 20mm antiaircraft guns. This was our first exposure to the navy and the first thing that struck us army guys was how young the sailors looked. And clean. And we also noted their superior food, which was served cafeteria style and eaten at tables sitting down! While aboard, we of course had the same routine. And we noted that, among other things, beans were always served at breakfast. I was assigned a bunk somewhere below decks. Before leaving Oujda, I was informed that I was to drive a command car across the beach. I had never driven the vehicle before and sought it out below decks and stowed some of my stuff in it. A command car can be described as an oversized jeep which rode quite high off the ground.
—Technician Fourth Grade Leonard Lebenson, Headquarters Company, 82nd Airborne Division

The airfield near Enfidaville is a beehive of activity as paratroopers receive instructions prior to moving to the aircraft on July 9, 1943. *United States Army Signal Corps photograph.*

July 9th started with an early breakfast and we were then issued a basic combat load of ammo, grenades and rations. We were issued two items that were unique to the Sicily operation, being Mae West life preservers and gas masks. —Sergeant William T. Dunfee, Company I, 505th Parachute Infantry

We had Mae West [life preservers] under our reserve chute with weapons and equipment some 120 to 150 pounds. We were instructed to unhook our harness and slip out of our chute just before a water landing. Our Mae West would then be inflated with a CO2 cartridge. —Sergeant Raymond F. Hart, Company H, 505th Parachute Infantry

I finished the last details on the sand table—McGuigan and Miller have nothing more to do but get ready. Everybody is calm about the jump and Gavin thinks it is still a dry run. —Private First Class Donald L. Adrianson, Headquarters Company, 505th Parachute Infantry

We studied maps and made sand tables. Intelligence officers briefed us on the enemy's strength. They told us that the mission would be no picnic. They were expecting an attack, and we would probably encounter a good deal of antiaircraft fire. The basic strategy was as follows: Paratroopers would jump behind enemy lines, disrupt enemy communications and cause as much damage as possible. The next morning at 05:00, a seaborne force would land at the city of Gela. We boarded C-47s with full combat gear, which included backpack with clothes and mess gear, canteen, M1 rifle, knife, and hand grenades. This was our first combat mission—the day we had anticipated since we began training a year and a half earlier. The mission of our unit, the 3rd Battalion, was to land near the high ground about fifteen miles northwest of Gela. The 505th Regiment was to land several miles behind the beach area, just north of Gela. —Lieutenant T. Moffatt Burriss, Headquarters Company, 3rd Battalion, 504th Parachute Infantry

These paratroopers with the 505th Parachute Infantry Regiment stand ready for an inspection after receiving Mae West life preservers, July 9, 1943. The trooper third from the right is a medic and is wearing a Marine medical drop kit on his chest. *Photograph courtesy of Daniel B. McIlvoy, Jr.*

This paratrooper is a rifle grenadier and holds his 1903 Springfield rifle with a grenade launcher attachment on the muzzle of the rifle in his left hand. In addition, he carries a personal weapon, an M1 folding stock carbine, which he holds in his right hand. A display of equipment for a rifle grenadier is shown on the next page. *United States Army Signal Corps photograph.*

The typical combat load carried by each paratrooper included a main parachute (top left), plus a reserve parachute (top right), an M1 Garand rifle, a Griswold case (left center), 168 rounds of .30-caliber M1 ammunition in clips of eight rounds each (lower center), four fragmentation grenades (right), one smoke grenade (lower right), plus a bayonet (right center), trench knife (lower center), and switchblade jump knife (bottom right). Along with their jumpsuit, each wore a helmet, helmet liner, and gloves (upper right), and carried a silk escape map and compass sown into the lining of the jumpsuit, wristwatch, combat harness (center), and a handkerchief. Extra clothing included two pairs of socks and one pair of under shorts. Each trooper was issued a musette bag that held a mess kit, several "K" and "D" rations, a tooth brush, tooth paste, a safety razor with five blades, a bar of soap, pencil, paper, ten packs of Camel cigarettes, matches, cigarette lighter, and Halazone tablets (for water purification). And finally, each load included a 30-foot rope (left), a blanket, shelter half, gas mask, entrenching tool, two first aid kits, flashlight (right center), compass (bottom right) and a canteen filled with water. Most carried extra .30-caliber machine gun ammunition or other special items such a machete (bottom left). Officers and NCOs carried a .45-caliber pistol (bottom center) with holster and ammunition. Officers carried hand held radios known as walkie-talkies (right center) and flares contained in canvas bags (left). The average combat load including the main and reserve parachutes, weighed around eighty to ninety pounds. *United States Army Signal Corps photograph, National Archives.*

This gear is typical for a non-commissioned officer, which included a Thompson submachine gun, binoculars (right), a map case (right center), and fighting knife (center). *United States Army Signal Corps photograph, National Archives.*

This demolitionist's gear includes a pack (top center) containing cans of C2 plastic explosives, detonator cord, and detonator caps. This photo shows a .45-caliber Thompson submachine gun with a fifty round drum instead of a twenty round clip. *United States Army Signal Corps photograph, National Archives.*

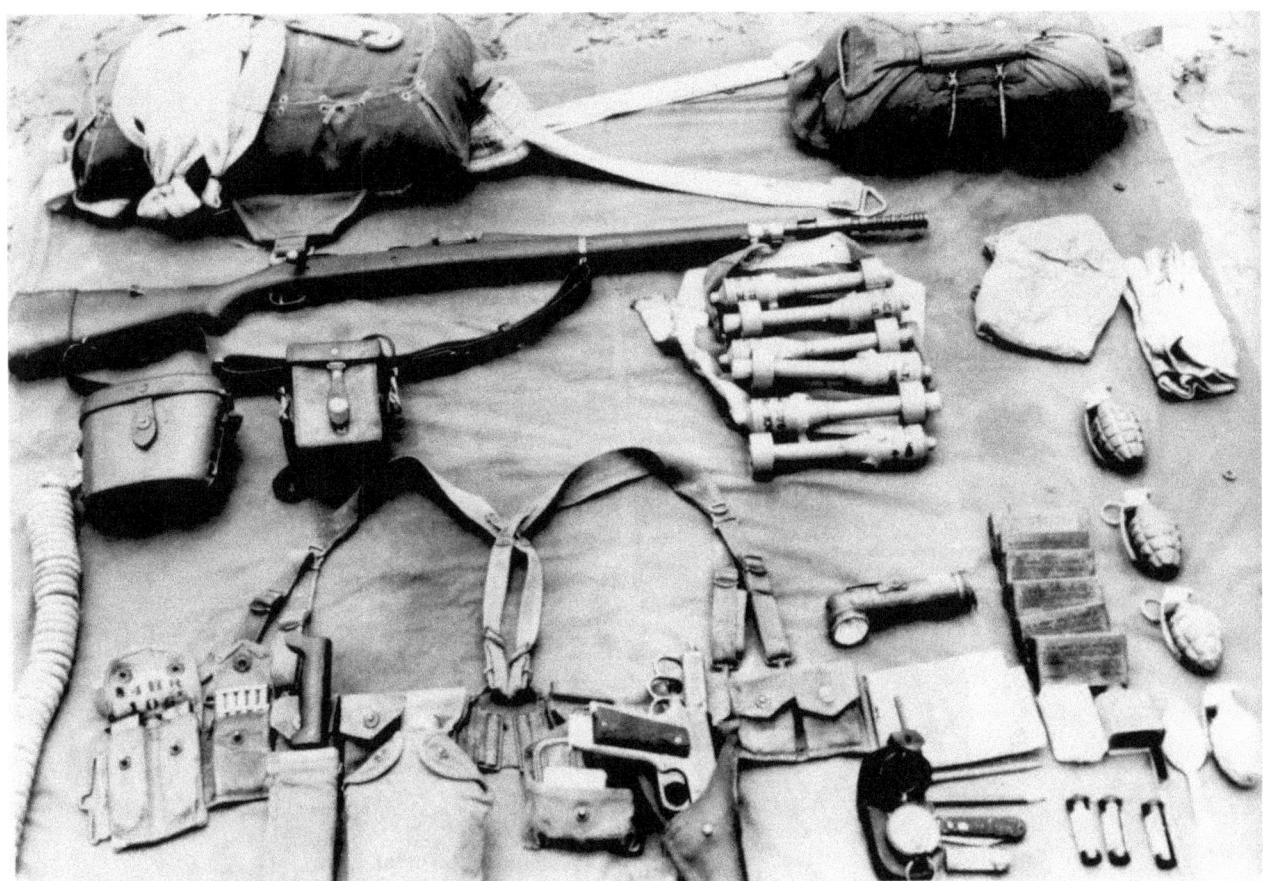

A rifle grenadier's equipment included a 1903 bolt action Springfield rifle with a grenade launcher attachment and six rifle grenades (right) as well as a .45-caliber pistol (bottom) or a folding stock carbine for personal protection. *United States Army Signal Corps photograph, National Archives.*

This bazooka gunner's equipment includes the rocket launcher (left), a rocket with six more in tubes in canvas bags (center), and a folding stock M1 carbine (right). *United States Army Signal Corps photograph, National Archives.*

Equipment bundles containing crew served weapons, ammunition, medical supplies, communications equipment, spare parts, and many other items are loaded under the belly of a C-47 troop transport aircraft at an airfield near Enfidaville, outside of Kairouan, Tunisia prior to the invasion of Sicily. *United States Air Force photograph, www.fold3.com.*

We had an early supper and at 16:00 hours trucks carried each group to their C-47's that were manned by the 52nd Troop Carrier Wing. After the equipment bundles were checked and loaded, we crawled under the wing, in the shade and relaxed. —Sergeant William T. Dunfee, Company I, 505th Parachute Infantry

We loaded the 75mm howitzer in six bundles underneath the plane and had a door load of a padded box, containing the sight and breach block and a bundle of the two wheels [of the howitzer] strapped together. —Private First Class Douglas Bailey, Battery B, 456th Parachute Field Artillery Battalion

Three men from the air corps were struggling on the tarmac to load one of our equipment bundles onto the plane. [Lieutenant Waverly W.] Wray was walking by at the time and observed them for a moment, then picked the [door bundle] up and hefted it inside, much to the amazement of the men. As he walked away, one of the men exclaimed, 'Geez, all you paratroopers that strong!' Well, no—as much as we'd like that image, we're not. He was strong, even for a paratrooper. He was an unusually strong man. I suppose he could, without exaggeration, be called 'powerful. —Private David V. Bowman, Company D, 505th Parachute Infantry

These troopers attach equipment bundles to racks beneath the aircraft. One of the paratroopers used switches located inside the aircraft near the door to release the equipment bundles carried on the racks during the jump. *United States Army Signal Corps photograph, National Archives.*

Private Thomas Lane, from Fort Worth, Texas and a member of Company I, 504th Parachute Infantry takes refuge from the stifling heat of Tunisia in the shade provided by a C-47 aircraft. An equipment bundle is secured to one of the plane's racks. *United States Air Force photograph, www.fold3.com.*

The assistant division commander, Brigadier General Charles L. "Bull" Keerans, Jr. extends his hand to wish Colonel Gavin good luck, July 9, 1943. *United States Army Signal Corps photograph, National Archives.*

Colonel Gavin shakes hands with General Keerans before leaving for Sicily, July 9, 1943. *United States Army Signal Corps photograph, National Archives.*

Colonel James M. Gavin (left), commanding officer of the reinforced 505th Regimental Combat Team, poses with Colonel Jerome B. McCauley (second from left), the commanding officer of the 316th Troop Carrier Group, who would fly the aircraft carrying Gavin and his stick of headquarters troopers; Jack "Beaver" Thompson, a war correspondent who worked for the *Chicago Tribune* newspaper; and an unidentified member of Gavin's stick prior to taking off for Sicily on the evening of July 9–10, 1943. *United States Army Signal Corps photograph, courtesy of William S. Mandle.*

At this time we were given the password, being 'George-Marshall' and told our destination by a mimeographed note given to each of us from Gavin. —Sergeant William T. Dunfee, Company I, 505th Parachute Infantry

Soldiers Of The 505th Combat Team

 Tonight you embark upon a combat mission for which our people and the free people of the world have been waiting for two years. You will spearhead the landing of the American Force upon the island of Sicily. Every preparation has been made to eliminate the element of chance. You have been given the means to do the job and you are backed by the largest assemblage of air power in the world's history. The eyes of the world are upon you. The hopes and prayers of every American go with you. Since it is our first fight at night you must use the countersign and avoid firing on each other. The bayonet is the night fighter's best weapon. Conserve your water and ammunition. The term American Parachutist has become synonymous with courage of a high order. Let us carry the fight to the enemy and make the American Parachutist feared and respected through all his ranks. Attack violently. Destroy him wherever found. Good landing, good fight, and good luck.

Colonel Gavin
Commanding

Colonel Gavin (standing, left) addresses the members of his stick prior to them putting on their parachutes and equipment and boarding their aircraft, July 9, 1943. *United States Army Signal Corps photograph, National Archives.*

Final briefings were held to reassure each man of his part in the overall plan. Invasion armbands, which bore the American flag, were issued to be worn by all personnel on their right arms, and strips of white cloth, which were to be worn on the left arm for night identification purposes, were also issued. Individual parachutes were issued and left in the planes for use that night. Pilot–jumpmaster conferences were held later in the day, at which time the complete air force and airborne plans for the drop were discussed. It was important that all airborne personnel knew the type of formation to be flown, checkpoints, air support, and air force instructions concerning the actual drop. It was at these conferences that all questions were answered and the air force-airborne team understood their mutual mission. It was at these conferences, also, that the airborne troop leaders found out that the objective area, which they knew so well, was located in Sicily. During the afternoon, the men dressed for combat. And after the evening meal, company commanders gave final briefings. —Lieutenant Robert M. Piper, Headquarters, 505th Parachute Infantry Regiment

At 6 p.m. we go to the airfield outside Enfidaville—a book on Sicily, a letter from the colonel and final instructions were provided. Campbell, the cameraman, is nervous as I adjust his chute for him. He can hardly breathe. It's his first jump, first night jump, first combat jump. But the rest of us are at ease. It's like the rest of the jumps. —Private First Class Donald L. Adrianson, Headquarters Company, 505th Parachute Infantry Regiment

A colonel who would lead the combat team into action was giving a last-minute briefing to enlisted men, officers, and one war correspondent who would ride and jump with him. It was a kind of sacred huddle—this briefing. The general's staff officers who came to wish them luck stood off to one side. It was a strange, fascinating sight—men with faces blackened and American flags freshly sewn on their sleeves gathered at the feet of their commander. The colonel, tallest of them all and his face more liberally smudged with blackening until he was darkest of them all, spoke his final commands: stowing of equipment, no smoking while in flight, the appointed rendezvous, timing of departure, time of replacing "Mae West" life jacket with chute, time over dropping zone. He outlined their procedure after hitting the ground. His words were calm, cool, and direct. The time for pep talks had passed. The operations had started. "You'd better do it in a hurry," the colonel added, "for there are going to be a lot of itchy trigger fingers." The briefing ended. The men had a few minutes for a smoke, a drink of water, and a little talk. —Sergeant Jack Foisie, correspondent, *Stars and Stripes*

Paratroopers assist one another in tightening the straps of their parachute harnesses to prevent injury during the opening of their canopies and other straps holding their equipment, ammunition, and weapons to prevent them being ripped from their bodies by the force of the parachutes' opening. *United States Air Force photograph, www.fold3.com.*

Africa was a living hell. We knew that Sicily couldn't be any worse. We were looking forward to it. By the time we were ready to go to Sicily, we were more than glad to go. —Private Russell D. McConnell, Company H, 505th Parachute Infantry

I struggled with all the equipment trying to get in the door. —Private Markus Rupaner, Company B, 505th Parachute Infantry

We didn't have too many thoughts—we were very quiet, loaded down with gear. Nobody said much. We knew we were finally getting into the war. —Staff Sergeant Joseph I. O'Jibway, Company B, 505th Parachute Infantry

No one knew what to expect or what was about to happen. Each was nervous and frightened. —Private Irvin W. "Turk" Seelye, Company E, 505th Parachute Infantry

"O.K., load up," ordered the colonel. The men drew the last puff of smoke, tightened the chin straps on their helmets and climbed aboard. One by one they disappeared into the cabin. Their commander saluted an assembled group then climbed inside, taking the seat nearest the door, since he would be the first to jump. The plane was piloted by Colonel Jerome C. McCauley of Denison, Texas. The copilot was Captain Albert Faby of Rome, Georgia. Upon their skill depended the initial success of the mission. The motors roared to life. All over the field motors of many transports filled with Yank paratroopers began roaring and the roar resounded over many other fields in North Africa. It was dusk and the wind still blew. From darkening corners taxied the transports. The colonel's plane rose gracefully like a bird and one by one the others nosed through the dust clouds and rose into the night air in smart formations of three each. Fighters hovered above them and above the fighters passed wave after wave of bombers. The sky was filled with planes as far as the eye could see. The liberation of Europe had begun. —Sergeant Jack Foisie, correspondent, *Stars and Stripes*

Paratroopers with the 505th Regimental Combat Team wait for the word to finish putting on their gear in preparation for the combat jump on the night of July 9–10, 1943. *United States Army Signal Corps photograph, courtesy of William S. Mandle.*

Information of the enemy indicated that the entire island of Sicily had been prepared for defense. Towns, consisting almost entirely of stone buildings, were reported organized as centers of resistance. All beaches were reported protected by batteries, pillboxes, barbed wire, and mines. Roads were understood to be blocked by antitank obstacles. Strength of the defenders was stated to be somewhat between 300,000 and 400,000 men. The plan for the invasion of Sicily provided for landings to be made on the southeastern extremity of the island, with British and Canadian forces on the east coast and American forces on the south coast. The American assault forces were to consist of the 3rd, 1st, and 45th Infantry Divisions, with attached units, which were to land in the Licata, Gela, and Sampiere vicinities, respectively, and parachute troops from the 82nd Airborne Division, which were to land inland from Gela. The plan of invasion called for one parachute combat team of the 82nd Airborne Division to drop just north of an important road about seven miles [north]east of Gela, between known large enemy reserves and the 1st Division's beaches, with the mission of preventing these reserves from interfering with amphibious landings. The assaulting paratroopers were the 505th Combat Team, commanded by Colonel James M. Gavin, reinforced by the 3rd Battalion, 504th Parachute Infantry Regiment, and their mission was thus stated in Field Order #6, issued by the II Corps: (1) Land during the night D-1/D in area N and E of Gela, capture and secure high ground in that area. (2) Disrupt communications and movement of reserves during night. (3) Be attached to 1st Infantry Division effective H plus 1-Hour on D-Day. (4) Assist 1st Infantry Division in capturing and securing landing field at Ponte Olivo. In compliance with Field Order #1, of Force 343 (Seventh Army), the division devised a movement table, under which the 504th Parachute Infantry Combat Team, as a second lift, was alerted for movement the evening of D-Day; or, in the event of negative instructions at that time, the evening of D plus 1, or any day thereafter. —Captain Adam A. Komosa, Headquarters Company, 504th Parachute Infantry

We loaded into the C-47 "Georgia Peach" and took off for our first combat jump, just as it was getting dark. For me, it was to be my thirteenth parachute jump and probably for a lot of the other guys. —Private Dennis G. O'Loughlin, Company E, 505th Parachute Infantry

These paratroopers are assisted in boarding by the aircraft's crew chief. The trooper climbing the ladder has chosen to secure his musette bag and shovel on his left hip and thigh. *United States Air Force photograph, www.fold3.com.*

Paratroopers with the 505th Parachute Infantry ready for takeoff for Sicily. They wore armbands with the American flag on their right arms and white armbands on their left arms for friendly identification. *United States Air Force photograph, www.www.fold3.com.*

This photo of troopers with the 3rd Battalion, 504th Parachute Infantry was taken shortly before takeoff. *Photograph by Robert Capa.*

Lieutenant Colonel Charles W. Kouns (standing), the commanding officer of the 3rd Battalion, 504th Parachute Infantry, talks to the men of his plane's stick shortly before takeoff for Sicily. *Photograph by Robert Capa.*

Troop carrier planes begin taking off from wide dirt runways with the C-47s staggered to avoid the dust clouds of planes taking off ahead of them. *United States Army Signal Corps film still image.*

By the takeoff time for Sicily, the men were so lean and tough, so mean and mad, that they would have jumped into the fires of torment just to get out of Africa. Gavin had done a prodigious job preparing for that attack, and we were ready, right down to the last round of ammunition. —Major General Matthew B. Ridgway, Headquarters, 82nd Airborne Division

At 19:30 hours 9 July 1943, the first of 226 planes carrying the paratroops began taking off from the dispersed airdromes. —Captain Edwin M. Sayre, Company A, 505th Parachute Infantry

The takeoff was without flaw— lots of dust, and it seemed all planes were soon airborne. There was a lot of chatter among troopers. "How the hell am I going to take a leak or a dump?" "What a relief to get out of A-rab country." "I wonder what Axis Sally looks like." "Does anyone still have a German propaganda (surrender) leaflet?" (No one did.) —Private Berge Avadanian, Headquarters Company, 2nd Battalion, 505th Parachute Infantry

The troop transport aircraft kick up huge clouds of dust behind them as they roll down one of the runways at an airfield outside of Enfidaville on the way to Sicily carrying paratroopers of the 505th Parachute Infantry; the 3rd Battalion, 504th Parachute Infantry; Company B, 307th Airborne Engineer Battalion; and the 456th Parachute Field Artillery Battalion. *United States Army Signal Corps film still image.*

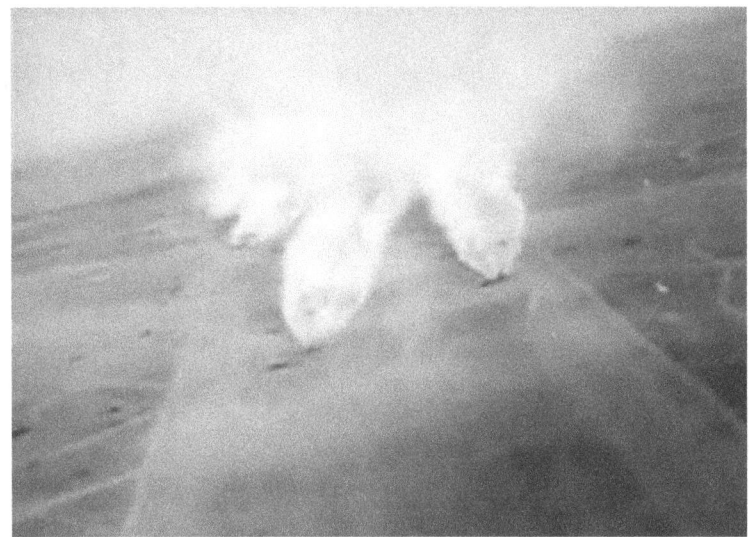

The sunset was beautiful as we climbed in a wide circle to gain altitude; below the shadows had lengthened and turned to darkness. In flock formation of three, we had joined the long line of planes and disappeared into the night out over a darkening sea. The troopers had settled down and I supposed their thoughts were much the same as mine. There was much of my past life I wanted to think over and put in place; it would be a long four hours, the time we were told it took before crossing the Sicilian coast over our destination. "Plenty of time to reminisce," I thought. —Sergeant Otis L. Sampson, Company E, 505th Parachute Infantry

As we took off and Africa fell away from us, we could feel the variety of moods. Some men were anxious, nervous, and sweating profusely, despite the chill in the night air. Others were pumped up with adrenaline and eager to engage the enemy. Still others dropped off to sleep, as if tomorrow were just another day. —Lieutenant T. Moffatt Burriss, Headquarters Company, 3rd Battalion, 504th Parachute Infantry

The air is choppy. We wonder how much ground wind there'll be, but nobody does much talking. The air is choppier when we get over the Mediterranean and [William B.] Drysdale, on my left, gets sick. He vomits so many times he just sits on the floor. So many guys get sick the smell nauseates me. I'm sleepy as the devil from being up the night before. It is a wonder all my buckles are fastened. —Private First Class Donald L. Adrianson, Headquarters Company, 505th Parachute Infantry

The first plane took off at 2010 hrs. and by 2116 the complete combat team was airborne. Since my squad was jumping [from] Captain [Willard R.] Follmer's plane, I was put at the end of the line being the last man out. I was concerned when Follmer put one of the new men between me and the rest of my squad. We had a direct order from Major [Edward C.] Krause to shoot any man that refused to jump. This presented an interesting problem, since had it occurred. My M1 was in a canvas container under my reserve chute. During most of the flight Captain Follmer was spending his time up front with the pilot. I recall asking him if he had them headed in the right direction, he grinned and nodded yes. The air corps was ordered to fly the mission two hundred feet above the water to avoid detection by enemy radio directional finders. The pilots were as green as ourselves and navigation at the time was pretty primitive. They established a heading and flew it for X number of minutes and made their turns as indicated to another heading. This did not take into account the thirty-five miles per hour gale we were experiencing. Consequently the flights became separated and many missed the checkpoints of the small island of Linosa and the larger island of Malta. —Sergeant William T. Dunfee, Company I, 505th Parachute Infantry

The first thought that all was not going just as planned came when the Island of Malta was not sighted on schedule. At about the time the planes should have passed over Malta, the formation ran into heavy headwinds and then began breaking up into small groups. The nine plane formation carrying the battalion commander's group and the 1st and 2nd Platoons and Company Headquarters of Company A managed to stay together. —Captain Edwin M. Sayre, Company A, 505th Parachute Infantry

Part of a nine plane V-of-V formation of C-47 aircraft flies eastward from Tunisia toward Malta, then northwest to Sicily as dusk turns to night on July 9, 1943. *United States Air Force photograph, www.fold3.com.*

Just as we reached the coast of Sicily, we ran into extremely heavy antiaircraft fire. The nervous guys sweated more profusely, the gung-ho types quieted down, and the sleepers woke up. We saw bursts of smoke all around us and heard the explosions. As a defensive maneuver, the formation split up. Our plane banked eastward instead of westward, and suddenly the red light came on. That meant ten minutes until jump time. I gave the order, "Stand up and hook up." Then, only a minute later, the green light flashed. I hadn't even given the command to check equipment, which was normal procedure, but we had no time. The green light meant that we were over the target area. If we didn't jump immediately, we would be too far away to carry out our mission. "Go!" I shouted. —Lieutenant T. Moffatt Burriss, Headquarters Company, 3rd Battalion, 504th Parachute Infantry

The pilot turned on the red light designating to me that we had five minutes before the jump. We stood up, had our equipment check procedure, and I was standing in the door as we approached the town of Gela. I would guess that our altitude was about eight hundred feet, because the scheduled jump height was five hundred feet. Suddenly we were in the center of what could best be described as a large Fourth of July fireworks celebration. Puffs of smoke and fireballs began to appear near our plane, and tracers could be seen headed our way. Our pilot must have decided that it was time to get out of there because he put the plane in a bank and steep climb mode that was so severe that I had to hang on to the sides of the open doorway to keep from falling down or out. Very shortly thereafter, the green light came on over the doorway indicating that it was time to jump. Before leaving North Africa, I had been given a landmark of a small lake [Lake Biviere] that was to indicate that we were near our jump area. I could not locate the lake, but decided that the pilot was better oriented than I, and so out we went. Our machine guns and ammunition were packed in bundles and fastened to the carriage underneath the C-47. The bundles each weighed three hundred fifty pounds and were carried by a twenty-four foot parachute, compared to our twenty-eight foot chute that supported a man and equipment of about two hundred fifty pounds. These bundles were released by the C-47's crew chief shortly after we started jumping. This was the highest jump I ever made—must have been up at least 2,000 feet. My chute opened and I was drifting in a bright moonlit sky. As I drifted in the breeze like a feather, I tried to keep track of our equipment that was dropping very rapidly straight down. I made my first tree landing in an olive tree. I didn't know how high I was off the ground. But after cutting off a few parachute suspension lines with my switchblade, my one foot touched the ground, indicating that I was only a couple of feet off of the ground. I unhooked myself from the parachute harness and stood there listening. The night was completely silent except for some dog barking some distance away. I started walking in the direction of where I assumed my men were. —Lieutenant Roy M. Hanna, Headquarters Company, 3rd Battalion, 504th Parachute Infantry

SICILY

At the time when the planes were supposed to be nearing the drop zone, antiaircraft fire could be seen coming up on the left side of the planes. This could only mean one thing: the planes were coming in on the wrong side of the island. The flight commander realized this and the formation was turned back out to sea in order to make another attempt to find the correct drop zone. After about an hour, a lake, which was the final checkpoint, was sighted. The planes turned over the lake in the direction to bring them over the drop zone in about two minutes. After proceeding about one minute and a half, the formation met heavy antiaircraft fire and began breaking up. One minute later the green 'go' light was given and the parachutists left the planes. I led my group out and a few seconds later disentangled myself from my parachute in a vineyard on the side of a very steep hill. —Captain Edwin M. Sayre, Company A, 505th Parachute Infantry

THE 505TH REGIMENTAL COMBAT TEAM
10-11 JULY 1943

This is an oblique view of a crossroads northeast of Gela where the north-south highway and east-west coastal highway intersected and led to the town. Concrete and stone pillboxes, dug in gun positions, and underground shelters connected by a trench system, overlooked the junction from the ridges paralleling the two roads. German and Italian reserve forces using these highways to counterattack the beach landings in the Gela sector would have to pass through this crossroads. The position was code named Objective Y. The 505th Regimental Combat Team's chief mission was to seize control of this crossroads and establish a blocking position to prevent enemy troops and armor from attacking the Gela beach landings. *United States Air Force photograph, National Archives.*

This view of a portion of the defenses at Objective Y shows an obsolete Italian field gun (left center) in an open concrete position flanked by concrete pillboxes on both sides. Another pillbox is on the ridge in the distance at the upper left of the photo. *United States Army Signal Corps photograph, courtesy of Martin K. A. Morgan.*

This is another of the line of concrete bunkers overlooking Objective Y with underground shelters dug in behind it on the reverse slope. *United States Army Signal Corps photograph, courtesy of Martin K. A. Morgan.*

This concrete and stone pillbox was a typical fortification found throughout much of Sicily. *United States Army Signal Corps photograph.*

The planes rocked back and forth because antiaircraft shells were exploding around them. When the pilot turned the red light on, we stood and hooked up. Some troopers lost their footing before they jumped, and because of the weight and bulk we were carrying, we had to help them back to their feet. When he turned the green light on, we jumped! I made my first combat jump and landed safely. I landed sixty miles from where I was supposed to be, but I was alive—now, I just needed to stay alive and find some fellow troopers. —Private Arnold G. "Dutch" Nagel, Company C, 505th Parachute Infantry

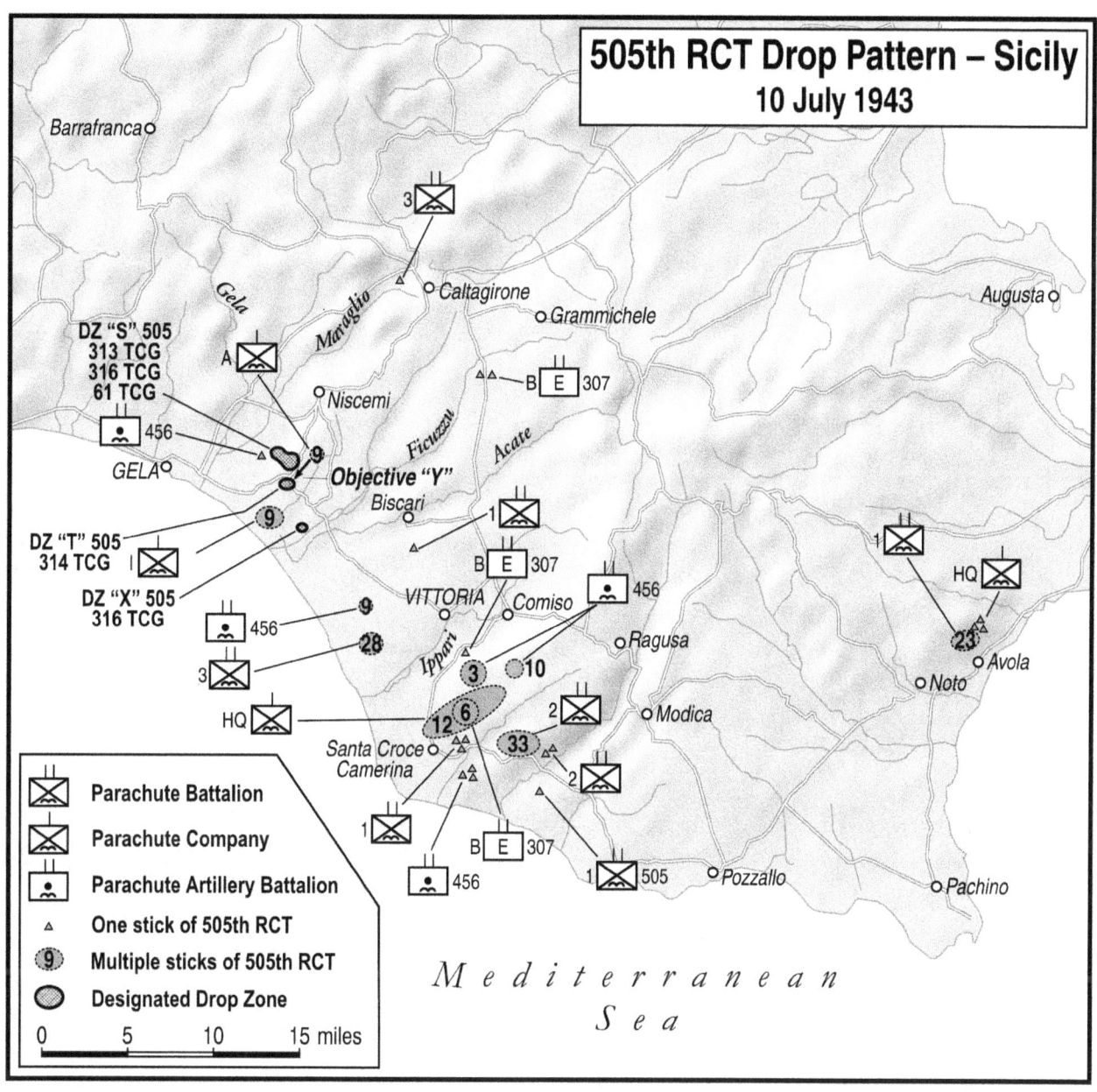

As we approached Sicily and for reasons unknown to this day, the rest of the 3rd Battalion flight turned back out to sea, subsequently returning to be dropped on the wrong D.Z. Pilot Bommar and Captain Follmer, seeing the Acate River in the distance, were satisfied we were on a proper course and the I Company flight proceeded toward Sicily. As we crossed the coastline Follmer told me to pass the word back to "Stand up, hook up and check equipment." This done, we sounded off equipment check, starting with me and moving toward the door. At about this time we were over Lake Biviere, Captain Follmer moving by me said, "About five minutes," and moved on back to his position at the door. Being crowded when we stood up and hooked up, it was necessary for me to step through the bulkhead into the radio operator's area. At this point, I noticed the new man in front of me had sat down. I told him to stand up and he started giving me conversation and I made it very clear to him in four-letter words that he damned well better stand back up. I had noticed the green light had been on for some time when Captain Follmer yelled, 'Let's Go!' and we started moving toward the door. For whatever reason the man in front of me went past the door into the tail section of the plane. I grabbed his backpack and pulled him back to the door. He started to back off again, so I grabbed the sides of the door opening and pulled us both out. I had no more than felt the shock of the parachute opening, when I was going through pine trees, hitting the ground going downhill. —Sergeant William T. Dunfee, Company I, 505th Parachute Infantry

Major General Ridgway (center with overseas cap with airborne patch) and a member of the 82nd Airborne Division staff on board the USS *Monrovia* observe other naval ships and landing craft. *Photograph, George S. Patton Scrapbook Collection, Library of Congress.*

As it became light, from our vantage point on the deck some distance, maybe a mile offshore, we could make out the smoke and sounds of battle. Reports were not circulated as to progress, but in the absence of negative news, everyone had the feeling the landings had been a success. No word at all about the airborne landings except we knew that they had happened. As for our little group, General Ridgway and his aide had managed to get taken ashore by landing craft early on. —Technician Fourth Grade Leonard Lebenson, Headquarters Company, 82nd Airborne Division

Troopers with the 505th Parachute Infantry who were misdropped in the British sector on the eastern side of Sicily riding in commandeered horse carts move through the city of Avola on July 11, 1943. *Forging Ahead in Sicily, British Pathé film still image.*

Another 505th paratrooper rides a beast of burden through the streets of Avola, July 11, 1943. *Forging Ahead in Sicily, British Pathé film still image.*

Troopers with the 505th arrive in the town square at Avola where they meet British troops who landed by sea the previous day. *Forging Ahead in Sicily, British Pathé film still image.*

This is a close up shot of 505th troopers riding in a horse cart to the town square at Avola. *Forging Ahead in Sicily, British Pathé film still image.*

Troopers gather in the town square of Avola. *Forging Ahead in Sicily, British Pathé film still image.*

Three 505th paratroopers pose for the camera in the town square at Avola, D+1, July 11, 1943. *Forging Ahead in Sicily, British Pathé film still image.*

A paratrooper with the 505th Parachute Infantry who had been dropped near the town of Avola, on the eastern coast of Sicily, some sixty miles from the drop zone enjoys a cigarette while conversing with two British soldiers on D+1, July 11, 1943. *Photograph, British Imperial War Museum.*

As we reached the outskirts of Avola, there was some outlying buildings there, a few little stores. And when we reached that point, an Italian soldier stepped out of the woods and fired a shot at the group, and then turned and ran down the street. The lieutenant, who was armed with a folding stock carbine, shouted, "He's mine. He's mine." And he started trying to shoot him and he made several attempts to fire the carbine, but he had not yet loaded it. The Italian soldier ducked between some carts that were against the building. These were little two wheel freight carts that could be pulled by a donkey or by a man, and he ducked between several of them. The lieutenant directed one of the other enlisted men to run down the street so he could see in this doorway. He said, "Go down the street until you can see in the blue doorway. I said, "No lieutenant, he didn't go that far. He didn't go in a door. He ducked between the carts. The lieutenant countermanded my order and directed him to go ahead as he had told him to do. Well, I realized that he was going to become a victim because the [Italian] guy was waiting behind the carts for someone to come into view. So I just shot through the carts, and this soldier pitched out in the street there, and the bullet had hit him through the chest. I was thoroughly provoked with the lieutenant then because he hadn't loaded his gun and he wanted to shoot this soldier in the back, running away, and because he hadn't organized the patrol. So I announced that I was going to part company with that group and go on further on my own and anyone who wanted to go with me was welcome to go. Several of them stepped out. Well, the lieutenant quickly began to apologize for the fact that they weren't well organized and promised to lead a well directed platoon and he started barking orders. He said, "You two guys will be on point, you go down the road two hundred yards. The rest of you divide up an equal number on both sides of the road, ten yards apart. He turned to me and said, "You, you'll be the rear guard. You stay two hundred yards to the rear. Well, I waited to see if the other guys were going to accept his command. Anyway they did; they began to form up. So I stood there until the platoon formed and moved out and they were in proper formation and he was walking in the middle of the road. I presumed we were going to give arm and hand signals. So I waited until they were down the road a couple of hundred yards, and then I started walking down [the road] and looking to the rear, walked backwards most of the time. After going a few hundred yards, I heard [noise in] a building that we had passed by, and it was a scraping sound. We hadn't seen anyone else except Italian soldiers, so I stopped to determine where the sound came from. I could tell it was coming from an upper story of a building that was built right up to the sidewalk, or right up to the street. I tried to get the attention of the rest of the patrol because there was a likelihood of a danger to their rear that they needed to be aware of. But, I couldn't get their attention—they kept walking. Finally, I found the source of the noise. The roof sloped down toward the street and there was a hole in the roof. I saw a hand pulling slate shingles enlarging the hole. He pulled a shingle out and placed it over, aside. I knew that he was in the attic and he was making a hole big enough that he could raise up through the hole. I had no idea who he was or anything other than that, but I had to wait because my obligation was to protect the patrols from the rear. So I stood there and waited, and soon a long rifle came out, and I knew that wasn't American. He laid the rifle down on that roof. Then a head came out—he had long hair and a beard—he hadn't shaved in weeks. He was obviously an Italian soldier and I shot him. I had imagined that he was in the attic standing on the ceiling, but when I shot him, I heard the body hit down at the ground floor. —Corporal Elmo E. Bell, Company C, 505th Parachute Infantry

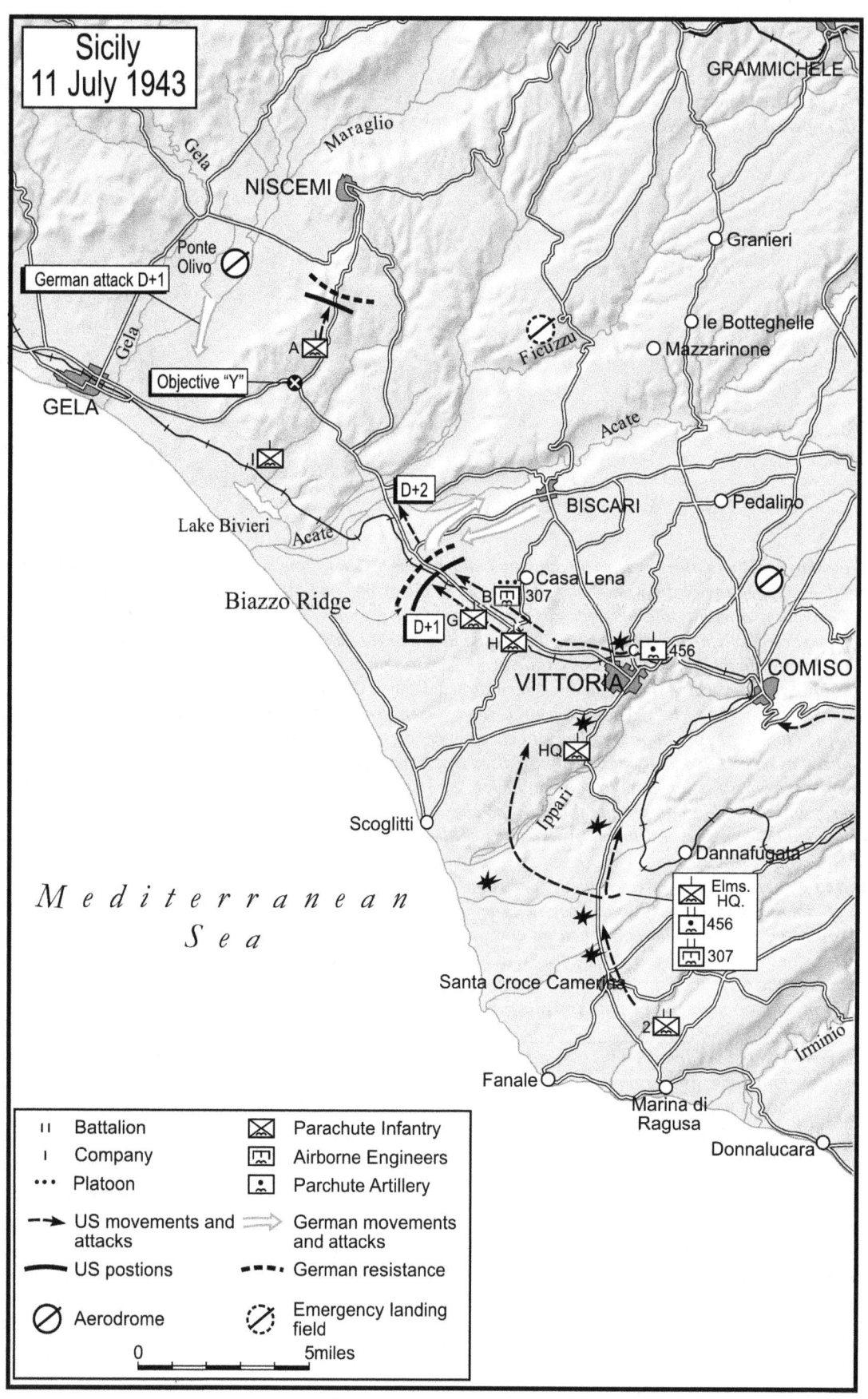

156　SICILY

Paratroopers with the 3rd Battalion, 505th Parachute Infantry moving northwest on Highway 115 from Vittoria toward Gela take a break at the gatekeeper's house where railroad tracks cross the highway, on the morning of July 11, 1943. *United States Army Signal Corps photograph, National Archives.*

I continued on toward Gela and to my surprise came across the 3rd Battalion of the 505th, in foxholes in a tomato field and just awakening. The battalion commander, [Major] Edward Krause, whose nickname was "Cannonball," was sitting on the edge of a foxhole, dangling his feet. I asked him what his battalion was doing. He said that he had been reorganizing the battalion and that he had about 250 troopers present. He had landed nearby and had rounded everybody up. I asked him about his objective, several miles to the west near Gela, and he said that he had not done anything about it. I said we would move at once toward Gela and told him to get his battalion on its feet and going. In the meantime, I took a platoon of the 307th engineers, commanded by Lieutenant [Ben L.] Weschler. Krause said that there were supposed to be Germans between where he was and Gela and that the 45th Division had been having a difficult time. Using the platoon of engineers as infantry, we moved at once on the road to Gela. We had hardly started when, as we went around a bend in the road, a German motorcycle with an officer in the sidecar drove up in the midst of us. We put our guns on him. He threw up his hands, said he was a medical officer, pointed to his insignia, and told us he wanted to be released at once. We were about to release him. He was the first live German we had seen in combat, and we noticed that he had grenades in the sidecar. Reasoning that an armed medic should not be let loose, we took the motorcycle and sidecar from him and started him to the rear on foot, disarming the driver, also. The medic said they had been moving down from Biscari toward Vittoria. We could hear a great deal of firing, so we continued. —Colonel James M. Gavin, Headquarters, 505th Parachute Infantry

Two members of the group, Jack "Beaver" Thompson (left), a war correspondent with the *Chicago Tribune*, and Colonel Jim Gavin (right), the commanding officer of the 505th Parachute Infantry, talk while standing next to a stone wall near the railroad gate. Thompson had jumped with Gavin's stick on the night of July 9–10, 1943. *United States Army Signal Corps photograph, National Archives.*

This group moves out from the gatekeeper's house toward Biazzo Ridge, a short distance away, which would become the scene of intense fighting a short time later. *United States Army Signal Corps photograph, National Archives.*

It was broad daylight, about 8:30 a.m. In less than a mile we reached a point where a small railroad crossed the road. On the right was a house where the gatekeeper lived. There was a striped pole that could be lowered to signal the automotive and donkey-cart traffic when a train approached. Just ahead was a ridge, about half a mile away and perhaps a hundred feet high. The slope to the top was gradual. On both sides of the road were olive trees and beneath them tall brown and yellow grass, burnt by the hot Sicilian summer sun. I told Lieutenant Weschler to deploy his platoon on the right and to move on to seize the ridge. In the meantime I sent word to Cannonball to bring his battalion up as promptly as he could. We moved forward. I was with Weschler, and in a few hundred yards the fire became intense. As we neared the top of the ridge, there was a rain of leaves and branches as bullets tore through the trees, and there was a buzzing like the sound of swarms of bees. A few moments later Weschler was hit and fell. Some troopers were hit; others continued to crawl forward. Soon we were pinned down by heavy small arms fire, but so far nothing else. I made my way back to the railroad crossing and in about twenty minutes Major [William J.] Hagan [III] joined me. He was the battalion executive officer for the 3rd Battalion. He said the battalion was coming up. I asked where Cannonball was, and he said that he had gone back to the 45th Division to tell them what was going on. I ordered Hagan to have the troops drop their packs and get ready to attack the Germans on the ridge as soon as they came up. By that time, we had picked up part of a company from the 45th Division that happened to be there, part of a company from the 180th Infantry. There was also a sailor or two who had come ashore in the amphibious landings. We grabbed them, also. —Colonel James M. Gavin, Headquarters, 505th Parachute Infantry

The same group ascends the eastern slope of Biazzo Ridge and move through the orchard to engage Kampfgruppe Links of Fallschirm-Panzer Division 1 Hermann Göring, on the other side of the ridge. This kampfgruppe consisted of two battalions of motorized infantry of Panzer Grenadier Regiment 1, two batteries of armored artillery battalion, and a company of Mark VI Tiger I tanks of Kompanie 2, Schwere Panzer Abteilung 504. *United States Army Signal Corps photograph, National Archives.*

The attack went off as planned, and the infantry reached the top of the ridge and continued to attack down the far side. As they went over the top of the ridge, the fire became intense. We were going to have a very serious situation on our hands. This was not a patrol or platoon action. Mortar and artillery fire began to fall on the ridge, and there was considerable machine gun fire. —Colonel James M. Gavin, Headquarters, 505th Parachute Infantry

They were at the crest of the hill. It amounted to a bayonet fight. They ordered us to fix bayonets and I said, "Oh Lord, help me." —Sergeant Hunter M. "Bill" Bishop, Jr., Company G, 505th Parachute Infantry

You could hear the German tanks milling about. All of a sudden they told us to charge up, and we all started running up over the ridge. —Private Russell D. McConnell, Company H, 505th Parachute Infantry

H Company came through us, since we had fought up to the crest of the hill, and they went over and engaged in a bayonet fight, and that was a bloody, terrible looking sight. I didn't see it, but could hear it. We saw it when we followed H Company, just mangled up bodies. [The Germans] had quite a few killed and they pulled out. —Sergeant Hunter M. "Bill" Bishop, Jr., Company G, 505th Parachute Infantry

The whole fight didn't seem to last too long until we drove them off. They were shooting at us, and we were shooting back at them. I saw dead Germans, but I don't know whether I hit anyone. —Private Russell D. McConnell, Company H, 505th Parachute Infantry

These troopers set up communications using a couple of radios as they try to get a view of the battle raging on the opposite slope and flat ground beyond. *United States Army Signal Corps photograph, National Archives.*

I saw one of our troopers draped over the limb of a tree, quite dead. Suddenly it started...unmistakable ripping noises that were bursts from a rapid-fire German machine gun. Having never heard the sound of 1,200 rounds per minute, I thought, "What was that?" But it took only a minute or two to figure it out. It was impossible to distinguish a single burst. Running down the embankment with the others, I lay prone there for most of the day. Initially, the Germans fired [white] phosphorous shells that started to burn the foliage and grass, but proved ineffectual. The Tiger tank got me in its sights, traversed its machine gun, fired a burst, then traversed three or four clicks and fired another burst. The first burst stitched up the ground inches from me on one side, while the next burst stitched up the ground inches from me on the other side. Any lesser clicks, traversing from left to right would have cut me in two. —Lieutenant Robert A. Fielder, Headquarters Company, 3rd Battalion, 505th Parachute Infantry

This ridge was a hard place to dig a foxhole, and I finally dug a slit trench. It was hard shale, and with extra hard work I finally got it about twenty inches deep, when I saw the tank. We had no idea the Germans [we had attacked] had tanks, let alone Tiger tanks. I saw the tank rotate its gun toward me and I jumped into the hole. It shot and hit an oak tree about twelve feet from my hole. It ran over me [while lying in the slit trench] and twisted [its treads] over the hole. I think I lost consciousness for a short period. I was completely covered with dirt. —Private First Class Cloid B. Wigle, Company H, 505th Parachute Infantry

An officer ventures forward to observe the fighting on the far slope. Two antennas indicate that radios are set up and the trooper at the left has a walkie-talkie sitting on the ground immediately in front of him. *United States Army Signal Corps photograph, National Archives.*

Me and a fellow named [Technician Fourth Grade Henry D.] Duke Boswell were lying within two or three feet of the tank treads in a small ditch. They would shoot at a single man with the 88s they had on those tanks. They killed a bunch of people with that 88. They ran over one man's legs. Of course, he died from shock. His name was [Sergeant] Gerald [L.] Ludlam. We had two bazooka men [Private First Class Earl H. Wright and Private Kenneth L. Harris] and they knocked the track off the first tank that pulled out of this little village. The second tank came around the disabled tank and luckily he jammed the turret and so he withdrew. The third tank saw what was happening and he too withdrew. Bazooka men were in great peril because the first thing they would try to knock out was the bazooka men. —Sergeant Hunter M. "Bill" Bishop, Jr., Company G, 505th Parachute Infantry

J. D. [Private James D.] Long and I were together. He was packing a bazooka. We spotted a German tank, and believing everything you were told in training, we thought we would be able to disable the tank with what equipment we were carrying. As we were running toward the tank, the turret swung around and they fired at J. D. They hit him dead center. They then started turning the turret in my direction. I dove behind a tree, its trunk at least two and one half feet in diameter. When they fired, they hit the tree about three feet above the ground, cutting it completely in two. The next thing I remember was trying to stop the flow of blood from my right arm or shoulder. I couldn't do it, so I thought it best if I could get to the aid station on my own. I knew where it was because we had come by it when we first got to Biazzo Ridge. —Private Richard E. "Pat" Reid, Company H, 505th Parachute Infantry

An 81mm mortar is set up in the orchard to the right rear of the troopers fighting for Biazzo Ridge to provide indirect fire support. *United States Army Signal Corps photograph, National Archives.*

I was worried about being enveloped on the right; some of the 45th Infantry Division should have been down on the left toward the beaches, but the right was wide open, and so far I had no one I could send out to protect that flank. If the German column was coming from Biscari, the tactical logic would have suggested that they bypass me on the right and attack me from the rear. At that time I had a few engineers I kept in reserve and two 81mm mortars. The first wounded began to crawl back over the ridge. They all told the same story. They fired their bazookas at the front plate of German tanks, and then the tanks swiveled their huge 88mm guns at them and fired at individual infantrymen. By this time the tanks could be heard, although I could not see any because of the smoke and dust and the cover of vegetation. [Major] Hagan came in, walking and holding his thigh, which had been badly torn by fire. Cannonball [Lieutenant Colonel Edward C. Krause] had gone forward to command the attack. It did not seem to be getting anywhere however, as the German fire increased in intensity and our wounded were coming back in greater numbers. The first German prisoners also came back. They said they were from the Hermann Göring Parachute Panzer Division. I remember one of them asking if we had fought the Japanese in the Pacific; he said he asked because the paratroopers had fought so hard. I went back a few hundred yards to check the 81mm mortars and to see what other troopers had joined us. A few had. Lieutenant [Robert L.] May had been hit by mortar fragments. I talked to the crews of the two pack 75mm artillery pieces and told them we were going to stay on the ridge no matter what happened. We agreed that they should stay concealed and engage the less heavily armored underbellies of the tanks when they appeared at the top of the rise. It was a dangerous tactic, but the only thing we could do, and tanks are vulnerable in that position. I was determined that if the tanks overran us we would stay and fight the infantry. —Colonel James M. Gavin, Headquarters, 505th Parachute Infantry

Paratroopers with the 505th Parachute Infantry examine one of the four Mark VI Tiger I tanks knocked out during the battle for Biazzo Ridge. Of particular note is the presence of four bazookas in the photo (upper right, right center, center, and lower left). That night, the Germans recovered three of the four tanks, including the one in this photo, leaving only the one in the following photos in possession by the Americans. *Photograph courtesy of Gilles Guignard.*

At about six o'clock I heard that Lieutenant Harold H. Swingler and quite a few troopers from regimental headquarters company were on the road. Swingler had been a former intercollegiate boxing champion; he was a tough combat soldier. He arrived about seven o'clock. In his wake appeared half a dozen of our own Sherman tanks. All the troopers cheered loud and long. It was a dramatic moment. The Germans must have heard the cheering, although they did not know then what it was about. They soon found out...By now no more wounded were coming back. A heavy pall of dust and acrid smoke covered the battlefield. I decided it was time to counterattack. I wanted to destroy the German force in front of us and to recover our dead and wounded. I felt that if I could do this and at the same time secure the ridge, I would be in good shape for whatever came next—probably a German attack against our defenses at daylight, with us having the advantage of holding the ridge. Our attack jumped off on schedule; regimental clerks, cooks, truck drivers, everyone who could carry a rifle or carbine was in the attack. The Germans reacted, and their fire increased in intensity. Just about two hundred yards from the top of the ridge, Swingler crawled up on a cut through which the paved road ran and saw a German Tiger tank with the crew standing outside, looking at it. He dropped a grenade among them and killed them, and thus we captured our first Tiger. There were several bazooka hits on the front plate with holes large enough to put one's little finger into them, but they went in only about an inch or so. The sloped armor on the Tiger was about four and a half inches thick. Soon we overran German machine guns, a couple of trucks, and finally we captured twelve 120mm Russian mortars, all in position with their ammunition nearby and aiming stakes out. Apparently the troopers had either killed, captured, or driven off the German crews. The attack continued, and all German resistance disappeared, the Germans having fled the battlefield. —Colonel James M. Gavin, Headquarters, 505th Parachute Infantry

The two photos on this page are differing views of the same Mark VI Tiger I tank. Captain Harold H. "Swede" Swingler, the commanding officer of Service Company, 505th killed the entire crew as they stood outside of the tank on Highway 115 on the southwestern side of Biazzo Ridge, July 11, 1943. *United States Army Signal Corps photographs.*

This still image of a United States Army Signal Corps film shows the Mark VI tank captured by Captain Swingler sometime after the prior photos as the tank's 88mm main gun muzzle brake has been removed from the barrel. *United States Army Signal Corps film still image.*

This is a second view of the tank with a DUWK driving west past it on Highway 115. *United States Army Signal Corps film still image.*

Major Edward C. Krause (left), the commanding officer of the 3rd Battalion, 505th Parachute Infantry, stands beside a 75mm PAK 40 antitank gun captured after driving a powerful German kampfgruppe from the field at Biazzo Ridge, July 11, 1943.

The photos above and below depict the terrible cost of the victory at Biazzo Ridge. The bodies of the paratroopers killed during the battle have been collected and await burial. *United States Army Signal Corps photographs, National Archives.*

German prisoners captured during the battle for Biazzo Ridge dig graves to bury the dead paratroopers in a small temporary cemetery at the edge of the ridge's orchard. *Photographs courtesy of Jerome V. Huth.*

Captain [Alexander P.] Pete Suer had taken over an ambulance from the 45th Division, and we used that to evacuate the men to the seacoast and to the navy. We had around forty-five killed and 150 wounded. Father [Captain Matthew J.] Connelly and Reverend [Captain] George [B.] Wood were quite busy consoling the men as well as burying the dead, and when they had the opportunity, also served as litter bearers and did their share of bandaging up the wounded. Father Connelly and Chaplain Wood buried sixty-seven on Biazzo Ridge. These great men can never secure the credit they so rightly deserve.
—Captain Daniel B. McIlvoy, Jr., Medical Detachment, 3rd Battalion, 505th Parachute Infantry

Sergeant [Tony] Castillo, first sergeant of G Company, was in charge of the burial detail. He was a Pueblo Indian from Colorado. German POWs were digging graves and Castillo gave them a rough time. —Sergeant Frederick W. Randall, Company H, 505th Parachute Infantry

When we marched past where their graves were, that's when it really hit. We had lost some of our closest friends. —Private Russell D. McConnell, Company H, 505th Parachute Infantry

We had triumphed, but there were no pats on the back; we had a long way to go yet and some of the men would accompany us no more. —Sergeant Frank M. Miale, Company B, 307th Airborne Engineer Battalion

We moved to a bivouac north of Gela several miles where a reorganization took place. We were still having men come in. The combat team remained there for about three days when we moved up the southwest coast in division reserve.—Colonel James M. Gavin, Headquarters, 505th Parachute Infantry

Paratroopers pose with a captured German Mark IV tank. This photo has been identified as being a captured Mark VI Tiger tank after the battle at Biazzo Ridge, but the sprocket wheel of the tank reveals it to be a Mark IV, which makes the more likely location Piano Lupo, where less than one hundred Company A and Headquarters Company, 1st Battalion, 505th paratroopers captured the regimental objective, a key road junction codenamed Objective Y.

We had been on the hill for about an hour when we were hit by a heavy German tank attack. Six tanks were coming directly toward the battalion positions and about twenty more hitting the 26th Infantry about four hundred yards to the battalion's rear and left flank. The rawness of the replacements of the 2nd Battalion [16th Infantry, 1st Infantry Division] now became evident for the first time. When most of them saw the tanks coming, they jumped from their foxholes and started running to the rear. About one-third of that battalion and all of the parachutists stuck to their positions. The tanks were soon on top of the battalion positions. The troops were fighting back desperately with rocket launchers, rifle grenades, machine guns, rifles, pistols, and throwing hand grenades. One of the tanks was knocked out by [Lieutenant] Colonel [Arthur F.] Gorham with a rocket launcher. Two officers of the 2nd Battalion managed to get a 57mm gun, which had been deserted by its crew, into action. They also knocked out a tank. When this tank was knocked out, the remaining tanks withdrew to the battalion's left flank. The desperate fighting of the American troops denied them the only covered route of approach to the beaches of the 1st Division. As the tanks could not take the covered route, they continued to the left flank and pushed on toward the beaches. In order to get to the beaches, the tanks were forced to cross a wide open flat piece of terrain about three miles from the beaches. As the tanks started across this open ground, they were taken under fire by U. S. Navy destroyers in the landing area of the 1st Division. When the smoke cleared away, more than fifteen of the enemy's heavy tanks had been knocked out and the others forced to withdraw. Because the 2nd Battalion now only had about two hundred men, [Lieutenant] Colonel [Joseph] Crawford [the commanding officer of the 2nd Battalion, 16th Infantry] decided to withdraw to a hill about five hundred yards to the rear. This hill was almost inaccessible to tanks and gave the battalion a chance to round up their men and reorganize. Many of the men who ran had abandoned crew-served weapons and these all had to be redistributed. The parachutists had picked up six Browning Automatic Rifles and were happy to have them. —Captain Edwin M. Sayre, Company A, 505th Parachute Infantry

We were going to reinforce the 505th Regimental Combat Team, who had jumped on Sicily during the night 9–10 July and as we were to jump behind friendly lines, the operation was supposed to be a milk run. —Private First Class Larry Reber, Battery C, 376th Parachute Field Artillery Battalion

THE 504TH REGIMENTAL COMBAT TEAM
11–12 JULY 1943

A stick of paratroopers with the 504th Parachute Infantry pose in front of their C-47 aircraft prior to gearing up for a combat jump by the 504th Regimental Combat Team on the night of July 11–12, 1943. *Photograph courtesy of Adam A. Komosa.*

We drew our chutes and checked all our equipment. We packed our big equipment, like radios, machine guns and wire equipment in para-packs, which were attached to the bottom of the planes, to be dropped like bombs. That night, sleep was scarce; all the boys' nerves were on the edge. Finally, morning came; we all loaded our equipment on the trucks and left for the airport. We were scattered on several different fields. We loaded the planes up and waited all day for the takeoff. We played cards, sang and told jokes under the wings of the plane Number 63. Some of the boys just sat around in silence, smoking one cigarette after another. —Private Henry D. Ussery, Jr., Headquarters Battery, 376th Parachute Field Artillery Battalion

We moved to the airport and the day was spent busily preparing the final details for the coming night's work. Before you knew it they were serving supper and surprisingly everyone had enough good food to eat. The past weeks had been spent in the desert and the food had not been too palatable. At the signal from the CO we moved to the planes to await zero hour. At the planes we made a final check on the men's equipment and weapons. We made sure that the extra machine guns and ammunition on the [planes'] racks were securely fastened. Then we just sat and waited. It was interesting to listen to the men and the subjects they discussed at this thoughtful hour. Some described in lengthy detail the prettiest girl they had ever seen. Others expressed a wish for a good drink, or a dish of ice cream, or a good cold bottle of beer before they would go. All the men enjoyed the questions and complimenting remarks of the ground crew that would be left behind. The signal came at last. We took our places in the planes and we checked to make sure we had all our men and that we were in the correct places. We also made a final check on the equipment. Whether we knew it or not, we were about to begin the most exciting night of our lives. —Lieutenant Robert D. Condon, Company A, 504th Parachute Infantry

Brigadier General Maxwell D. Taylor (left), the commanding officer of the 82nd Airborne Division artillery, speaks with Colonel Reuben H. Tucker, III, the commanding officer of the 504th Parachute Infantry Regiment, shortly before the 504th Regimental Combat Team (less the 3rd Battalion, 504th Parachute Infantry) took off for Sicily on July 11, 1943. *United States Army Signal Corps photograph, courtesy of William S. Mandle.*

In the photos above and at right, paratroopers fasten the straps to their parachutes and gear as they ready themselves for the combat jump on July 11–12, 1943 near Gela, Sicily. *United States Army Signal Corps photograph above courtesy of William S. Mandle. United States Army Signal Corps photograph at right courtesy of Jan Bos.*

With their jumpsuit pockets bulging, 504th Parachute Infantry paratroopers put on their parachutes before all of the other equipment they have to carry into battle on July 11, 1943. *United States Army Signal Corps photograph, courtesy of Jan Bos.*

Bright sunlight illuminates medics with the 504th Parachute Infantry, who are putting on their gear in preparation for the jump during the night of July 11–12, 1943. *Photograph courtesy of William S. Mandle.*

Paratroopers with the 504th Regimental Combat Team consisting of the 504th Parachute Infantry (less the 3rd Battalion), the 376th Parachute Field Artillery Battalion, and Company C, 307th Airborne Engineer Battalion, begin the process of putting on their gear in preparation for the jump in Sicily on July 11, 1943. *United States Air Force photograph, www.fold3.com.*

At our airfield in Tunisia, we were still calibrating and packing our radios and taking care of the myriad other last minute details. The time went fast and I know that I was tired when I finally boarded. —Captain Paul D. Donnelly, Headquarters Battery, 376th Parachute Field Artillery Battalion

We were [assigned] in sections to each plane: a lieutenant, Sergeant Karl [Claus H. Karlson] and me. I do not remember their names. But there was about ten men in our plane, loaded with 75mm ammunition and radio equipment. I was Number 1 at the door. —Sergeant Elfren Solomon, Battery C, 376th Parachute Field Artillery Battalion

The basic load of combat equipment for the individual parachutist was checked. The bundles and equipment were complete and the aircraft were dispersed according to the parking plan at the departure airfields. The equipment bundles were raised and hooked into the para-packs under the bellies of the planes. Plane loads were lined up near their respective planes. The chutes of each individual were checked by each plane jumpmaster. The troops then emplaned thirty minutes before takeoff. The planning for the final takeoff had been complete and thorough, which, with the execution of the final plans, were probably the outstanding features of the entire airborne operation. Bundle and para-pack loading, dispersal arrangements and parking plans all went off like clockwork. Allowance was not made for the time required to inform all shipping and shore batteries of the impending flight. Ground units beyond the 1st Division knew nothing of the operation. The 504th RCT was familiar with the situation or countersigns of units on the flanks of the 1st Division area. —Captain Adam A. Komosa, Headquarters Company, 504th Parachute Infantry

Paratroopers put on their main and reserve parachutes. One of the two troopers at the left holds the reserve parachute for his buddy to secure on his chest. His musette bag is worn over the midsection, below the reserve chute. *United States Air Force photograph, www.www.fold3.com.*

I was thirteenth man in the stick and I didn't relish the thirteenth spot. When we first got to the airfield while warming up the plane, the chute of [one of] the equipment bundle[s] underneath started to open. I gave my reserve chute up and we put it on the bundle and I was moved up to fifth man—that made me feel real good. I do remember the plane's crew was helpful to us troopers. I couldn't get to my cigarettes and the crew chief got a cigarette and lit it for me.—Private Dennis T. Speth, Company A, 504th Parachute Infantry

A rattling of equipment rippled down the line of planes as we began to get into our harnesses. A sigh—half relief, half desperation—ran through the men. Main pack on, leg straps buckled, chest straps fast, static line loose from back, anchor line snap fastener handy, now reserve chute, both hooks snapped. "Fasten belly band, buddy!" "Okay, Joe! You fasten mine!" Rifle in case, grenades in pockets, bandoleers already around chest beneath chute, Mae West over neck, gas mask hung on, dispatch case hung on other side. Rations, maps, bailout kit in it. "Okay, all set. Good luck, pal. See ya in Sicily." "Okay, climb in the plane in order of jumping. Men, you know what to do. Go out fast when I give the word. Jump at ten forty-three on green light. Got that? Okay, sit down. Smoke after the takeoff." One engine starts, now the other. The motors warm up. The roar deadens and numbs your thoughts.—Corporal Ross S. Carter, Company C, 504th Parachute Infantry

The paratrooper at the far left carries his musette bag underneath his reserve chute. The barrel of the rifle of the trooper boarding the aircraft can be seen at his left. Some troopers chose to jump with their assembled rifles carried diagonally across their chests under their reserve chutes in order to be ready to use them immediately upon landing. Two equipment bundles are visible beneath the fuselage of the airplane. *United States Air Force photograph, www.www.fold3.com.*

As shadows lengthen on the airfield, paratroopers board their C-47 troop transport aircraft for the combat jump in Sicily on the night of July 11–12, 1943. *United States Army Signal Corps photograph, courtesy of William S. Mandle.*

The African sun, like a bloody curious eye, hung on the rim of the world as one hundred and forty-four planes coughed into life, spewing miniature dust storms across the flat wastes of desert airfields. Thin aluminum skins of C-47s vibrated like drawn snare drums and, as paratroopers sought their predesignated seats, they wrinkled their noses at the smell of gasoline and lacquer that flooded the planes' interiors. The takeoff proceeded in three plane V formations as planned. Flights, squadrons, and groups assembled at rendezvous points. By dusk, the planes were airborne and the formations started flying their course for Sicily. —Captain Adam A. Komosa, Headquarters Company, 504th Parachute Infantry

Propellers whip up clouds of dust. Hot breezes pour through the plane which taxies onto the runway as the motors step up to stupendous, ear-shattering roars. It's moving, picking up speed, pouring the desert by the little windows…airborne! We are in the air, we are going! We're off to Sicily! We gain altitude and circle. Beneath us on the airport a C-47 takes off every few seconds. Others keep taxiing up to the takeoff point. Our sky train grows like assembling flocks of migrating geese as more and more planes join our vast circling sweeps. We begin to fly over larger areas of desert. The planes jockey into V echelons. A plane noses into place about one hundred yards to our left rear; another noses into our right rear. Our platoon in the V echelon is complete. Looking out the leering door, I could see the sky train quit circling, whip into line, and become one long air fleet with one directing head. We were headed for the turquoise Mediterranean. The time was an hour before sundown. The desert, spotted with Arab villages whose dwellers peered up bug-eyed at the spectacle flowed smoothly under the air fleet. Camels, goats, horses, cacti, and wheat fields alternated with airports whose Spitfires, Wellingtons, trucks, jeeps, and gasoline drums perched insect-shaped on the desert floor. I sat opposite the door and saw the white beaches of the seashore and then Africa recede into the sunset. At last only water was visible. —Corporal Ross S. Carter, Company C, 504th Parachute Infantry

The last troopers board the aircraft and take their seats in preparation for the flight to Sicily, July 11, 1943. *United States Army Signal Corps photograph, courtesy of William S. Mandle.*

After circling in the air for about an hour the armada of planes was in line. As I leaned out the door and looked to the rear I saw a sight that I shall never forget. The large C-47s were in flights of three in a V formation as far as the eye could see. It was immense almost to the point of being unnatural. It was the beginning of the African July and the sun was just setting. As I watched these countless planes my heart filled and I choked up. My thoughts were that all these planes held the same load that mine did. Twenty-two of the best trained, best fit, and courageous men that the army has. They were just American boys, but they were picked men and they possessed just a little more of that indefinable something that distinguishes the best from the good. As we flew north toward Tunis and the coast I continued to stand in the door. The Arabs were finishing up their evening chores. But as the great spectacle passed over their quiet evening they stopped to stare up at us in wonder. The ground itself looked like a little kid's garden that he has under his Christmas tree. And I thought of Christmas and wondered if I would ever see another one. I looked at the men, who sat quietly smoking and wondered if they were thinking the same things that I was. I tried to read their faces, but they were lacking in expression. They just sat and smoked. As I looked from one to the other I thought how young they looked; how proud their mothers would be if they could see them. They must be thinking the same things I am, "Will I be afraid? Will I get killed? I hope to hell I don't!" Then I noticed the sun. It was in the final stages of setting and the sky seemed to be more beautiful than ever before. I wondered if I would see it set again.
—Lieutenant Robert D. Condon, Company A, 504th Parachute Infantry

I flew in the leading plane of the first serial and reached the coast of Sicily near Punta Socca at approximately 22:30 hours, thence flew in a northwesterly direction along the coast toward Gela. The left wing plane flew just over the water line, and the squadron of nine planes continued perfect formation up the coast at an altitude of approximately nine hundred feet.
—Captain Willard E. Harrison, Company A, 504th Parachute Infantry

Colonel Tucker steps on to his C-47 aircraft carrying his folding stock M1 carbine, which was found to be severely deficient in combat by the 82nd Airborne Division and was subsequently almost universally replaced by the reliable M1 Garand rifle, despite the table of equipment. *United States Army Signal Corps photograph, National Archives.*

Tracers arc into the night sky as the Allied naval ships fire on the troop carrier aircraft transporting the 504th Regimental Combat Team during the night of July 11–12, 1943. *Photograph courtesy of Jan Bos.*

I was on board of Colonel Reuben Tucker's plane when we jumped into Sicily. There were seventeen or eighteen paratroopers in the airplane scheduled to jump. I think it was seventeen, because prior to jumping, the procedure was a "count off" order and with Colonel Tucker at number one and me to be the last one out, my recollection is that I was number seventeen. Thirty seconds after I got out of my seat, it seemed all hell broke loose. Ack-ack was going off all around and tracer bullets were tearing thru the plane. This was it, boy. I was not afraid. For some reason I felt secure. I joked with a lieutenant beside me and hooked up my static line. Just then a gob of shells came up through the seat I had just left and tore out thru the top of the big transport airplane. They also tore up the seat next to mine. The airplane would lurch back and forth and we had to hang onto our static lines to keep balance. The captain, Air Corps (not the pilot) asked the colonel if he was going to jump into this and was promptly told "Hell yes, our orders are to jump on Sicily, take us back over the island." This was after turning away from the island and the first ack-ack fire. There were three casualties in our plane before we jumped. In such a case, the casualty is unhooked and laid over on the seats and the stick closes up. One senior officer who was wounded was Major [Julian A.] Cook (at that time S-4 supply officer of the 504th). Whether Cook (seriously wounded) returned to Africa with the airplane or jumped, I do not recall. Colonel Tucker jumped—by insisting that the pilot who wanted to avoid the severe flak and not return over the drop zone (which was the airport at Gela) must again seek to get the airplane over the designated drop zone which he courageously did do—after three passes back and forth over the area. The flight through the A.A. fire seemed endless and actually was rather long, because the pilot made three shots at the drop zone before he finally found it. Finally, the spot was hit and out we went, into the moonlight. My main interest was still the opening of that parachute and when it opened with its usual neck-breaking jerk, I felt relieved. I was floating peacefully, alone, that ground down there was Sicily, about thirty seconds away yet. My main interest still was to get down without breaking an ankle or leg, at least to be in sound physical condition. The ground was nearing, so I prepared for the landing and took it in stride with a front tumble. Oh boy, I was not hurt and a great hurdle was gone. I lay still a moment and listened. All was quiet, I struggled out of my parachute harness, looked about me and saw no one. I then made an answer to a seemingly sudden call of nature. That completed I began looking for other troopers from my plane, picked up a couple, determined a direction, started for the assembly point. Just then some tanks came around a corner, fifty yards away; we hit the dirt, sneaked our way to some bushes. Then I was scared. I pulled my pistol, cocked it, and lay motionless with my finger on the trigger guard. Three tanks buzzed by without seeing us and opened up with machine gun fire on another planeload a couple hundred yards away. We crawled down a ditch to an assembly point where we joined the rest of the combat team, within our own lines, awaiting orders and without having joined in a real fight. —Major Robert H. Neptune, Headquarters, 376th Parachute Field Artillery Battalion

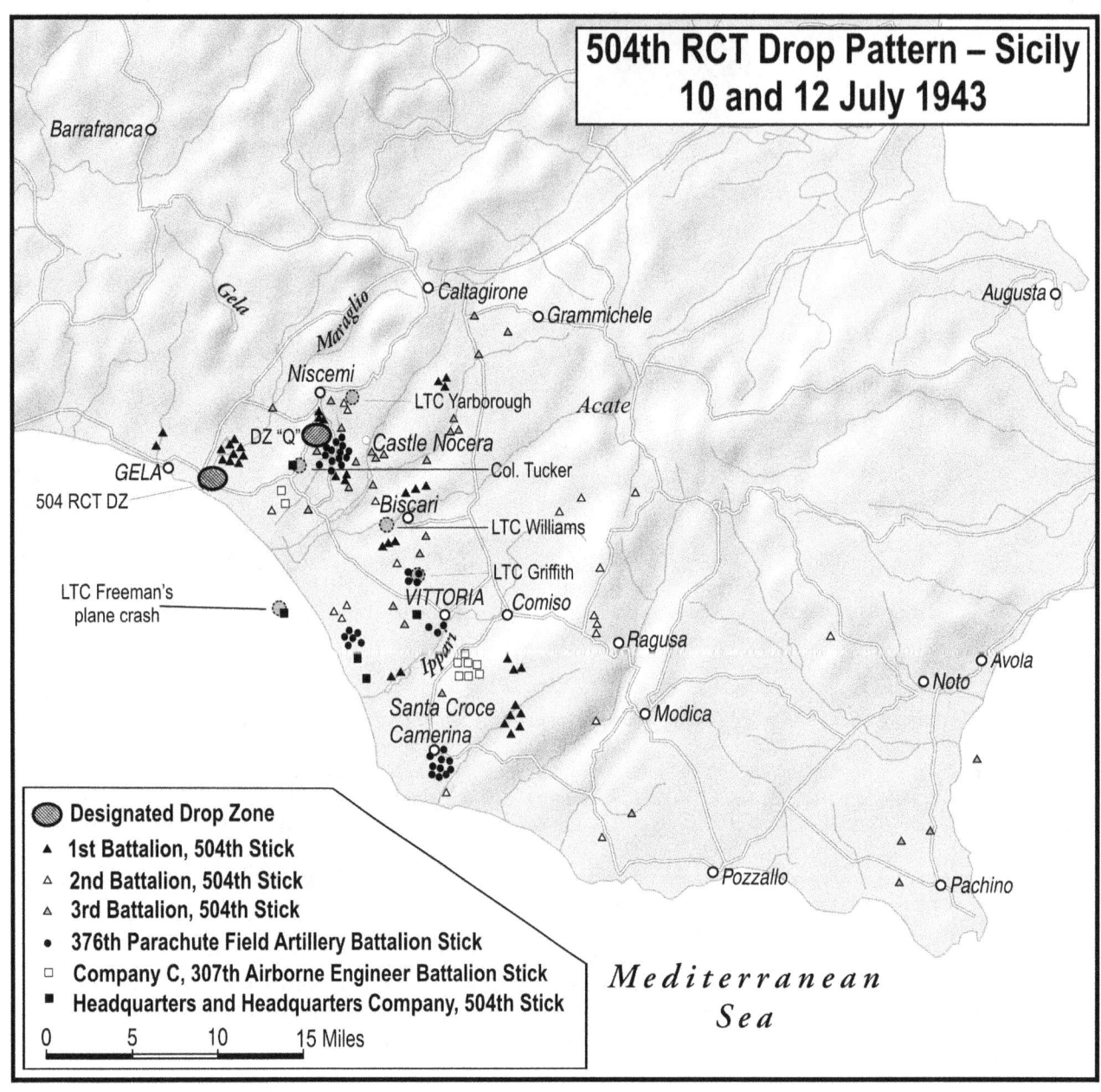

A gradual buildup of fire red tracers from below was engulfing our formation. I felt a shimmy go through our plane and then pandemonium reigned, as antiaircraft guns of our own forces at sea and on the beaches were blasting our slow flying aircraft. As my plane flew through the heavy flak, I could hear the hits as they penetrated. From my door position, I scanned the sky for other planes, but could see only those going down in flames. My plane developed a distinct shudder and banked away from the flak with one engine starting to sputter. I had my men stand up and hook up then, before going forward to talk with the pilot. I instructed my platoon sergeant to get the men out fast if the plane started to go down before I returned. From the pilot I learned he had lost the formation and had a damaged starboard engine. We decided since there was land below, that he would stay our present course and allow me a few seconds to return to the door, then turn on the green light. We both realized that with the heavy load he had, it would be difficult for him to fly back to North Africa. I rushed back to the door yelling to my men to get ready to jump. As I arrived, the red light came on, followed within seconds by the green light just as I hooked up. I immediately released the equipment bundles from under the plane then jumped into darkness with my men following. —Lieutenant Edward J. Sims, Company F, 504th Parachute Infantry

THE SICILY CAMPAIGN
15–23 JULY 1943

Paratroopers with the 505th Parachute Infantry who had been misdropped in the British sector of Sicily arrive at Tripoli, Libya, after being evacuated by the British Royal Navy. *United States Army Signal Corps photograph, National Archives.*

The British were planning to send the Americans back to North Africa. The American officers, all of us lieutenants, went to see the British major in charge. "Sir," we said, "we'd like to find our outfits and continue to fight. That's why we're here." "Sorry chap," he said, "but we've already made arrangements. You'll be escorting a load of Italian prisoners back to our POW [prisoner of war] camp in Tripoli. Leaving immediately. Rum thing." We argued with him but to no avail. —Lieutenant T. Moffatt Burriss, Headquarters Company, 3rd Battalion, 504th Parachute Infantry

Only people of company headquarters and 1st Platoon landed anywhere near our drop zone. Lieutenant [James M.] Irvin went to the British sector near Noto and picked up a few men. The bulk of B Company were in the British zone and were sent back to North Africa. —Sergeant Harvill W. Lazenby, Company B, 505th Parachute Infantry

On July 18, the 504th Regimental Combat Team, led by the 2nd Battalion, with the 82nd Armored Field Artillery Battalion and Batteries A and B, 83rd Chemical Mortar Battalion attached, relieved the 39th Regimental Combat Team of the 9th Infantry Division at Realmonte around noon. The 504th then moved west and secured a crossing of the Canne River and the high ground to the west by dark. It captured Montallegro by 3:00 a.m. on the 19th and by 9:00 a.m., the 2nd Battalion had reached the Platani River. It crossed the Maggazolo River by 10:15 a.m. and by noon it secured the town of Ribera. By about 9:00 p.m., the 504th RCT was stopped by an order from corps at a phase line about halfway between Ribera and Sciacca. The major obstacle was a blown bridge at the Canne River. The 307th Airborne Engineer Battalion solved this with the rapid construction of a temporary bridge strong enough to support heavy vehicles, completing it by 4:00 a.m. on July 19. In this photo, Major General Geoffrey Keyes (left), commanding officer of the Provisional Armored Corps, Ridgway (center), and Colonel Reuben Tucker (right), commanding officer of the 504th Parachute Infantry, confer outside of the town of Ribera, July 19, 1943. *United States Army Signal Corps photograph.*

Following Gavin's and Tucker's ill-starred parachute operations, the division slowly assembled in the Gela area. Most of the scattered parachutists gradually rejoined their units... The 82nd, along with the 3rd Division and part of the 9th, was assigned to a provisional corps under the command of Major General Geoffrey Keyes, which on July 19, moved west from Gela with the mission of attacking Palermo from the south and southwest. My light airborne artillery was reinforced by the attachment of the 155mm howitzer battalion of the 9th Division... —Brigadier General Maxwell D. Taylor, Headquarters, 82nd Airborne Division

General Ridgway confers with a member of his staff near Ribera, Sicily, July 19, 1943. Staff Sergeant Frank G. Farmer, Ridgway's driver is sitting behind him. Ridgway's 1903 Springfield rifle (left) sits in a holster on the right side of the jeep. *United States Army Signal Corps photograph, National Archives.*

Our first assignment was to clear the area west of the 1st Division, and then to attack westward and clear that end of the island. This was the first time the units of the division had been committed to action and many rough spots immediately became apparent. The one that was the most noticeable to me, as division commander, was the caution of the advanced elements. As soon as they came under fire, they would stop and ponder the situation, and I finally found out that the best way to keep them moving was to be right up there with them, moving with the point of the advanced guard, and that's where I spent my daylight hours during that drive to the west. Once I was told that General Patton, looking at an overlay map, told one of his staff, "That damned Ridgway has got his CP up where his outposts ought to be. Tell him to get it back." Coming from George Patton, who was not much of a man to hang back when there was shooting going on, I considered this to be more of a compliment than a rebuke. There was no strong resistance to the division in its drive to the west. We were running into Italians, not Germans, and we had a fairly easy time of it, for they would stand for a while and fight a brief, delaying action, then pull out, though they did cause us some casualties. Day after day, the spirit and confidence of the troopers increased, and pretty soon I didn't have to do much urging to get them to drive through the rough places. Little incidents come to mind that illustrate the spirit of the division. Once, I remember, when an element of the leading battalion was passing along on a hard-surfaced road through a narrow defile, a mortar shell burst right among us. Several men went down, killed or seriously wounded. I ran to the nearest and knelt down beside him. He turned his face toward me, and I could see at once that his eyes had been shot out. "Who's that?" he said. "General Ridgway," I told him. "Oh," he said, "I'm glad to see you, General." Each passing day the division grew more battle wise, more confident. Lead elements weren't stopping now when they got a little fire. They fanned out, flanked the pockets of resistance, overcame them and moved on. —Major General Matthew B. Ridgway, Headquarters, 82nd Airborne Division

General Ridgway (left) rests his hand on the metal stock of Brigadier General Maxwell Taylor's folding stock M1 carbine and watches as Taylor, the division's artillery commander, studies a map with an overlay on July 19, 1943 near Ribera, Sicily. *United States Army Signal Corps photograph, National Archives.*

I think I know Ridgway as well as anybody alive, because I spent lots of time with him in combat, under the most difficult circumstances. I've seen the guy under great pressure and stress. He's a man of extreme personal integrity. So much so that people would call him flinty, hard to get along with. Once he makes up his mind about something, look out, he's gone. Even with the Wehrmacht, it was always Ridgway versus the Wehrmacht in my mind. He'd come up to the front and go around the road bend and stand and urinate in the middle of the road. I'd say, "Matt, get the hell out of there, you'll get shot." No, he was defiant. —Colonel James M. Gavin, Headquarters, 505th Parachute Infantry

Ridgway was always very courteous. He never raised his voice—at least not to me. When he raised his voice, whoever he raised it to, boy you were dead from that time on. There was no forgetting...He was brilliant. He was a military man in every way. I never, ever saw him cross his legs. Unbelievable! No matter how soft the chair was, somehow the chair stiffened up when he sat in it. He would walk into a room and he would create a presence by being in that room. He didn't have to say anything. When his eyes would go over a room, everyone was instantly drawn to him, just like that. He didn't have to say a word. But when he spoke, he had a commanding voice...He was intense. I think he slept that way. He was a very determined person. He knew what he wanted. He wouldn't tolerate anything that was not right up to perfection. When things were not to his liking, just his look told you everything. His appearance in itself, his facial expressions, his use of eyes, perhaps his raising his eyebrows, said one hell of a lot more than any words that he could have come out with. He was just a remarkable person... He was always very nice. He was very demanding. He wanted everything just so and he wanted it right now. —Captain Arthur G. Kroos, Jr., Headquarters, 82nd Airborne Division

General Ridgway (left center) with his aide Captain Don Faith (left), an unidentified member of his staff (right center), and the division G-3 plans and operations officer, Lieutenant Colonel Richard K. Boyd (right) on July 19, 1943 near Ribera, Sicily. *United States Army Signal Corps photograph, National Archives.*

We were joined in the early days [of the campaign] by the balance of our G-3 group who were flown over and air landed on captured airfields. Sicily was a breaking in period for us and we started developing the skills needed to operate in battle. We quickly found out the things we needed and those that could be discarded. We put out situation reports under time pressure and gradually came to do a passable job. Fortunately for this breaking in, the battle area assigned to us after the first few days was relatively free from heavy confrontation with the enemy, and what we learned most of all was how to set up our operating location [command post], break it down quickly and move to another location as the battle progressed. —Technician Fourth Grade Leonard Lebenson, Headquarters Company, 82nd Airborne Division

[Captain] Don Faith—I don't know when he joined Ridgway as aide de camp. He was an attractive looking young fellow. He was smart. I'm surprised he wasn't West Point...I always felt that Ridgway had mentally adopted Don Faith...I had the feeling right after I joined Ridgway that in no way could I or would I ever replace Don Faith. Every time he mentioned Faith, it was always very nice and complimentary. —Captain Arthur G. Kroos, Jr., Headquarters, 82nd Airborne Division

General Ridgway points out the advance of his troopers in the distance to First Sergeant Frank L. Morang, a motion picture cameraman with the 3131st Signal Service Company, United States Army Signal Corps near Ribera, Sicily on July 19, 1943. Morang jumped with the 505th Parachute Infantry on the night of July 9–10, despite never previously having made a parachute jump. *United States Army Signal Corps photograph, National Archives.*

The usual action of the Italians was to fire a few shots, rifle and machine gun, cause the AG [advance guard] to deploy, and then surrender as soon as pressure was brought to bear on them. It made for treacherous action, even the white flag could not be trusted...During this advance extending over three days and stopping just short of Menfi, the 504 lost two-thirds of its effective strength from stragglers. I have never seen anything like it. This thing must be licked; all of us were ashamed of them. All along the roads they were bumming under trees, around houses, and in fields. On the march, officers and men alike would leave ranks to pick grapes, melons, and get water. Probably one of the greatest sources of losses was in capturing vehicles. Every wreck and abandoned vehicle that had not the slightest chance of ever operating again was the center of a group of from three to six parachutists who upon being questioned said they were getting it ready to run for use for the regiment. This had the sanction of the regiment in its desperation to get transportation. Our experience was that even the good serviceable vehicles soon broke down and became more of an automotive liability than asset. Orders were accordingly issued forbidding troops from leaving the ranks to capture vehicles. —Colonel James M. Gavin, Headquarters, 505th Parachute Infantry

Troopers and vehicles move along the highway leading to the town of Sciacca, which sits on the ridge in the distance. The 2nd Battalion of the 504th Parachute Infantry seized the coastal town on July 20, 1943. *United States Army Signal Corps photograph, National Archives.*

This ancient castle overlooking the valley and the highway below guarded the approach to Sciacca, but was not used by Italian soldiers to defend the town. *Photograph courtesy of www. http://sciaccaunavolta.altervista.org.*

As we approached Sciacca, I was leading with my platoon when I noticed smoke rising from the road ahead, so I dispersed my platoon into firing positions and went forward to check out the smoke. The road had been mined with antitank mines, and a two-wheeled cart, driven by an old man with a young child, had set off one mine, killing both of them and the mule that was pulling the cart. To our left on the crest of a small rise were a number of pillboxes with white flags being waved from the gun ports. We advanced cautiously and flushed out a large group (about one hundred) of Italian soldiers who wanted to surrender. After disarming them, they were sent under guard to our rear. We cleared Sciacca, then headed for Marsala.
—Lieutenant Edward J. Sims, Company F, 504th Parachute Infantry

Paratroopers commandeer captured Italian light armored vehicles and a bus for the movement to secure the western side of the island. *United States Army Signal Corps photograph, National Archives.*

A group of paratroopers pose with a Sicilian man and boy during the advance across Sicily. *United States Army Signal Corps photograph, National Archives.*

Paratroopers with the 504th Parachute Infantry move through one of the many villages that lie along the route of advance of the 82nd Airborne Division along the western portion of Sicily. *Photograph courtesy of William S. Mandle.*

These paratroopers are using a captured Italian tankette towing several trailers for transportation through the rolling hills of western Sicily. *United States Army Signal Corps photograph, National Archives.*

These Italian soldiers surrendered to elements of the 82nd Airborne and gladly marched into captivity. The 82nd reported capturing 11,265 enemy troops from July 19–26, 1943. *United States Army photograph, courtesy of William S. Mandle.*

Sicilians turn out to greet the division as it moves through their town during the advance up the western side of the island. *United States Army Signal Corps photograph, courtesy of William S. Mandle.*

Citizens of Marsala crowd around an 82nd Airborne Division jeep after the town was secured by the 504th Parachute Infantry, July 20, 1943. *United States Army photograph, courtesy of William S. Mandle.*

It never rained, so the campaign progressed rapidly. There was plenty of wine. Cantaloupes, tomatoes, and grapes abounded. At night we slept where we stopped. Occasionally an enemy plane flew overhead or dived down and strafed, but did little damage. Life was wonderful. We were convinced that war had never been like this in the history of the world. Cheering crowds greeted us in the towns. Peasants brought food and drink when we stopped. Barbers shaved us for a cigarette. Many girls could fall in love for a chocolate bar or a few cigarettes. We took more Italian prisoners than we could feed. On seeing us coming they cheered and hastened to surrender. —Corporal Ross S. Carter, Company C, 504th Parachute Infantry

My feet were so sore, and my buddy [Private James H.] Legacie, a BAR man, was hurting, too. So we dropped off the side of the road and sat down in a vineyard, took our dusty jump boots off, and tried to take care of our feet. We would reach up and grab a grape, but they were not ripe yet. We figured we would grab a ride on some vehicle and catch up to our company. Along comes a half-track—it stopped—an officer yelled to us, "What outfit you soldiers in?" We said, "504 Parachute Infantry." The officer said, "You guys hungry?" "Yes, sir," we said. He throws down a box of ten-in-one rations. We had heard about them, but we had never had any. I knew the box contained a can of bacon and my mouth was watering. Legacie and I opened up the box and I got the can of bacon. One of my prize possessions was a Coleman stove. I probably stole it somewhere. Now, how are we going are cook it? Out comes my entrenching tool, I shoved it into a sandy soil a few times, wiped it on my backside, lit the stove and cooked the bacon on the shovel. Man, did that taste good. —Private First Class Lawrence H. Dunlop, Company H, 504th Parachute Infantry

Paratroopers pack into the back and onto the front hood of a 2 ½-ton army truck for movement forward during the long advance across the western coastal area of Sicily. Shortages of transportation forced shuttling of troopers behind the forward elements of the advance. *United States Army Signal Corps photograph, National Archives.*

As the heavily laden truck drives away, troopers unable to board it await a truck to transport them forward to join their unit. *United States Army Signal Corps photograph, National Archives.*

A long column of 2½-ton trucks transporting elements of the 504th Parachute Infantry move through a village as its citizens wave to the troopers. *United States Army Signal Corps photograph, courtesy of William S. Mandle.*

Italian and German army trucks captured during the campaign in Sicily were pressed into service to provide transportation for the paratroopers as the division moved northwest toward Trapani. *United States Army Signal Corps photograph, courtesy of William S. Mandle.*

This is an aerial reconnaissance photo of the airfield at Trapani, Sicily, which was overrun and captured along with the town by the 505th Parachute Infantry Regiment during the division's last action in Sicily. *United States Air Force photograph, www.fold3.com.*

Our final action on Sicily was in taking the town of Trapani. It was an Italian naval and marine base, and we were not real sure of the number of defenders to expect. Having superior numbers and their backs to the sea they just might fight like hell. We had formed up at the edge of an olive grove looking out on a plain that was about a mile to the foothills overlooking the harbor. I Company moved out of the cover of the grove and immediately drew artillery fire. On hearing incoming mail, we would hit the deck and move forward after the explosions. Hearing incoming rounds, we had just hit the deck, when Major [Edward C.] Krause drove up in his jeep. He had not heard the incoming rounds and started giving us hell. As luck would have it, at this very moment two rounds bracketed his jeep, and to quote from that era: He hauled ass out of there. We continued forward under constant but moderate artillery fire. When we started up the hill the artillery ceased, and mortar rounds took over. Small arms fire was quite intense, but we had ample cover in the form of large rock formations. As we neared the crest we were ordered to fix bayonets. We continued our advance and the mortar fire became only an occasional round and the rifle fire diminished. In short order white flags appeared and for these Italians the war was over. —Sergeant William T. Dunfee, Company I, 505th Parachute Infantry

This is a view from an Italian Army gun emplacement on the high ground outside of Trapani, which was assaulted by the 505th Parachute Infantry during the final actions of the Sicily campaign. *United States Army photograph, courtesy of William S. Mandle.*

A few miles out of the city of Trapani, resistance began to stiffen. Artillery fire, fairly heavy, began to fall in fields on either side of the road along which we were moving. I was up with the advance guard, expecting momentarily to get a salvo on the road, when I looked around to see General Maxwell Taylor, my division artillery commander, standing by my side, watching the shell bursts casually, with an artillery man's appraising eye. Max was also serving as assistant division commander, for the original ADC, General Keerans, who had been lost when friendly fire brought down the twenty-three planes of the 504th. It distressed me to see Max up there, for one shell could easily have gotten us both, leaving the division without a top command. So I told Max, by God, he was to get back and stay back until I sent for him. I didn't want the division commander and the second in command wiped out at once. I talked pretty strongly to Max, for I knew he had all the courage in the world, and would be right up there with the point, with the first rifleman, if I'd let him. But somebody had to stay back at the CP and I knew it wasn't going to be me. That's one of the privileges of rank you can go where you think you can do the most good. I always felt my place was up where the heaviest action was not interfering with the commander who was actually doing the fighting, but looking over the situation and helping him as I could. In this particular action, I felt the best thing I could do to help was to get some guns up there. So Max, with his fine spirit, went back and borrowed a battery of 155 howitzers from the 9th Division, and shoved them up there, and we soon blasted the Italians out of their nests and went on into Trapani. —Major General Matthew B. Ridgway, Headquarters, 82nd Airborne Division

The advance led through Sciacca to Castelvetrano, then to Marsala and Trapani, which the division captured on July 23, after a march of about 150 miles in six days. Most of the way it was as pleasant a campaign as one is likely to find in war. No one was very angry at anyone. The Italians had no desire to die for the King [Victor Emmanuel III] or [Marshal Pietro] Bagdolio, much less Hitler. In the towns we passed through, the villagers greeted us as liberators and many rushed up to ask in broken English about relatives in America…In Sicily, our division lost some two hundred killed, including the airborne losses of the 504th and 505th Regiments, but, in turn, it took over 20,000 prisoners. While [Lieutenant General George S.] Patton was most flattering in his comments on the behavior of our troops, the scattered drop of the two parachute regiments put a damper on the airborne movement both in the army and in the air force. It was clear that the joint training of our parachute troops with the troop carrier units of the air force had been deficient and that the navigational equipment and methods of the air force were inadequate to assure accurate parachute drops at night. —Brigadier General Maxwell D. Taylor, Headquarters, 82nd Airborne Division

In its drive to the west the division moved 150 miles in six days, capturing fifteen thousand prisoners. We moved on foot, at a pace which astonished even General Patton. Late in the campaign, I remember, one little incident occurred which vastly amused the whole division. As we moved on Palermo, we received orders to get the hell off the roads and let the 2nd Armored [Division] through so they could administer the coup de grace to this big town on the north shore. So we got off the roads with none too good grace, and the 2nd Armored came tearing through and went roaring into the center of Palermo to find troopers of the 82nd applauding them derisively from the sidewalks, where they had been for hours, cutting the dust from their throats with wine. The 2nd Armored wasn't very happy about that, and some harsh words were passed. —Major General Matthew B. Ridgway, Headquarters, 82nd Airborne Division

OCCUPATION DUTY
24 JULY – 18 AUGUST 1943

On July 24, 1943, members of the 505th Parachute Infantry Regiment came upon this German Mark VI Tiger I tank and several destroyed American Sherman tanks several hundred yards beyond on this road which led from Trapani to Gela. The 504th and 505th Regimental Combat Teams spent the following three and a half weeks performing occupation duty in Sicily. Meanwhile, the 325th Glider Infantry and the other glider-borne units of the division remained in Tunisia. *United States Army Signal Corps photograph, National Archives.*

Company H, 504th Parachute Infantry troopers Private Daun Z. Rice (left) from Gary, Indiana, Corporal John Fowler (center), from Pittsburgh, Pennsylvania, and Private F. S. Cole (right) from Brooklyn, New York enjoy ice cream in Palermo, after its capture. Sadly, Rice would be killed in action later in the war in Holland on September 26, 1944. *United States Air Force photograph, www.fold3.com.*

Castellammare de Golfo (upper left) was located on the northern shore of the island between Trapani to the west and Palermo to the east. The villa (upper right) overlooking the town became the command post for the 504th Parachute Infantry. A closer view of the villa may be seen in the photo below. *Photographs courtesy of William Mandle.*

Jack "Beaver" Thompson (left), a correspondent with the *Chicago Tribune*, and who had jumped with the regiment, listens as Emmitt C. Shirley (back to camera), with Service Company, 505th; Major Mark J. Alexander (third left), the commanding officer of the 2nd Battalion, 505th; Colonel Jim Gavin (fourth left), the commander of the 505th; and Major Ed Krause (right), the commanding officer of the 3rd Battalion, 505th engage in a discussion at the regiment's encampment near Trapani. *Photograph courtesy of John Sparry.*

This is the enclosure at Trapani set up by the 82nd Airborne Division to hold enemy prisoners of war captured during the drive up the western coast of Sicily. *Photograph courtesy of Daniel B. McIlvoy, Jr.*

In Trapani, we inherited the duty of giving medical care for all the prisoners we had picked up, which numbered almost in the thousands. We had a terrific number of Italians in the prisoner of war camp that was established there. They had their own medical officers and with the Italian boys as aid men, saw to it that they quite adequately took care of their men. —Captain Daniel B. McIlvoy, Jr., Medical Detachment, 505th Parachute Infantry

Next Page Top and Bottom Photographs: The enemy prisoners of war, almost exclusively Italian army troops, sleep in tents or on bedrolls on the grounds of the walled enclosure. The medical detachment of the 505th Parachute Infantry, under the command of Captain Daniel B. McIlvoy, Jr., provided medical care and worked to prevent the spread of any diseases until the prisoners could be evacuated to more permanent prisoner of war camps in the United States. *Photographs courtesy of William S. Mandle.*

These troopers sit in the back of a truck near Trapani awaiting departure to perform occupation duties. *Photograph courtesy of Jerome V. Huth.*

The division staff in Trapani, Sicily in July 1943 (left to right) consisted of Lieutenant Colonel Frederick M. Schellhammer, G-1 (personnel); Lieutenant Colonel George E. Lynch, G-2 (intelligence); Colonel Ralph P. Eaton, Chief of Staff; Lieutenant Colonel Richard K. Boyd, G-3 (plans and operations); and Lieutenant Colonel Robert H. Wienecke, G-4 (logistics and supply). *United States Army photograph.*

A trooper talks with a British soldier driving a lorry through the town of Gibellina, east of Marsala, July 29, 1943. *United States Army photograph, courtesy of William S. Mandle.*

The American cemetery near Gela, Sicily was the burial place for many of the 82nd Airborne Division paratroopers who were killed during the invasion. *United States Air Force photograph, www.fold3.com.*

The airfield at Ponte Olivo north of Gela was used by the 52nd Troop Carrier Wing in support of Allied landings at Salerno, codenamed Operation Avalanche. *United States Air Force photograph, www.fold3.com.*

This is another view of the Ponte Olivo airfield, located north of Gela. *United States Air Force photograph, www.fold3.com.*

A practice jump is conducted near the airfield at Ponte Olivo, Sicily. *United States Air Force photograph, www.fold3.com*.

The pathfinder school at the Comiso airfield developed the procedures and trained the pathfinders who marked drop zones and guided the aircraft approaching Paestum, Italy during the Salerno, Italy jump in the first use of pathfinders by the United States Army. *United States Air Force photograph, www.fold3.com*.

Technician Fifth Grade Jerome V. Huth, an original pathfinder with Headquarters Company, 505th Parachute Infantry holds an equipment bundle containing a Eureka transponder beacon. A pathfinder school was established at the Comiso airfield to train teams to guide incoming serials of aircraft containing the main body to the proper drop zones. *Photograph courtesy of Jerome V. Huth*

General Ridgway and Brigadier General Ray A. Dunn, the commanding officer of the 51st Troop Carrier Wing, confer during training exercises. Navigational aids to improve the accuracy of the drops were implemented through the formation of a pathfinder school at Comiso, Sicily. Training was conducted by the British regarding the use of the Eureka–Rebecca beacon system. Experimentation was conducted with Halophane lights to provide a visual signal to pilots as they approached a drop zone. These lights could be seen from the air, but not from the ground. *United States Air Force photograph, www.fold3.com.*

PREPARING FOR THE NEXT OPERATION

After the arrival of the 52nd Troop Carrier Wing preparations at airfields in Sicily began for a planned combat jump and air landing operation near Rome, Italy. *United States Air Force photograph, www.fold3.com.*

A Sicilian views the spectacle of troop transport aircraft parked at an airfield prior to the invasion of Italy. *United States Air Force photograph, www.fold3.com.*

Troop transport aircraft are queued up at one of the airfields in Sicily prior to the invasion of Italy. *United States Air Force photograph, www.fold3.com.*

The 52nd Troop Carrier Wing moved from airfields near Kairouan, Tunisia to airfields in Sicily prior to the planned combat jump near Rome, Operation Giant, which was cancelled shortly before the aircraft were scheduled to takeoff on September 9, 1943. *United States Air Force photograph, www.fold3.com.*

Young Sicilians marvel at the sight of troop transport aircraft and the glider troopers and paratroopers of the 82nd Airborne Division at one of airfields. *United States Air Force photograph, www.fold3.com.*

A glider trooper speaks with curious Sicilian kids at an airfield in Sicily. *United States Air Force photograph, www.fold3.com.*

Paratroopers with the 2nd Battalion, 509th Parachute Infantry Regiment (redesignated on December 10, 1943 as the 509th Parachute Infantry Battalion), prepare for a training jump in Sicily prior to the invasion of Italy. The 509th was attached to the 82nd Airborne Division in French Morocco and was held in reserve at Kairouan, Tunisia during the Sicilian campaign. *United States Air Force photograph, www.fold3.com.*

The 2nd Battalion, 509th Parachute Infantry had small American flags sewn on the left shoulders of their jumpsuits, making them easily identifiable. *United States Air Force photograph, www.fold3.com.*

This paratrooper with the 2nd Battalion, 509th Parachute Infantry adjusts the straps of his parachute harness in preparation for a training jump in Sicily. *United States Air Force photograph, www.fold3.com.*

This 509th trooper holds his M1 rifle which indicates that he will not be jumping with it disassembled and contained in a Griswold case. Most veterans of prior combat jumps preferred to jump with their weapons assembled and loaded, ready for immediate use upon landing. *United States Air Force photograph, www.fold3.com.*

Paratroopers with the 2nd Battalion, 509th finish putting on their parachutes and equipment prior to boarding troop transport aircraft for a practice jump in Sicily. *United States Air Force photograph, www.fold3.com.*

One of the two 509th paratroopers checks the parachute of the other to insure that the risers of his main parachute are routed properly on the back of the parachute pack. *United States Air Force photograph, www.fold3.com.*

This paratrooper is checking the parachute of his fellow 509th trooper. *United States Air Force photograph, www.fold3.com.*

These two 509th paratroopers have conducted equipment checks and relax before boarding their plane for the practice jump. *United States Air Force photograph, www.fold3.com.*

Lieutenant Colonel Harry Lewis (center), the commanding officer of the 325th Glider Infantry, addresses the officers of the regiment at the port of Licata, Sicily prior to embarkation on September 13, 1943 for the voyage to Italy. The 325th was transported to Palermo, Sicily, where it spent the night of September 14–15, 1943, before sailing to the Salerno beachhead. *United States Army Signal Corps photograph, courtesy of William S. Mandle.*

Glider troopers of the 325th wait to board their landing craft at the harbor at Licata. *Photograph by Robert Capa.*

Glider troopers await loading for Operation Avalanche at the docks at Licata, Sicily, September 13, 1943. *United States Army Signal Corps photograph, courtesy of William S. Mandle.*

A United States Army Signal Corps jeep drives aboard an LST (Landing Ship Tank) which will transport it to the beaches of Salerno as part of Operation Avalanche. *United States Army Signal Corps photograph, courtesy of William S. Mandle.*

Equipment bundles are loaded under the wings of C-47 aircraft in preparation for a combat jump on the Salerno beachhead on the evening of September 13–14, 1943. *United States Air Force photograph, www.fold3.com.*

Mark Clark's Fifth Army hit the beaches at Salerno, drove inland against fierce opposition, and by nightfall were clinging by teeth and fingernails to a dominating ridge line overlooking the beachhead area. The Germans struck hard in counterattack, hitting the left flank of the VI Corps, driving it back to the Albanella River. Several days later it began to appear that the German onslaught might drive clear through to the beach, split our forces there, and push us into the sea. I knew none of this at the moment. At scattered airfields in Sicily, the 82nd, rested and refitted, was waiting for whatever mission might be assigned us. No plans for future operations were at that moment on the books. At noon on September 13, I left the airfield at Licata to make an inspection swing over the 82nd's bivouac areas. About fifteen minutes out, the navigator of my C-47 came back and told me that there was an urgent message for me back at Licata. He had no information as to who the sender was, nor what the nature of the message might be. This presented quite a problem of decision, for I was on fairly urgent business of my own. However, some sixth sense must have told me that this thing was important, for I gave orders to return. We landed at Licata about 2:00, and there I found a tired, begrimed P-38 pilot bearing a personal letter from Mark Clark. Even through the formal official phrases I could read my old friend's deep concern. The gist of the message was that unless we could get help to him and get it there fast, the landing in Italy might be turned into another Dunkirk. It was absolutely essential, he wrote, that we drop strong forces within the beachhead area that night. Word was sent at once to Troop Carrier Command, and I took off immediately for south central Sicily, where Reuben Tucker's fine 504th was in bivouac. To Tucker and his staff I quickly outlined the plan. Within two hours the men were assembling at their aircraft in full combat gear. Maps were spread over the tail surfaces of the C-47, and there on the field the units of the regiment were given their missions. —Major General Matthew B. Ridgway, Headquarters, 82nd Airborne Division

Troop Carrier pilots are briefed on the afternoon of September 13, 1943 for the operation to drop elements of the 504th Parachute Infantry that night near Paestum, Italy to reinforce the Salerno beachhead. *United States Air Force photograph, www.fold3.com.*

Pilots of the 52nd Troop Carrier Wing listen intently to the briefing prior to takeoff to drop paratroopers on the night of September 13, 1943 within the beachhead at Salerno, Italy. *United States Air Force photograph, www.fold3.com.*

Maps are spread on the side of a C-47 shortly before takeoff to allow orientation of 504th Parachute Infantry jumpmasters and aircrews as to the route to the Salerno area and the location of the drop zone at Paestum. The 1st and 2nd Battalions of the 504th Parachute Infantry; Company C, 307th Airborne Engineer Battalion, less the 1st Platoon; and a detachment of the 82nd Airborne Reconnaissance Platoon would make the jump on the night of September 13–14, 1943. *United States Air Force photograph, www.fold3.com.*

The commander of the 504 Parachute Infantry, Colonel Reuben H. Tucker, who had happened to be at Licata airfield was directed to get the 504th alerted and off as soon as troops were ready and troop carrier aircraft were assembled. At Comiso field the 1st Battalion received a warning order about 14:00. The battalion, commanded by Lieutenant Colonel Warren R. Williams, was made as ready as it could. Bundles were rolled, combat gear was checked, and ammunition was issued. All was in readiness except for the questions: Where? What? Who? Late in the afternoon the battalion commander and his officers were briefed in the bombed out hanger at Comiso field. The mission outlined was to parachute onto a secured drop zone about two miles south of Paestum, Italy and report to a representative of VI Corps, who would be there with further instructions. The troops were briefed with the aid of flashlight and the only available maps, of scale 1/1,500,000. Only in a cursory manner was the situation on the Salerno beachhead known. Company planes were assigned and units began to load bundles. All did not move too smoothly. The last seven planes for B Company did not arrive until 21:00 hours. As B Company rapidly loaded into planes, the pilots were being briefed. Shortly after 21:00 the first elements of the battalion were moving down the runway. —Lieutenant John S. Lekson, Headquarters, 1st Battalion, 504th Parachute Infantry

The original 504th pathfinder team was the first United States Army pathfinder team to be used operationally in combat during the jump at Paestum, Italy on the night of September 13, 1943 to reinforce the beach landed forces at Salerno. The team of 504th Parachute Infantry pathfinders in this photo was formed in October 1943 at the pathfinder school at Comiso airfield in Sicily. The team members were (front row left to right) Lieutenant Bruno J. Rolak, Company C; Technician Fourth Grade Robert W. Lowery, Company C, Eureka operator; Corporal Carlos B. Guttry, Company C, assistant Eureka operator; (back row left to right) Private First Class Thomas J. McCarthy, Company A; Private First Class John W. DeCoursy, Company B; Private First Class Valentine Dobrychlop, Company B; Private Eugene R. Elliott, Headquarters Company, 1st Battalion; Private First Class William L. Clay, Company B; and Private First Class James J. Adams, Company A. *Photograph courtesy of Robert W. Lowery and Mike St. George.*

Plans for lighting the drop zone came with Clark's letter. The troops on the ground were to fill oil cans with sand soaked with gasoline, arrange the cans in a big "T", and as the first drop plane drew near, the "T" would be lighted. Every plane would spill its stick to fall on this flaming beacon. We also had Clark's assurance that along the corridor we would fly, not a gun on the ground would fire. Eight hours after the pilot had handed me General Clark's letter, planes of the 52nd Troop Carrier were lifting from the Sicilian fields, carrying the 504th Regiment, plus Company C of the 307th Airborne Engineers.
—Major General Matthew B. Ridgway, Headquarters, 82nd Airborne Division

The plane from which my [pathfinder] radar team jumped was jump mastered by [Lieutenant] Colonel Charles Billingslea. As our plane approached the DZ, a flaming cross was ignited on the ground as a signal to us. As soon as the green light went on, out we went. No sooner had our chutes opened, when the troops on the ground began firing at us. I could hear the bullets whistling around me and could see tracers clearly. At this time, a loud voice below bellowed, "Cease fire, you ___ers, they are American troops," but this did not stop the firing. Instead of releasing the seventy-five pound Eureka from my right leg, I hit the ground with silk in my hand and the Eureka still attached to my leg. Momentarily, I thought that I had a broken leg, but that was not the case. I set up the Eureka immediately and with Colonel Billingslea beside me, we could hear the planes triggering in on the set. The main body of troops began to jump right over the set. What a beautiful sight to behold! —Sergeant Regis J. Pahler, Headquarters Company, 1st Battalion, 504th Parachute Infantry

A lieutenant (standing at left) checks on the paratroopers of his stick prior to takeoff for Paestum, Italy to reinforce the Salerno beachhead. Note the folding stock carbine the officer is carrying under his reserve chute and the trooper sitting second from the right with his M1 rifle fully assembled instead of carrying it disassembled inside a Griswold case. *United States Air Force photograph, www.fold3.com.*

The regimental lift proceeded across the Tyrrhenian Sea without enemy interference. Approximately halfway out the formation ran into a cloudbank. Elements were above, below, and to either side of the battalion's S-3 plane. As the lift neared Agropoli, several C Company planes flying too close to shore were fired upon by single small caliber weapons with no effect. Then the red light switched on. Parachutists hustled as they fastened harnesses. Bundles were pushed into the door. Snap fasteners clicked onto the anchor line and down the line came the "readies". Underneath was Agropoli, then the sea, then a shore, and a stream. —Lieutenant John S. Lekson, Headquarters, 1st Battalion, 504th Parachute Infantry

A "T" designated the field clearly. We jumped at 23:35, assembled on the blinker, and moved to the road where trucks were waiting. We were the first elements of the regiment to arrive with the exception of the pathfinder group, which we met on the field. —Lieutenant Chester A. Garrison, Headquarters, 2nd Battalion, 504th Parachute Infantry

We didn't fly over the Navy at all. We came up from the south. We stayed over the sea. The south end of the Bay of Salerno juts out, so we flew over that; and when we came over that we could see the drop zone. We dropped between six and eight hundred feet. —Lieutenant Reneau G. Breard, Company A, 504th Parachute Infantry

As the green light switched on, a large flickering "T" appeared [on the ground] below. Out into space went the bundles and, after it, parachutists snapped out one behind the other. The air was crowded with troops and bundles. Below, the 2nd Battalion was already moving on the drop zone toward a bright light. The drop zone was black specked, dotted with masses of rocks and small trees. —Lieutenant John S. Lekson, Headquarters, 1st Battalion, 504th Parachute Infantry

SALERNO

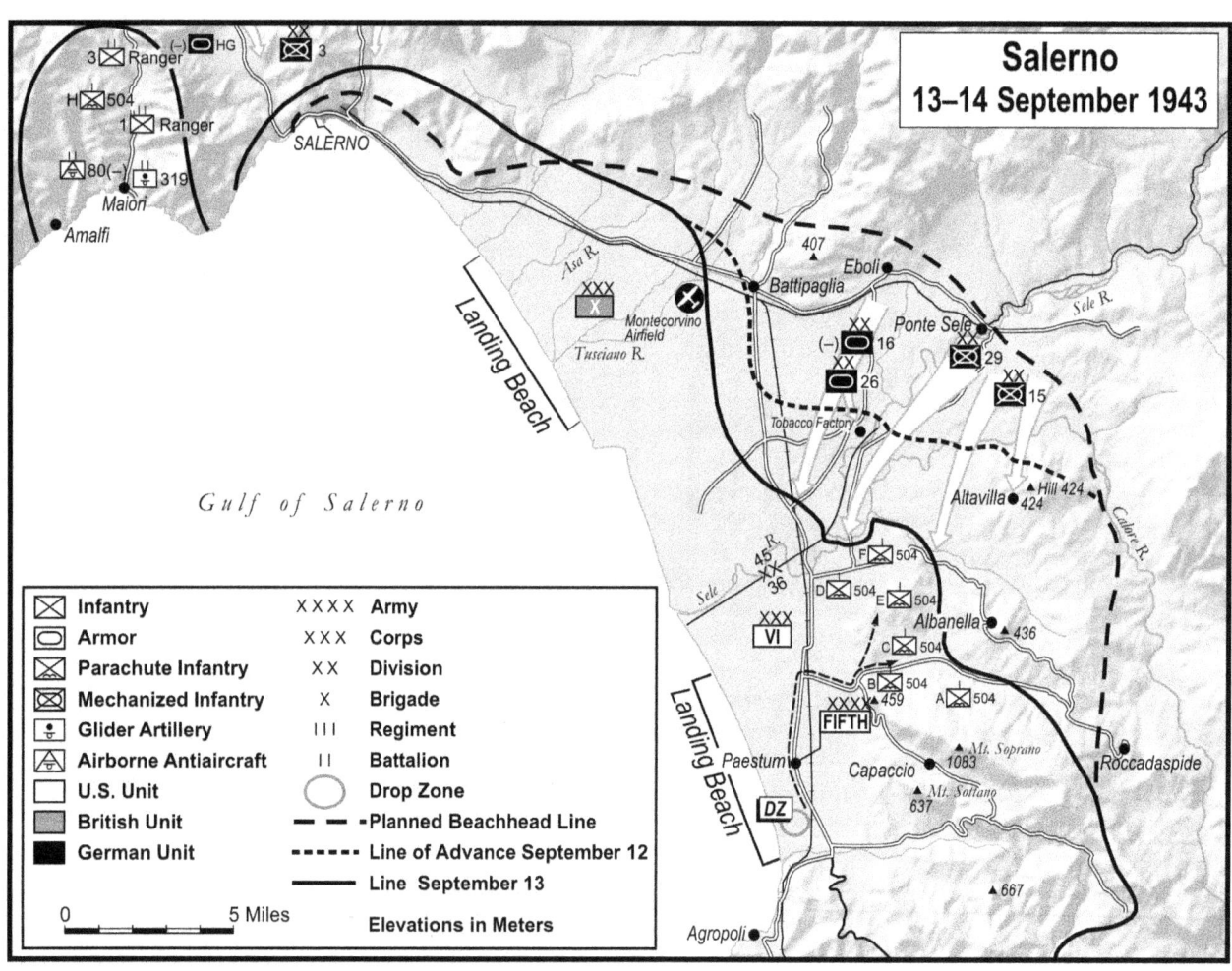

SAVING THE BEACHHEAD
13-18 SEPTEMBER 1943

This is an aerial photo of Maiori on the coast of the Sorrento Peninsula on the north side of the Salerno Bay. On September 9, 1943, a force of U.S. Army Rangers landed by sea at Maiori and captured the Chiunzi Pass and the mountains which overlooked it, and also seized the coastal highway to Salerno, securing the left flank of the Salerno landings. The next day, Company H, 504th Parachute Infantry; the 319th Glider Field Artillery Battalion; plus Batteries D, E, F, and Headquarters of the 80th Airborne Antiaircraft (Antitank) Battalion; a platoon of Company A, 307th Airborne Engineer Battalion; and two platoons of the 813th Tank Destroyer Battalion landed by sea at Maiori to reinforce the Rangers. *United States Army Signal Corps photograph, National Archives.*

On our way to Salerno, Company H was given a new mission to land at Maiori, Italy. We had to coordinate by radio with the U.S. Rangers who would land in the same area on September 9, 1943. The following day, we landed unopposed on the narrow stone coastal area near Maiori, which is nine miles west of Salerno and part of the Sorrento Peninsula. After landing, we moved inland and went to the mountains where we seized some high ground near the Chiunzi Pass area, including a vital tunnel. Two battalions of U.S. Rangers moved north to positions that commanded the Pagani-Nocera Pass. Another battalion moved into the Amalfi area. My platoon occupied positions at the [Agerola–Gragnano] tunnel on the right flank of the company. The company commander borrowed a truck from a local citizen to use for mobility in order to cover the wide area (about five miles) we had to defend. Our company strength at that time was about 120 men. This rugged mountain area was not difficult to defend because the heavy equipment of the Germans was restricted to road use. There were two roads that had to be considered—one from Gragnano through the tunnel and the other through Sorrento and Amalfi. It was our job to prevent German forces from using these roads to get through to Salerno. Certain local Italians in the area had friends in Castellammare di Stabia, with whom they had phone contact. When a German unit passed through Castellammare, the locals were supposed to be called and informed which road they were using. This information was to be relayed to the company commander, but it my belief that his alliance did not work. During the ten days we defended in this area, the Germans made a number of attempts to get through, but were repulsed. They did get a few small patrols into our position and on one occasion, took two of my men prisoner. During part of the time in this position, we received supporting fire from a 4.2" Chemical Mortar unit and from the 319th Glider Field Artillery Battalion. For our action here, the company was awarded the Presidential Unit Citation, which was among the first to be awarded to units of the 82nd Airborne Division.
—Lieutenant Edward J. Sims, Company H, 504th Parachute Infantry

This is a photograph of the Amalfi coast taken in 1943. *Photograph courtesy of William S. Mandle.*

We landed at night. We came ashore at Maiori beach unhindered and were stopped vocally by a Ranger for the password and were welcomed to land. I was at a roadblock on the mountain road. At that time, no Rangers were near us. —Staff Sergeant Bernard P. Wenneman, Battery D, 80th Airborne Antiaircraft (Antitank) Battalion

They had no assigned forward observers, so I volunteered to go with them [319th Glider Field Artillery Battalion]. There were, I believe, six of us from the 456th and 376th Parachute Field Artillery [Battalions]. We landed there with no opposition. We joined the Rangers at the Chiunzi Pass. —Lieutenant Robert S. Hutton, 376th Parachute Field Artillery Battalion

We started up the mountain that night. On the way out of town I picked up an Italian carbine. It was lying by some Ginzo soldier that must have been killed by Darby's men. I kept it, it was better than mine. I hid it and brought it with me. Ammunition was no problem since cartridges of all kinds were plentiful and some Kraut ammo fit it. —Technician Fourth Grade Edward R. Ryan, Battery C, 319th Glider Field Artillery Battalion

I was told to take my platoon and establish guiding lights for bombers. This was done on a mountain with ammo cans filled with dirt and gasoline. I was told to take my platoon and check out a monastery on a mountain which was being used by the Germans as an OP [observation post]. After a four or five hour climb, we reached the monastery and were told they had not seen a German in weeks. During my time there [in the mountains] I only recall receiving mortar and artillery fire. —Lieutenant Floyd N. Dixon, Battery E, 80th Airborne Antiaircraft (Antitank) Battalion

This photograph of the area of the Salerno landings at Paestum was taken on September 9, 1943 during the landing of the 36th Infantry Division. The hills overlooking the beach and flat ground in front of them provided excellent observation for German artillery. *United States Air Force photograph, www.fold3.com.*

This is an aerial photo looking northeast of the beach at Paestum and beyond. It shows the almost tabletop nature of the terrain in front of the hills. *United States Army Signal Corps photograph, National Archives.*

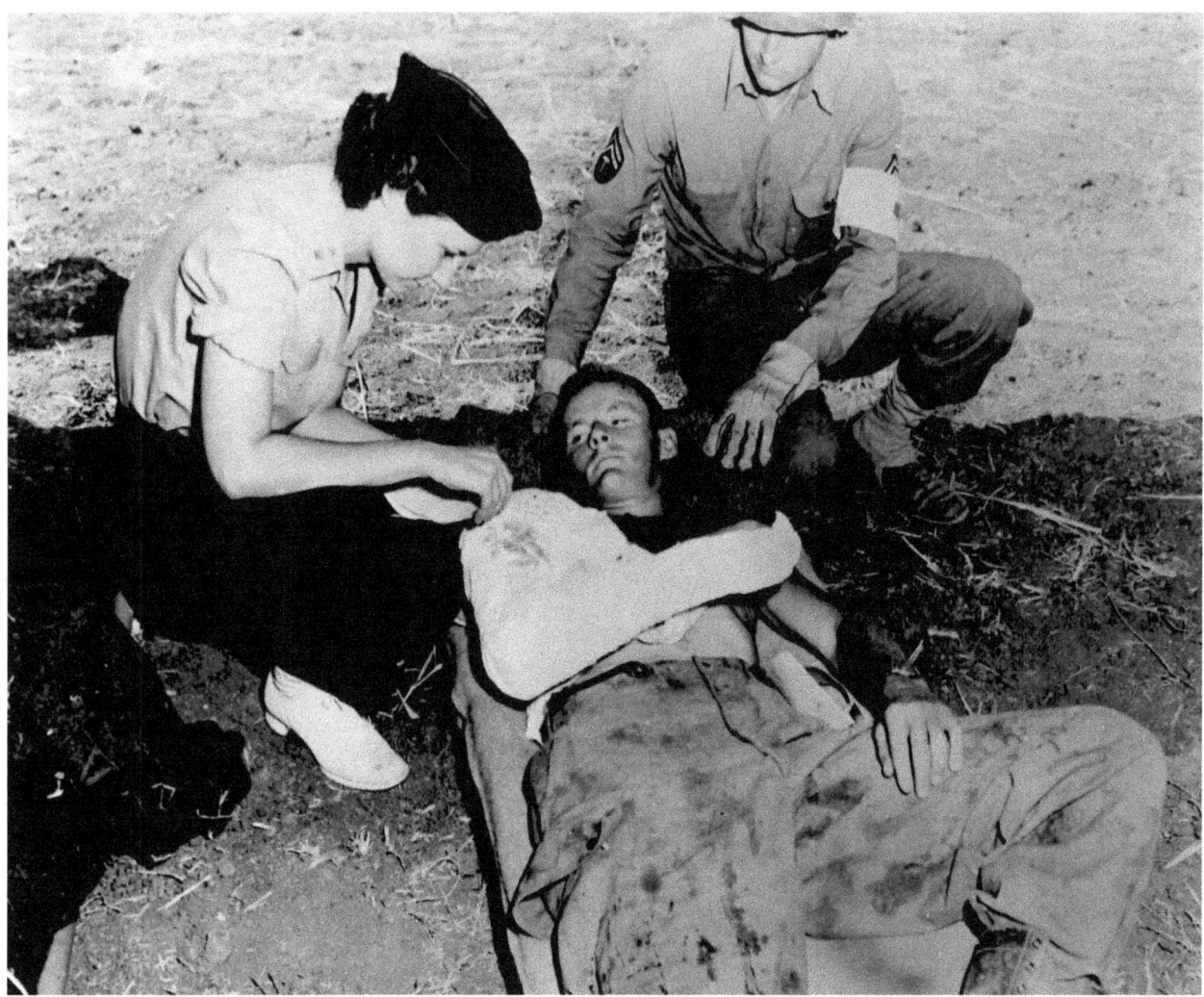

Verona Savinski (left), a nurse with the 802nd Medical Air Evacuation Transport Squadron and Technician Fifth Grade Claude W. Thomas (right), with the 3rd Auxiliary Surgical Group, attend to Private First Class Joe Hirsch, with Company A, 504th Parachute Infantry, who was wounded during a strafing by German aircraft while moving to the front line after jumping at Paestum, September 13, 1943. *United States Air Force photograph, www.fold3.com.*

A Lieutenant Colonel [Wiley O'Mohundro] of VI Corps began to review the situation in the VI Corps sector. He told of the troops that had been cutoff at Altavilla, and of a gap that existed in the VI Corps line into which the regiment, led by corps guides, would move. The regiment would "hold to the last man and last round." Troops were to be warned that men of the 36th Division would undoubtedly be drifting through the lines. Then Colonel Tucker made his assignments. The 2nd Battalion would defend the left sector; the 1st Battalion, the right, extending up the slope of Mount Soprano. Then came the order to move out. North and east toward Mount Soprano went the convoy until, some eight miles from the drop zone, it halted. The position to be defended was a flat valley floor and the north slopes of Mount Soprano. Ahead some fifteen hundred yards was La Cosa Creek. At 02:00 14 September, troops unloaded from the trucks... —Lieutenant John S. Lekson, Headquarters, 1st Battalion, 504th Parachute Infantry

Probably due to an insufficient briefing, the pilot of the lead plane gave B Company a green light over the mountains some six miles south of the drop zone. Upon landing Captain [Charles W.] Duncan failed to recognize any landmarks and decided to form a perimeter with his group of four officers and eighty men. When dawn came this group could see the Paestum beaches to their north. At once, they moved off toward the beaches. Near the regimental drop zone they were able to obtain truck transportation and a guide who led them to the battalion defense position. With the coming of B Company, C Company moved to the north and B Company filled in the center of the battalion sector, astride the road, tying in with A Company on the right. —Lieutenant John S. Lekson, Headquarters, 1st Battalion, 504th Parachute Infantry

A 504th paratrooper has set up his temporary home on the south bank of the Sele River, using a portion of his parachute canopy and his shelter half to cover his slit trench. The sign reads, "Cozy Cove." *Photograph courtesy of William S. Mandle.*

Great numbers of retreating 143rd Regiment [36th Infantry Division] men are being attached to us in E Company—about 130 enlisted men and two officers by noon. E Company has advanced to the forward slope of its hill. Our artillery in our vicinity set up a heavy pounding at noon. All the attached men are being sent forward to the 141st Regiment which is to our left. F Company was withdrawn from the Sele River where, with tank destroyers, they had been keeping the Germans from making a river crossing. —Lieutenant Chester A. Garrison, Headquarters, 2nd Battalion, 504th Parachute Infantry

Paratroopers prepare to fire a bazooka round at an enemy position in the hills overlooking the beach. *United States Army Signal Corps film still image.*

The back blast from the bazooka obscures the paratroopers as the bazooka round explodes a short distance away prior to an assault on an enemy position. *United States Army Signal Corps film still image.*

The troopers immediately rise to their feet to assault the enemy position as the smoke and debris from the bazooka round hangs in the air. *United States Army Signal Corps film still image.*

Troopers rush forward to assault the enemy position. *United States Army Signal Corps film still image.*

The paratroopers continue to advance across a terraced field in the hills above the beaches of Salerno. *United States Army Signal Corps film still image.*

Paratroopers fire an 81mm mortar concealed in the natural vegetation of the area. *United States Army Signal Corps film still image.*

Paratroopers manning a Browning .30 caliber light machine gun fire across a low hedge as a mortar round explodes just ahead of them. *United States Army Signal Corps film still image.*

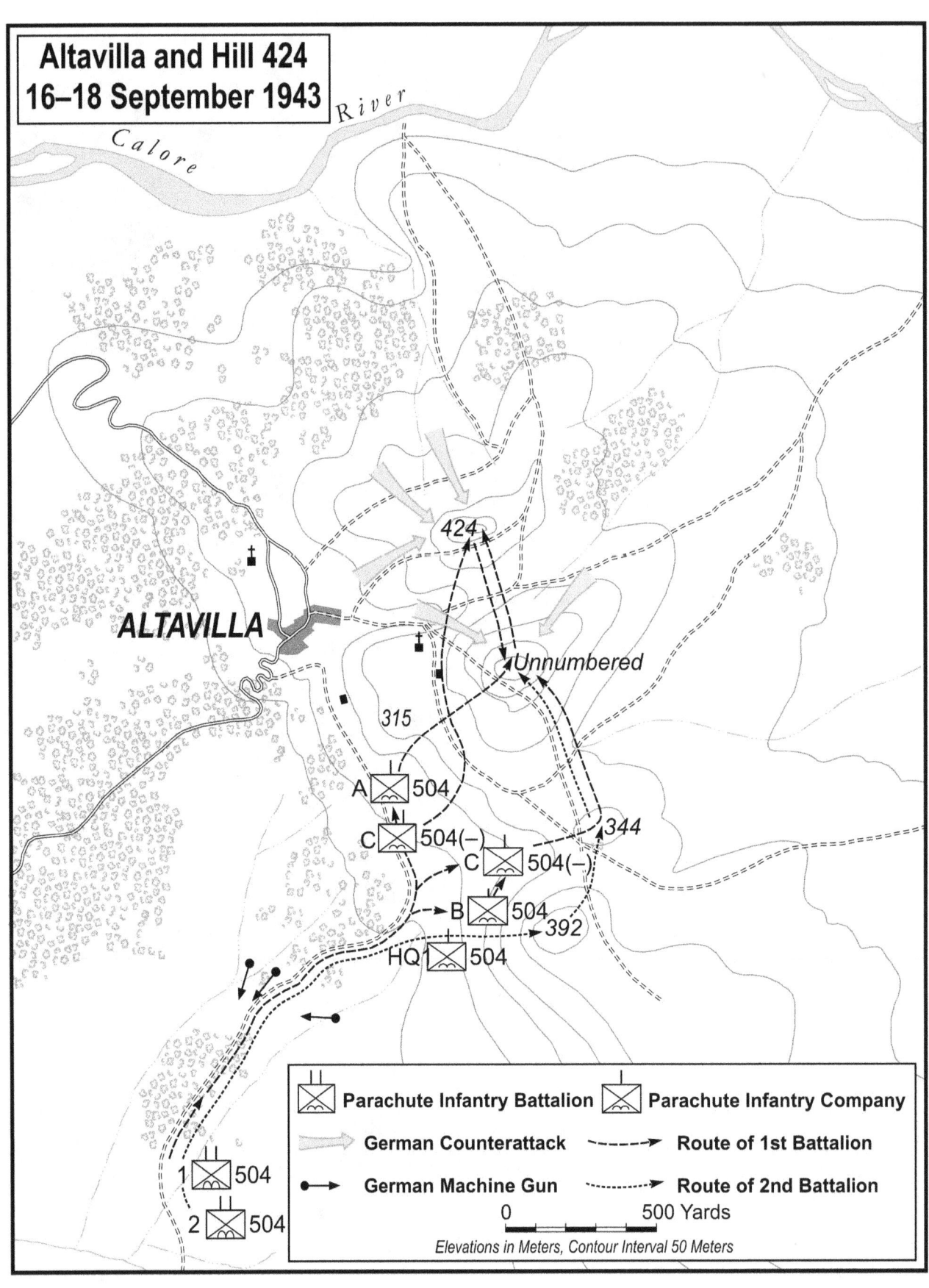

This photograph was taken on one of the hills near Altavilla captured during a night assault by the 504th Parachute Infantry and held against enemy counterattacks until relieved by elements of the 36th Infantry Division. It purportedly shows two dead paratroopers (center and upper left) with a third trooper sitting near a tree to the right of the trooper at the upper left. Neither of the dead troopers is wearing jump boots and the trooper in the center's musette bag appears to have been emptied, which lends credence to them being dead. *Photograph courtesy of William S. Mandle.*

At the northeastern edge of Altavilla, on the road that ran east along Hill 424 could be seen three German tanks. All three tanks soon began to fire into foxhole after foxhole along the northwest slope on the hill. The tanks first fired on the foxholes on the western edge of A Company, then along the 2nd and 3rd Platoons of B Company. A direct hit on a bazooka position of the 2nd Platoon, B Company blasted two men out of the position. The platoon leader of the 2nd Platoon of A Company and his aid man ran down. They were joined by the 1st Platoon leader and his platoon sergeant. Another shell burst wounded the A Company platoon leader before the bazooka team could be evacuated. On the right flank of the 2nd Platoon, B Company, was a company strongpoint dug in among a cluster of trees. Two shell bursts killed six men there. As the tanks fired, a German attack was launched from the northwest along the draw against the 1st Platoon of A Company. In a short firefight, the German force was driven back with some loss. Though the German tank support had hit the battalion northwest perimeter hard, the 1st and 3rd Platoons of A Company had not been affected by the tank fire. While the tanks had been active, the artillery observer had gained radio contact. Soon, VI Corps artillery was firing on Altavilla and on the tanks. As the German tanks and infantry withdrew, enemy artillery began to pound the hill. I, with a command post detail, moved to the aid station to collect ammunition from the wounded. Some of the troops had reached a critical low in small arms [ammunition]. In the aid station was some twenty wounded. About ten had been killed so far in the morning's action. —Lieutenant John S. Lekson, Headquarters, 1st Battalion, 504th Parachute Infantry

Troopers with Company A, 504th take a break in a ravine on Hill 424. *Photograph by Corporal John E. Thawley, courtesy of William Mandle.*

Private Robert Larsen with Company A, 504th Parachute Infantry guards one end of the ravine on Hill 424 while other troopers of his unit take a much needed break. *Photograph by Corporal John E. Thawley, courtesy of William S. Mandle.*

Troopers drive to their assigned aircraft in preparation for being flown to Italy. Elements of Headquarters Company, 82nd Airborne Division and divisional special troops were flown from an airfield near Licata, Sicily on September 18, 1943 and air landed at an airfield constructed near Paestum, Italy. *United States Air Force photograph, www.fold3.com.*

Troopers load C-47 aircraft at the airfield near Licata, Sicily in preparation for being flown to an airfield near Paestum, Italy. *United States Air Force photograph, www.fold3.com.*

Troopers and air corps personnel use a ramp to load a jeep into a C-47 at the airfield at Licata, Sicily prior to being flown to Italy where elements of Headquarters Company, 82nd Airborne Division and divisional special troops were air landed on September 18, 1943. *United States Air Force photograph, www.fold3.com.*

Musette bags are transferred from a ¼-ton trailer onto a C-47 in preparation for a flight from an airfield near Licata, Sicily to an temporary airstrip near Paestum, Italy on September 18, 1943. *United States Air Force photograph, www.fold3.com.*

An officer with Headquarters Company, 82nd Airborne Division (right center) fills out a Form B load manifest prior to takeoff for Paestum, Italy on September 18, 1943. *United States Air Force photograph, www.fold3.com.*

Master Sergeant Alvin Thornton fills out a Form B load manifest prior to the flight to an airfield near Paestum. *United States Air Force photograph, www.fold3.com.*

An officer (center) checks the manifest prior to departure for Italy where elements of Headquarters Company, 82nd Airborne Division and a detachment of divisional special troops were air landed near Paestum on September 18, 1943. *United States Air Force photograph, www.fold3.com.*

Troop carrier aircraft transport elements of Headquarters Company, 82nd Airborne Division and divisional special troops from the airfield near Licata, Sicily to an airfield constructed near Paestum, Italy, September 18, 1943. *United States Air Force photograph, www.fold3.com.*

Lieutenant General Mark Clark, the commander of the Fifth Army, expresses his thanks to 325th Glider Infantry troopers on September 23, 1943, for their part in holding Mount San Angelo on the left flank of the beachhead. *United States Army Signal Corps photograph, National Archives.*

Most of the 82nd Airborne Division's glider borne artillery, antitank, engineer, and medical units as well as the division's vehicles destined for Salerno departed by landing craft from the Termini-Imerese harbor, just east of Palermo, Sicily (above). This photo of LSTs (Landing Ship Tank) being loaded there was taken on September 13, 1943. The 320th Glider Field Artillery Battalion; the 376th Parachute Field Artillery Battalion; Batteries A, B, and C, 80th Airborne Antiaircraft (Antitank) Battalion, Headquarters and Headquarters Battery, Division Artillery; and the 307th Airborne Engineer Battalion, less Companies B and C departed this harbor by landing craft for the beach at the Sele River area, arriving on September 23. The 307th Airborne Medical Company; the Antitank Platoon, 325th Glider Infantry; the 82nd Airborne Military Police Platoon; a detachment of Headquarters Company, 82nd Airborne Division; and a detachment of Special Troops, 82nd Airborne Division departed from Termini-Imerese for Maiori, arriving on September 30, 1943. *United States Army Signal Corps photograph, National Archives.*

The [376th Parachute Field Artillery] Battalion moved from Kairouan to Bizerte, then back to Sicily in the area of Gela. From Gela to Palermo by motor convoy. From Palermo by LST to Salerno. We landed from LSTs at Salerno and waded ashore, but did not occupy any firing positions. —Private Herman Swope, Battery C, 376th Parachute Field Artillery Battalion

For the Italian campaign we sailed from Termini on an LST to the Salerno beachhead on 23 September 1943. The 504 and 505 jumped at Salerno and we came in by LST. There was artillery fire on the beach.—Sergeant James F. Crosbie, Battery B, 376th Parachute Field Artillery Battalion

Most of the division's vehicles landed on September 23, 1943 along with the 320th Glider Field Artillery Battalion; the 376th Parachute Field Artillery Battalion; Batteries A, B, and C, of the 80th Airborne Antiaircraft (Antitank) Battalion; the Division Artillery; the 307th Airborne Medical Company; and Headquarters, Service Company, and Company A, 307th Airborne Engineer Battalion. *United States Army Signal Corps photograph, courtesy of William S. Mandle.*

An ambulance assigned to the 307th Airborne Medical Company disembarks from LST 372 on September 23, 1943. *United States Army Signal Corps photograph, courtesy of William S. Mandle.*

Troopers wait on the beach for the vehicles to be unloaded and assembled before moving to join elements of the division already ashore, September 23, 1943. *United States Army Signal Corps photograph, courtesy of William S. Mandle.*

THE LIBERATION OF NAPLES
28 SEPTEMBER – 1 OCTOBER 1943

General Ridgway, with his 1903 Springfield rifle in a holster on the right side of his jeep, is driven by Staff Sergeant Frank Farmer, who also served as his bodyguard. Once the division's vehicles arrived at the Salerno beachhead, first with jeeps for Headquarters and Headquarters Company personnel as well as the division reconnaissance platoon on September 18 by air, then the bulk of the trucks, jeeps, trailers, artillery, and antitank guns on September 23 by sea, the division prepared to lead the drive north to liberate Naples. *United States Army Signal Corps photograph, courtesy of William S. Mandle.*

With the whole 82nd in the Salerno beachhead, General Clark committed us as a division, giving us the mission of moving westward, close to the coast, and seizing the dominating high ground that overlooked the Naples plain. —Major General Matthew B. Ridgway, Headquarters, 82nd Airborne Division

As we moved northward, our route took us along the Amalfi Peninsula, which is the spectacular southern side of the Sorrento Peninsula. It was gorgeous, but a hell of a place to fight a war because the steep mountains and deep gorges were perfect for defense. But the Germans apparently planned to make their defensive line further north. They withdrew slowly and grudgingly, but withdrew they did. I remember coming into the seaside town of Maiori, where some of our troops had come in on naval landing craft. Maiori was at the base of a mountain system rising from the sea which led to the Chiunzi Pass, on the other side of which led down to the plains below the city of Naples, which was a major objective of ours. Some of our troops and also some Rangers under the command of the legendary Colonel [William O.] Darby were dug in at the summit near the pass and on the flanks of the mountain below. —Technician Fourth Grade Leonard Lebenson, Headquarters Company, 82nd Airborne Division

Paratroopers with the 505th Parachute Infantry emerge from the Agerola–Gragnano tunnel in the mountains of the Sorrento Peninsula as they begin the advance toward Naples on September 27, 1943. The tunnel is located north of the town of Agerola. *Allies Enter Naples, British Pathé film still image.*

After leaving the tunnel, the 505th troopers ascend the pass along a winding road. *Allies Enter Naples, British Pathé film still image.*

The 82nd Airborne Division was moved to Amalfi, and the 505th Parachute Infantry moved up the mountain road from Amalfi to the top of the Sorrento Peninsula. There, near the small town of Agerola, where the Amalfi–Castellammare road goes through the tunnel at the top of the mountain, I established my command post. We were at one end of the tunnel and the Germans were at the other. On September 28, I climbed to the top of the Sorrento Peninsula and there had my first view of Naples. Billowing black clouds of smoke covered the waterfront, and buildings were burning throughout the city. A pall of smoke and dust, so characteristic of a battlefield, hung over the area. I was told to attack and seize the town of Gragnano at the foot of the mountain the following morning. I had never fought in such terrain, and looking back, I realize that if the plan I prepared had been carried out, it probably would have been a disaster. I had three separate columns moving down spurs of the mountains with the mission of making a combined attack on the hill overlooking Gragnano, about five miles away. Fortunately, at daylight on September 29, I learned that the Germans had withdrawn. I moved at once down the road into the town and then on to Castellammare [di Stabia]. —Colonel James M. Gavin, Headquarters, 505th Parachute Infantry

Paratroopers with the 307th Airborne Engineer Battalion construct a temporary platform to bridge a gap across an ancient stone bridge blown by the German army's rear guard to slow the Allied advance toward Naples. *United States Army Signal Corps photograph, National Archives.*

The Allied vehicle convoy begins to cross the repaired bridge on the way to liberate Naples. *United States Army Signal Corps photograph, National Archives.*

This is an aerial view of the volcanic Mount Vesuvius (lower left) and the coastline to the north toward Naples. *United States Air Force photograph, www.fold3.com.*

Troopers and a couple of British soldiers view Mount Vesuvius from the Sarno Plain. *Allies Enter Naples, British Pathé film still image.*

Private First Class Ervin L. Prechowski (left), Private Ellis A. Starling, (center), and Sergeant Bertram J. "Jack" Bishop (seated drinking from canteen cup) are among the Company A, 504th troopers taking a break outside of the city of Castellammare di Stabia on the morning of September 29, 1943. *Photograph by Sergeant Albert B. Clark, courtesy of William S. Mandle.*

Company A, 504th Parachute Infantry troopers bivouac in an orchard outside of Castellammare di Stabia, on September 29, 1943, during the division's advance toward Naples. *Photograph by Sergeant Albert B. Clark, courtesy of William S. Mandle.*

Troopers view an amphitheater at Pompei during a short break before resuming the advance to Naples. *Allies Enter Naples, British Pathé film still image.*

We spent one night in Castellammare, which was picturesque and relatively undamaged by the war. The great beauty of this part of the world could not escape me. There were gardens and citrus fruits on the side of the mountains that seemed to take a perpendicular climb from the sea. The people were surprisingly friendly. When there was no artillery exchange or mortar fire, they would come out and throw grapes in our jeeps as well as walnuts. The children would yell for "bon bons". September 29th, the division passed through Vesuvius and Pompei. The ruins were slightly damaged by mortar fire, but remained essentially intact. Our headquarters stayed long enough for me to look briefly at Pompei.—Lieutenant James E. Baugh, Headquarters, 80th Airborne Antiaircraft (Antitank) Battalion

Troopers inspect the ruins at Pompei before resuming the drive to Naples. *Allies Enter Naples, British Pathé film still image.*

Pompei would later become one of the options for troopers on leave during the occupation of Naples because of its interesting ruins and history. *Allies Enter Naples, British Pathé film still image.*

I was standing with the advance guard, discussing the situation, when the Regimental S-3, Major Jack Norton approached. "Colonel," he said, "We are to wait until a triumphant entry is organized." "A triumphant entry!" I exclaimed. "How in the world can we organize such a thing? It takes participation of the natives." I had never put anything like that together in my life, and visions crossed my mind of Napoleon's colorfully clad soldiers entering European capitals that had just capitulated, beautiful nubile women leaning over the balconies tossing flowers, much waving of handkerchiefs, and bands playing. And I recalled the entry of Allenby into Jerusalem – and here I was told to organize a triumphant entry. Word came down that General Clark was going to come to the head of the column and that he would lead the triumphant march into the city. Then word arrived that we were to lead them to Garibaldi Square. I found it on the map; it was in front of the railroad station. But suppose instead of people tossing flowers there were Germans tossing grenades from the rooftops. And in any event, the masses of people milling around in the streets and throwing candy and offering bottles of wine to the troops all had to be dealt with. —Colonel James M. Gavin, Headquarters, 505th Parachute Infantry

Paratroopers with the 3rd Battalion, 505th Parachute Infantry mount British armored vehicles as troopers in a jeep pass by for the movement through Naples to Garibaldi Square, October 1, 1943. *Allies Enter Naples, British Pathé film still image.*

The division reconnaissance platoon riding in jeeps modified with armor plating on the front and sides of the driver and front passenger compartments passes crowds of jubilant citizens, many of them armed with rifles. *Allies Enter Naples, British Pathé film still image.*

Crowds cheer the division reconnaissance platoon as it drives past them in armored jeeps. *Allies Enter Naples, British Pathé film still image.*

Paratroopers with the 3rd Battalion, 505th Parachute Infantry, riding on British trucks, follow the jeeps, while scanning the windows and rooftops above and the crowds for signs of German troops and die hard Italian fascists. *Allies Enter Naples, British Pathé film still image.*

Young Italian men attempt to climb aboard the trucks as paratroopers with the 3rd Battalion, 505th riding on top keep their attention focused on the windows and rooftops for signs of enemy troops. *Allies Enter Naples, British Pathé film still image.*

Riding in jeeps and atop British armored vehicles, the first troopers arrive at an almost empty Garibaldi Square, October 1, 1943. Riding in a British armored car (center), Generals Ridgway (left) and Clark (right) can be seen standing up in it as the convoy enters the square. *Allies Enter Naples, British Pathé film still image.*

THE LIBERATION OF NAPLES

Troopers gather at the base of a statue of Giuseppe Garibaldi, October 1, 1943, where a large crowd was expected to welcome General Mark Clark, but they had gathered at Plaza Plebisceto instead. *Allies Enter Naples, British Pathé film still image.*

The citizens of Naples welcome their liberators. *Allies Enter Naples, British Pathé film still image.*

Crowds of ecstatic citizens of Naples soon converge on the troopers as they celebrate the city's liberation. *Allies Enter Naples, British Pathé film still image.*

Jubilant crowds rush toward the column of vehicles as the 82nd Airborne Division moves through the heart of Naples on October 1, 1943. *United States Army Signal Corps photograph, National Archives.*

Paratroopers with Headquarters Company, 2nd Battalion, 505th Parachute Infantry move into the outskirts of Naples, Italy on October 1, 1943. *United States Army Signal Corps photograph, National Archives.*

Headquarters Company, 2nd Battalion, 505th Parachute Infantry paratroopers wait for the order to move forward into the center of Naples on October 1, 1943. *United States Army Signal Corps photograph, National Archives.*

Paratroopers march into the heart of Naples through the rubble strewn streets, October 1, 1943. *Allies Enter Naples, British Pathé film still image.*

Citizens of Naples welcome troopers of the 82nd Airborne Division as they enter the city. *Photograph courtesy of William S. Mandle.*

Crowds welcomed the troopers of the 82nd Airborne Division as liberators. *Photograph courtesy of William S. Mandle.*

Major General Ridgway (left) stands by as Lieutenant General Mark W. Clark (center), commander of the Fifth Army, prepares to board his plane to return to the Fifth Army headquarters after his "triumphant entry" into Naples, October 1, 1943. *United States Army Signal Corps film still image.*

Wrecked German vehicles, including a prime mover (left) used for towing artillery and antitank and antiaircraft guns litter a plaza in Naples with damaged buildings in the background. The damage was most likely caused by bombing by Allied aircraft prior to the liberation of the city. *Photograph courtesy of William S. Mandle.*

The town was pretty much destroyed, including the public water system and everything useful. This was done by the Germans on their way out of town. G Company spent the night in a bombed out railroad station. The next day we moved to a bombed out theater where we were organized into patrol groups. My group was assigned to the area near the docks, which by this time was beginning to unload supplies. Our biggest problem was controlling the bread lines at bakeries, where there was a limited amount of bread being produced due to the limited supplies. —Sergeant William L. Blank, Company G, 505th Parachute Infantry

Damaged buildings were found throughout Naples, especially near the harbor, where Allied bombing had been concentrated. *Photograph courtesy of William S. Mandle.*

A partially submerged ship lies in the Naples harbor, which was largely destroyed by retreating German troops. *Photograph courtesy of William S. Mandle.*

Troopers patrol the bomb damaged streets of Naples. *Photograph courtesy of William S. Mandle.*

Three troopers pose with children during the division's occupation of Naples. *Photograph courtesy of William S. Mandle.*

This man offered carriage rides through the streets of Naples. *Photograph courtesy of William S. Mandle.*

A trooper poses prior to taking a carriage ride through the streets of Naples. *Photograph courtesy of William S. Mandle.*

A trooper gets his jump boots shined in Naples. *Photograph courtesy of William S. Mandle.*

A German time bomb detonated in the basement of the central post office building in Naples on October 7, 1943, killing over one hundred people, most of whom were homeless and living in the building. In this photo, smoke is still rising from the building as troopers rush to aid the dying and wounded. A United States Army Signal Corps film photographer happened to be nearby when the bomb exploded and captured the bloody scene. *United States Army Signal Corps film still image.*

American and British ambulances arrive on scene to transport the wounded to a military hospital. *United States Army Signal Corps film still image.*

Victims of the bombing are placed on stretchers and loaded into ambulances. *United States Army Signal Corps film still image.*

Allied troops and Naples policemen congregate around the site of the massive bombing. *United States Army Signal Corps photograph.*

Troopers clear rubble from the street after a German time bomb detonated in the Naples post office. *Photograph courtesy of William S. Mandle.*

A church service for troopers of the 82nd Airborne Division is conducted in one of the beautiful churches in Naples. *United States Army Signal Corps photograph, courtesy of William S. Mandle.*

On Sunday morning, I went with General Clark to services at the cathedral, and while we were there we heard a tremendous dull explosion. We left at once, to find that the barracks where the engineer battalion had been quartered had blown up. I will never forget the tragic sight. Arms and legs of American soldiers, killed in their sleep, were sticking pitifully out of the rubble of the second floor. Twenty men were killed, and many more were wounded. We were never able to establish definitely whether the explosion was the result of a time device left by the Germans, or whether some of the engineers' own demolitions went off by accident. I still believe, though, that it was the result of a German booby trap. —Major General Matthew B. Ridgway, Headquarters, 82nd Airborne Division

Troopers and Naples policemen enforce order at a bakery. Food shortages caused chaos as desperate citizens competed for the limited supplies of bread. *The Path to Rome 1943–1944 Reel 2, British Pathé film still image.*

It was necessary to have guards at water points and at the bakeries. I saw one woman very badly cut-up with a broken gallon jug, because she tried to cut into the waiting line. I also saw a woman who appeared to be pregnant [in order] to get in the bread line and another woman pulled a knife and slit the first woman across the abdomen. I held my breath until I saw the feathers fly, the pregnancy turned out to be a pillow.
—Private First Class Reed S. Fassett, with Battery A, 376th Parachute Field Artillery Battalion

The glider troopers manage to get an orderly queue established and reduce the level of anxiety among the city's civilians. *The Path to Rome 1943–1944 Reel 2, British Pathé film still image.*

The troopers deal firmly with anyone who threatens to cause a disruption. *The Path to Rome 1943–1944 Reel 2, British Pathé film still image.*

THE 504TH INTO THE MOUNTAINS
27 OCTOBER – 27 DECEMBER 1943

The town of Arnone (upper right), located on the Volturno River, and was captured by the 2nd Battalion, 505th Parachute Infantry on October 5, 1943. The railroad yard, the scene of intense fighting by Company E is located at the left center of the photo. *United States Air Force photograph, National Archives, courtesy of Mark Sparry.*

We arrived at about 18:00 hours with the mission to drive to the Volturno River, about fifteen miles to the northwest, to save five canal bridges in route to the Volturno River and the village of Arnone on the southwest bank of the river. The bridges were essential to the movement of the [British] armored brigade and eventual crossing of the Volturno River. Rather than wait until morning, I directed two platoons of about twenty-four men each to move out as fast as possible in the dark to take the first two bridges. Each platoon had a light machine gun and a bazooka team. The battalion followed in column on both sides of the road. —Lieutenant Colonel Mark J. Alexander, Headquarters, 2nd Battalion, 505th Parachute Infantry

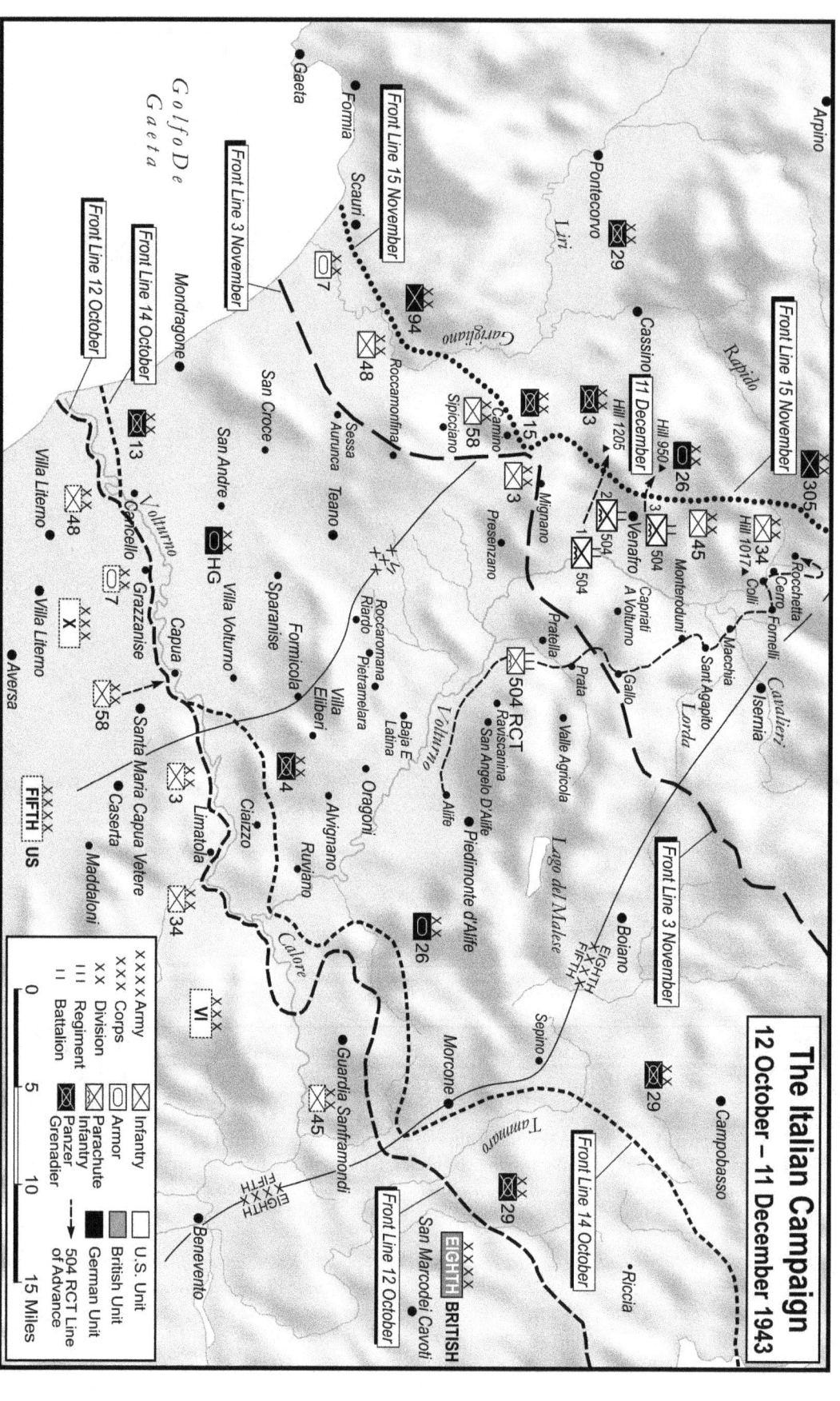

The Italian Campaign 12 October – 11 December 1943

The 504th Regimental Combat Team was detached from the 82nd Airborne Division and was put to work in mountains northeast of Naples on October 27, 1943. On November 18, 1943, the 82nd Airborne Division, less the 504th RCT, sailed from Naples on its way to Northern Ireland and then to England to prepare for the invasion of Normandy.

Paratroopers with the 376th Parachute Field Artillery Battalion, concealed under camouflage netting, fire their 75mm pack howitzer in support of the 504th Parachute Infantry during the drive in the hills and mountains north of the Volturno River. *Photograph courtesy of William S. Mandle.*

Artillerymen with the 376th Parachute Field Artillery Battalion eat from mess kits in the muddy quagmire during the fall of 1943. *Photograph courtesy of William S. Mandle.*

Private Dickie L. Hensley, with Battery B, 376th Parachute Field Artillery Battalion, from Mexia, Texas, tenderly holds a young girl who was one of eight civilians killed when German troops blew up a roadblock in the village of Prata, Italy on November 1, 1943. *United States Army Signal Corps photograph, National Archives.*

Our job was to protect the right flank of the U.S. Fifth Army and to maintain contact with the British Eighth Army on our right. We were restricted to movement by foot and had to carry our equipment and ammunition. The few mules we had were a big help, but progress was slow in these treacherous mountains. The numerous booby traps and destruction of trails made it more difficult. German resistance was sporadic, but by October 29, 1943, we had passed through Valle Agricola, Letino, and seized Gallo. From October 20 to November 12, 1943, we moved higher into the Apennines toward Isernia. On our way we cleared the villages of Macchia, Fornelli, Cerro, and Rochetta. Near Colli, Company H was ordered to attack and seize Hill 1017. The attack started by fording a raging stream, then up the south slope of the hill. Resistance was moderate, but the entire area had been heavily mined with personnel mines (S-mines). The first casualty was the company commander who had his heel blown off. The officer who then took command, within minutes, fell from the cliff when he attempted to avoid incoming artillery, and broke his leg. At that point, I assumed command of the company and continued to direct the attack. Due to enemy fire and personnel mines, we had to proceed slowly and cautiously. While doing so, many S-mines were activated causing a number of casualties Of the three mines I stepped on, the first one angled up under a mule in front of me and demolished his rear end, the second one while I was carrying a wounded man, exploded in the ground when it failed to bounce up and the third mine bounced up but failed to explode. By late afternoon, we were able to take the hill and set up a defense. I ordered everyone to stay in place until I could get our engineers up to clear the mines from the area.
—Lieutenant Edward J. Sims, Company H, 504th Parachute Infantry

This 81mm mortar squad loads the heavy weapon onto two mules for transport through the Apennine Mountains north of the Volturno River. *United States Army Signal Corps photograph, courtesy of William S. Mandle.*

A 504th officer (left) and one of his troopers (center) have carried the body of their dead comrade on a blood stained stretcher down the slope of one of the hills secured by the 504th and have secured it to a mule for the Italian soldier (right) to take to a graves registration vehicle at the bottom of the hill. *United States Army Signal Corps photograph, National Archives.*

The trooper makes a last check of the ropes securing his comrade's dead body before the Italian soldier leads it to the graves registration vehicle. *United States Army Signal Corps photograph, National Archives.*

Troopers send and receive radio messages using Morse code. Units, officers, objectives, and other key names were assigned code words to prevent radio intercepts from being useful to the German army. The trooper at right has a code book and keys outgoing messages while the trooper in the center is operating a hand crank to provide electrical power to the radio, and the trooper on the left listens on headphones and writes down incoming messages. *United States Army Signal Corps photograph, courtesy of William S. Mandle.*

President Franklin D. Roosevelt congratulates Colonel Reuben Tucker after awarding the Distinguished Service Cross to him during a ceremony at an airfield near Castelvetrano, Sicily on December 8, 1943. *United States Air Force photograph, www.fold3.com.*

Citation: Reuben H. Tucker, (O-19894), Colonel, 504th Parachute Infantry, for extraordinary heroism in action. On 17 September 1943, about one-half mile northeast of Altavilla, Italy, Colonel Tucker, commanding officer of the 504th Parachute Infantry, observed that the enemy was digging in on Hill 424, Army objective of the 1st Battalion of his regiment, the advance of which had been delayed by terrain. Colonel Tucker organized a small group of twenty-three men, and with utter disregard for his own safety, Colonel Tucker led this small group through heavy enemy artillery fire, attacked and drove the enemy from Hill 424. In this action five of the men became casualties, but Colonel Tucker and the remaining eighteen men held Hill 424 against enemy counterattacks and against enemy forces that were retreating in front of the 1st Battalion, until the 1st Battalion was able to occupy and hold the hill. By his heroic actions, Colonel Tucker enabled the 1st Battalion to attain its important army objective. Entered United States Military Academy from Ansonia, Connecticut.

Headquarters, Fifth Army, General Orders No. 71 (September 30, 1943)

President Roosevelt awards the Distinguished Service Cross to Lieutenant William W. Kellogg, with Company C, 307th Airborne Engineer Battalion during a ceremony conducted at an airfield near Castelvetrano, Sicily on December 8, 1943. General Dwight D. Eisenhower is the far right of the photograph. *United States Air Force photograph, www.fold3.com.*

Citation: William W. Kellogg (O-446618), First Lieutenant, 307th Airborne Engineer Battalion, 82nd Airborne Division. For extraordinary heroism in action, 15 September 1943 to 28 September 1943, between Paternapoli and Montello, Italy. As leader of an airborne platoon, Lieutenant Kellogg landed with his men forty miles behind enemy lines and for a period of thirteen consecutive days, in the face constant danger and overwhelming enemy odds, courageously conducted outstandingly successful operations in enemy territory. During this period, Lieutenant Kellogg personally led his men in disrupting telephone, power and railroad lines, and demonstrated outstanding bravery and aggressiveness in his constant harassing of the enemy. In one night's action against superior enemy forces, Lieutenant Kellogg gallantly led his band in the ambush of an enemy convoy, destroying two troop carriers and inflicting many casualties on the enemy. On September 24, he demonstrated personal heroism of the highest type in rescuing a severely wounded Allied airman whose plane was shot down behind enemy lines. In close proximity to the enemy and under intense aerial bombardment and a hail of fire from enemy guns, Lieutenant Kellogg, with utter disregard for his own life, made his way to the wounded man on an open hillside, carried him to cover, and succeeded in delivering him to friendly hands. Lieutenant Kellogg's outstanding personal valor, his inspirational leadership despite hunger, thirst, fatigue, and constant danger, and his exceptional devotion to duty no matter what the odds reflect the highest traditions of the army of the United States.

Headquarters, Fifth Army, General Orders No. 84 (November 11, 1943)

President Roosevelt congratulates Lieutenant Kellogg after awarding him the Distinguished Service Cross at a ceremony held an airfield near Castelvetrano, Sicily on December 8, 1943. *United States Air Force photograph, www.fold3.com.*

Next Page Top Photo: President Roosevelt poses with the recipients after awarding each of them the Distinguished Service Cross during a ceremony conducted at an airfield near Castelvetrano, Sicily on December 8, 1943. The recipients from left to right are Lieutenant General Mark W. Clark, the commanding officer of the Fifth Army; Colonel Reuben H. Tucker, III, commanding officer of the 504th Parachute Infantry Regiment; Lieutenant Colonel Joseph P. Crawford, the commanding officer of the 2nd Battalion, 16th Infantry Regiment; Lieutenant William W. Kellogg, with Company C, 307th Airborne Engineer Battalion; Lieutenant Thomas F. Berteau, with Company A, 101st Military Police Battalion; and Lieutenant Edwin F. Gould, with the 27th Armored Field Artillery Regiment. *United States Air Force photograph, www.fold3.com.*

The recipients are (from left to right) Lieutenant General Mark W. Clark, Colonel Reuben H. Tucker, III, Lieutenant Colonel Joseph P. Crawford, Lieutenant William C. Kellogg, Lieutenant Thomas F. Berteau, and Lieutenant Edwin F. Gould. *United States Air Force photograph, www.fold3.com.*

The town of Venafro sits at the base of Mount Croce (upper left). The 504th Parachute Infantry bivouacked there prior to moving to the San Pietro area for combat on Hills 1205 and 950. *United States Army Signal Corps photograph, National Archives.*

A religious service is conducted in the field for troopers of the 504th Parachute Infantry prior to going into combat. *Photograph courtesy of William S. Mandle.*

A 60mm mortar crew practices firing near Venafro in December of 1943, prior to going into combat. *United States Army Signal Corps photograph, National Archives.*

It was after Thanksgiving Day that the 504th received badly needed replacements. Rivers [Lieutenant Richard G. LaRiviere] and I were in that group. I will always remember the night we reported for duty to the 504th regimental headquarters [in Venafro] just to the rear of the mountains in a small blacked-out house with a deep cellar. We reported to the regimental commander, Colonel Reuben Tucker, who was seated behind a desk in a dimly lit room. He was an impressive looking man who had a deep voice and wasn't given to small talk. As he welcomed us, he talked about what we would be up against: rugged terrain and a determined enemy giving up ground only grudgingly and at a high price. The sounds of incoming and outgoing artillery permeating the air made the briefing short. For me, I had found a home after eighteen months of frustration trying to become part of a combat unit. I would not be reassigned again, nor would I be with any other unit for the balance of my nearly four years of active duty. I could not have been assigned to a better fighting unit than the 504th Parachute Regiment. Lieutenants Richard G. LaRiviere (Rivers), Peter Gerle, and I were sent to H Company along with a number of enlisted men, including James Musa, John Granado, and Valentine Maliborski. From that point until the end of the war, H Company, 504th, would be the mailing address for Rivers and me. When we reported, staff sergeants had taken over when the platoon officers became casualties. Staff Sergeant Tom Harmon had the platoon to which Rivers was assigned. Harmon was later given a battlefield commission. I was sent to the 3rd Platoon, then being led by Staff Sergeant Michael "Mike" Kogut, who reverted to platoon sergeant. Mike was an original member of the 504th; a combat veteran of the jump in Sicily, the landings at Salerno, Maiori, Chiunzi Pass, and Naples; and the crossing of the Volturno River. It was good fortune to be with him during my baptism of fire. I learned from him some of the tricks of staying alive and how to lead men, not command them. At six foot three, Mike was an impressive figure, but his stature was based on the respect his men had for him more than his physique. As a replacement officer in combat for the first time with a lot to learn, I relied heavily on Mike's advice and assistance. Being an officer and a platoon leader did not automatically command the respect of the men. It had to be earned, and that could be done only by leading. —Lieutenant James Megellas, Company H, 504th Parachute Infantry

Monte Summacro, designated on maps as Hill 1205, the highest elevation facing the German Gustav Line, had a clear view across the valley of the abbey on Monte Cassino, the strategic town of San Pietro (right center), and Highway 6 (foreground). The 1st and 2nd Battalions, 504th Parachute Infantry relieved the 1st Battalion, 143rd Infantry Regiment, 36th Infantry Division on Monte Summacro on December 11–12, 1943. *United States Army Signal Corps photograph, National Archives.*

We got off the trucks under the rocky slopes of the biggest mountain we ever saw in Italy and set up a bivouac in some olive trees. Dozens of 105 howitzers and 155 long toms and other breeds of howitzers were all around us. They fired day and night. A man had to be stone deaf to get any sleep. Plenty of tanks were all around. It looked like something big was going on, something bigger than anything we'd seen so far. We were about two miles from Venafro. The Fifth Army had pushed up the peak, which was 3,613 feet high, barren of vegetation and composed of tricky masses of rotten stone given to easy landsliding, boulders, and cliffs. The 36th Division, the 1st, 3rd, and 4th Ranger Battalions, the 1st Special Service Force, and the Legion [504th Parachute Infantry] took the hill. I don't want to leave any outfit that was there out of the story because any man who lived through that scrap ought to get credit for it. Hill 1205, called Monte Summacro, turned into one of the bloodiest hills seen in Italy up to that time We stayed in the olive grove a couple of days…Personal past experience filled us with dread and foreboding as we sat scrutinizing the gray, weathered, rotten, landsliding, precipitous, ledge-covered, waterless, barren mountain. On the peak Krautheads were hidden in the caves, grottoes, camouflaged pillboxes, foxholes, and behind the rocks. Big artillery sat leashed like giant dogs awaiting the signal to tear us to death. The Rangers, who had fought that way to the top in a few spots, had suffered fifty percent casualties. We were going to relieve them. It was clear to us, as we sat amid the reverberating thunder of our own artillery that we would die in heaps on that hideous pile of elevated stones. Early one afternoon we began the seven hours' climb, our hearts as heavy as our backloads of ammo, guns, and rations. After two hours of steady climbing we reached a small rocky plateau. From this point we followed a shepherd's path along which lay blood-stained bandages, belts, mangled boots, abandoned stretchers and helmets with no holes in them—a veritable trail of blood. Farther up a dead trooper (3rd Battalion man) lay by the trail, his skin a waxy yellow, his eyes sunk back in his head. He lay flat on his back with his right hand, like a yellow claw, reaching for the sky. —Corporal Ross S. Carter, Company C, 504th Parachute Infantry

Troopers share K-rations in the shade of the trees prior to moving out to relieve elements of the 36th Infantry Division and the 3rd Ranger Battalion on Hills 1205 and 950, December 11, 1943. *United States Army Signal Corps photograph, courtesy of William S. Mandle.*

Cleared the area at 17:30 in the order of F, D, battalion CP, Headquarters, and E Companies. Left the road and started to climb at 18:45, continued to slowly climb a long, muddy torturous trail with all equipment back-carried. Destination—Hill 1205, Mount Summacro. The night was as black as could be, with a mist setting in early and turning to rain. When at 03:00 a place was reached where the ascent was possible only by pulling oneself up by a long rope, the battalion stopped for a few hours' sleep. Loose and rolling rocks also hampered the climb. In the dark, it was almost impossible to find a nook or cranny large enough to lay down on a level. Most of the men slept where they were able to sit and still keep from sliding down the mountainside. Little sleep was had. Moved about two hundred yards further up the mountain and established a battalion CP. The battalion is in the same area as personnel of 143rd Infantry (36th Division) perched atop the mountains in the rocks—impossible to dig in. The 3rd Battalion is to the right [on Hill 950]. Lieutenant Colonel [Emory S. "Hank", Jr.] Adams [was] at the CP during the afternoon. D and F Companies are on the ridge line with one 81mm mortar attached to each. Two platoons of E Company are at the bottom of the mountain for purposes of ration carrying (round trip)—took six hours. The 1st Battalion is in reserve. An intense enemy artillery barrage beginning 15:00 and lasting one hour—dislodged rocks which rolled dangerously; several broken legs, hips, etc. —Lieutenant Chester A. Garrison, Headquarters, 2nd Battalion, 504th Parachute Infantry

Engineers with Company C, 307th Airborne Engineer Battalion and the Demolition Platoon, Headquarters Company, 504th Parachute Infantry used metal detectors to clear a slope of enemy antipersonnel mines on December 11, 1943. *United States Army Signal Corps photograph, National Archives.*

After a mine is detected, a combat engineer digs around it and carefully lifts what appears to be an S-mine, known as the Bouncing Betty, because when triggered it would launch up to about three feet in the air before exploding. *United States Army Signal Corps photograph, National Archives.*

Mules were employed by the 504th Parachute Infantry to haul their .30 caliber machine guns, mortars, ammunition, and other heavy gear up the slope of Hill 1205, on December 11, 1943. *United States Army Signal Corps film still image.*

Troopers finish securing a .30 caliber machine gun to the back of this mule before moving out. *United States Army Signal Corps photograph, National Archives.*

Paratroopers with the 504th prepare to move up the slope of Hill 1205, which overlooked San Pietro. *United States Army Signal Corps film still image.*

Boxes of .30 caliber machine gun ammunition are secured to the back of this mule. *United States Army Signal Corps film still image.*

These mules were fitted with padded blankets and wooden frames with which to secure the troopers' equipment, weapons, ammunition, water, rations, and various other supplies. The mules would carry casualties down the hills for medical treatment or burial. *United States Army Signal Corps film still image.*

The long column of 504th troopers ascends the lower slope of Hill 1205. *United States Army Signal Corps photograph, National Archives.*

Troopers and their mule trudge up the rocky trail created atop a rock terrace on the lower slope of Hill 1205 on the afternoon of December 11, 1943. *United States Army Signal Corps photograph, courtesy of William S. Mandle.*

With mules and their handlers leading the way, troopers continue up a steep trail in single file toward the top of Hill 1205. *United States Army Signal Corps photograph, courtesy of William S. Mandle.*

Communication wire was laid from the 376th Parachute Field Artillery Battalion positions to the 504th positions on Hills 1205 and 950 to facilitate fire support. Field telephones provided a more reliable connection than radios in the mountainous terrain. *United States Army Signal Corps photograph, courtesy of William S. Mandle.*

An officer crouches on the forward slope of a rocky hill to observe enemy positions and movement in anticipation of a counterattack. *Photograph courtesy of William S. Mandle.*

There was not a speck of anything green and growing. Artillery had pounded the life out of it. From our left around to our right was a desolate, steep, mountain. On our right was a peak shaped like an upside down ice cream cone. The whole area was echoing with the screech and explosions of hundreds of shells. It was obvious that this was not a neighborhood in which to raise children. The ice cream cone was to be ours—Hill 950. The bursting flowers of flame could be nothing but hand grenades, which meant very close contact with the enemy. We started up. My old friend [Sergeant Floyd V.] Engebritzen was waiting for me, but we hadn't gone far when a grenade exploded next to his thigh, giving him a very nasty wound. After calling a medic, I moved on. It was so steep that you had to use your hands as well as your feet. I got to the top where my squad was digging in. How do you dig in on a forty-five degree slope of solid rock? —Private Francis W. McLane, Company I, 504th Parachute Infantry

Italian troops lead mules loaded with supplies along the road from Venafro to the 504th positions on Hills 950 and 1205, December 12, 1943. *United States Army Signal Corps photograph, courtesy of William S. Mandle.*

Mule teams bring supplies for a short way from the road (an Italian outfit is used expressly for this purpose), but most of the carrying is done on the backs of the men. —Lieutenant Chester A. Garrison, Headquarters, 2nd Battalion, 504th Parachute Infantry

Rocky [Private Rockwell R. Easton] and I became close friends the first day I was with the 504 in Italy, on a trail going up Hill 1205. Enemy mortar fire was following the trail down the hillside perfectly, curve for curve, bend for bend. I was carrying a five-gallon water can on my backpack and I fell to find cover. In doing so, I lost my helmet and was in the middle of the trail with no cover at all. Shells were [exploding] within five feet of me and all of a sudden, I felt "something" fall on me. That "something" remained on me until the barrage moved downhill. I felt the 'something' move from my back and a voice said, "I think its okay now! Let's get the hell out of here!" The "something" that I felt save my life was Rockwell Easton. —Private Jack L. Bommer, Headquarters Company, 504th Parachute Infantry

Carrying parties, each paying a death toll, shuttled water, ammunition, food, and supplies up the trail increasingly scattered with new dead men and their equipment. The living, far too tired to pay attention to the deceased, merely stepped across their bodies and pushed on with their loads. —Corporal Ross S. Carter, Company C, 504th Parachute Infantry

Paratroopers move along the debris strewn and cratered road from Venafro toward San Pietro, which was abandoned the previous night of December 16, 1943 by German troops. *United States Army Signal Corps photograph, National Archives.*

A knocked out Sherman tank lies abandoned on the road as a patrol from the 504th Parachute Infantry moves along the road to San Pietro on December 17, 1943. *United States Army Signal Corps photograph, courtesy of William S. Mandle.*

A patrol of the 504th Parachute Infantry moves into San Pietro on December 17, 1943. *United States Army Signal Corps photograph, courtesy of William S. Mandle.*

Troopers with the 504th Parachute Infantry and the 143rd Infantry, 36th Infantry Division move through the rubble of San Pietro, December 17, 1943. *United States Army Signal Corps photograph, National Archives.*

Two paratroopers with the 1st Battalion, 504th Parachute Infantry fire a machine gun from a gap in a stone wall on Monte Summacro, designated as Hill 1205, on December 18, 1943. *United States Army Signal Corps photograph, National Archives courtesy of Martin K. A. Morgan.*

Troopers with the 504th and their mules wind their way down the slope of the hill they had fought so hard to secure after being relieved in late December 1943. *United States Army Signal Corps photograph, National Archives.*

This photograph of the same troopers and mules was taken shortly after the photo above. The mule on the left is carrying an 81mm mortar tube and base plate while the mule behind it is carrying the mortar's ammunition as the column makes its way down one of the hills northwest of Venafro. *United States Army Signal Corps photograph, National Archives.*

ANZIO

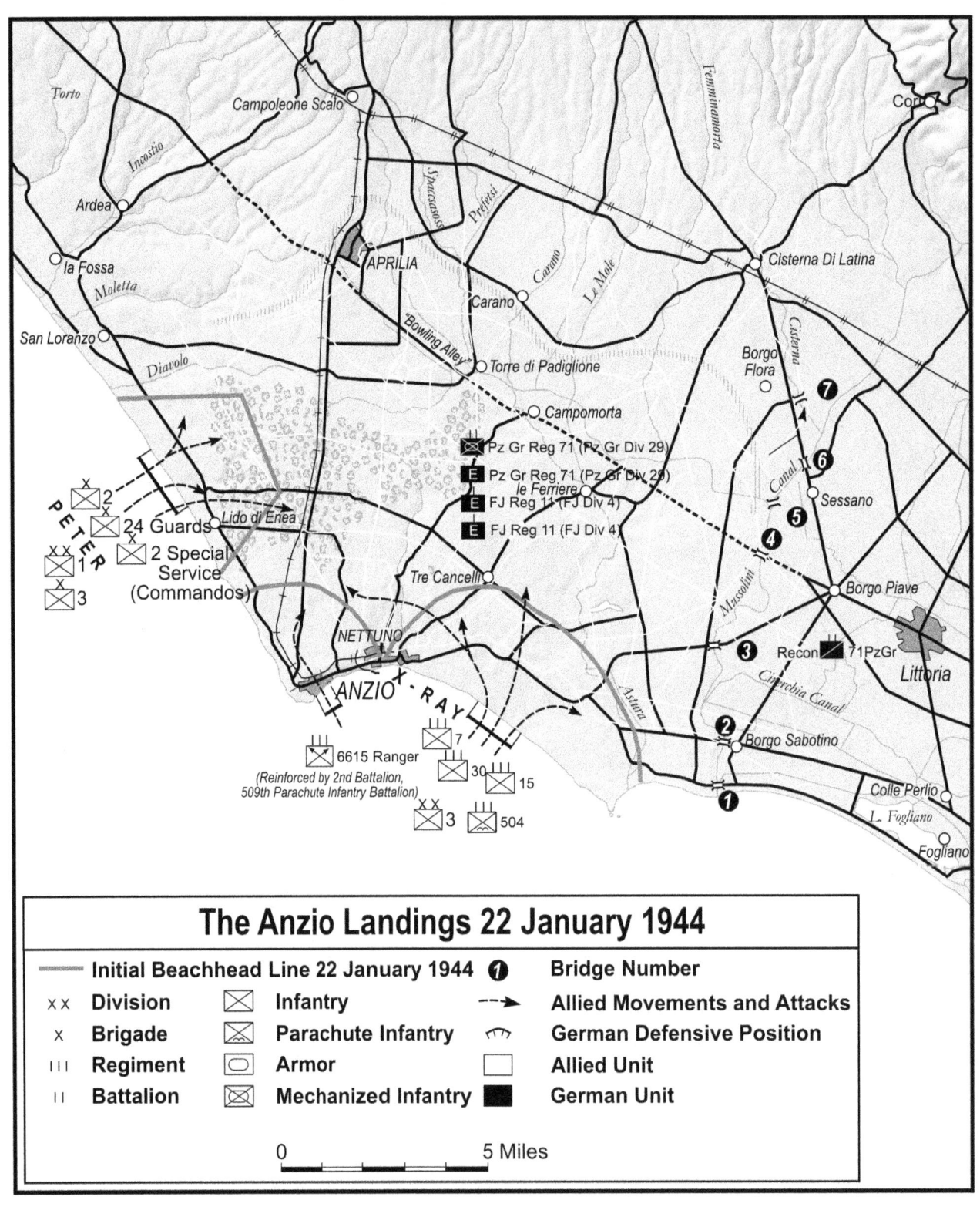

THE 504TH BEACH LANDING
22 JANUARY 1944

This is the beach south of Anzio where American forces would land. The town of Anzio is in the far distance to the northwest (upper left). *United States Army Signal Corps photograph, National Archives.*

A trooper stands on the deck of an LCI (Landing Craft Infantry) moored in the harbor at Pozzuoli, north of Naples, where the 504th Regimental Combat loaded for the voyage to Anzio and Operation Shingle. *Photograph courtesy of William S. Mandle.*

These 504th paratroopers relax on the deck of one of the thirteen LCIs (Landing Craft Infantry) transporting the regiment to Anzio. *Photograph courtesy of William S. Mandle.*

These troopers pose for a photo aboard ship on the way to Anzio. The two standing at left are wearing tankers overalls and jackets that were acquired during their time in the mountains of Italy. To the left of the troopers appears to be the rear of a 2½-ton truck, which would indicate these troopers are aboard a Landing Ship Tank (LST) and would therefore be members of the 376th Parachute Field Artillery Battalion. *Photograph courtesy of William S. Mandle.*

Troopers with the 504th Parachute Infantry wade ashore to the beach south of Anzio on January 22, 1944 from one of the thirteen LCIs (Landing Craft Infantry) transported the regiment. *United States Army Signal Corps, National Archives.*

Paratroopers with the 504th Parachute Infantry wade ashore at the Anzio beachhead. The trooper on the right is carrying a BAR (Browning Automatic Rifle) as the bipod can seen extending from the muzzle of the weapon. *United States Army Signal Corps photograph, National Archives.*

Smoke billows from the LCI which transported Company G, 504th Parachute Infantry after a German bomber scored a hit on it during the landing. Fortunately, most of the troopers had debarked from the landing craft when it was struck and there was only one man killed, but a number were wounded and blown overboard. *United States Army Signal Corps photograph, National Archives.*

I was blown into the water along with my forward observer members and several infantrymen. I lost my whole crew. Two of my men were seriously wounded. I was hurt in the knee and evacuated to a hospital in Naples. It was not serious and I was back to my battery in a few weeks. —Lieutenant Robert S. Hutton, 376th Parachute Field Artillery Battalion

THE BATTLE FOR THE MUSSOLINI CANAL
23–30 JANUARY 1944

An 81mm mortar crew relaxes on the reverse slope of the Mussolini Canal embankment. A mule is employed to haul the heavy weight of the mortar and ammunition. *United States Army Signal Corps photograph, National Archives.*

For the next several days, all three battalions of the 504th were engaged in action across the Mussolini Canal. We were supported by the navy. German resistance was fierce at times, because they used tanks and flak wagons. They counterattacked to regain lost ground. The 504th was successful in holding outpost positions, but after one week the main line of resistance (MLR) was still the Mussolini Canal. All along the 504th front, squads and platoons of riflemen were making contact with the German forces. Each small unit had its mission or objective, whether it was a patrol at night to secure prisoners or a daytime attack on an enemy outpost. Although the battle comprised small unit actions, taken collectively from the sights of the guns of the individual soldiers, it formed the big picture as seen in the higher commands. —Lieutenant James Megellas, Company H, 504th Parachute Infantry

This aerial view of the Mussolini Canal shows the positions of the 504th Parachute Infantry along the reverse slope of the western canal embankment. Fighting positions were located along the eastern canal embankment. Dugouts and shelters can be seen along the length of the canal. Located at the bottom right corner of the photograph is a fairly extensive position with camouflage netting. Farmhouses and a road can be seen at the top. *United States Army Signal Corps photograph, National Archives.*

The field hospital on the beachhead was a more dangerous place than the front line along the Mussolini Canal. German artillery shelled the hospital so heavily that it was known as hell's half acre. Even though the bottom portion of the tents were somewhat protected by earthen walls, they had no protection from aerial bursts from German guns. *United States Signal Corps photograph, National Archives.*

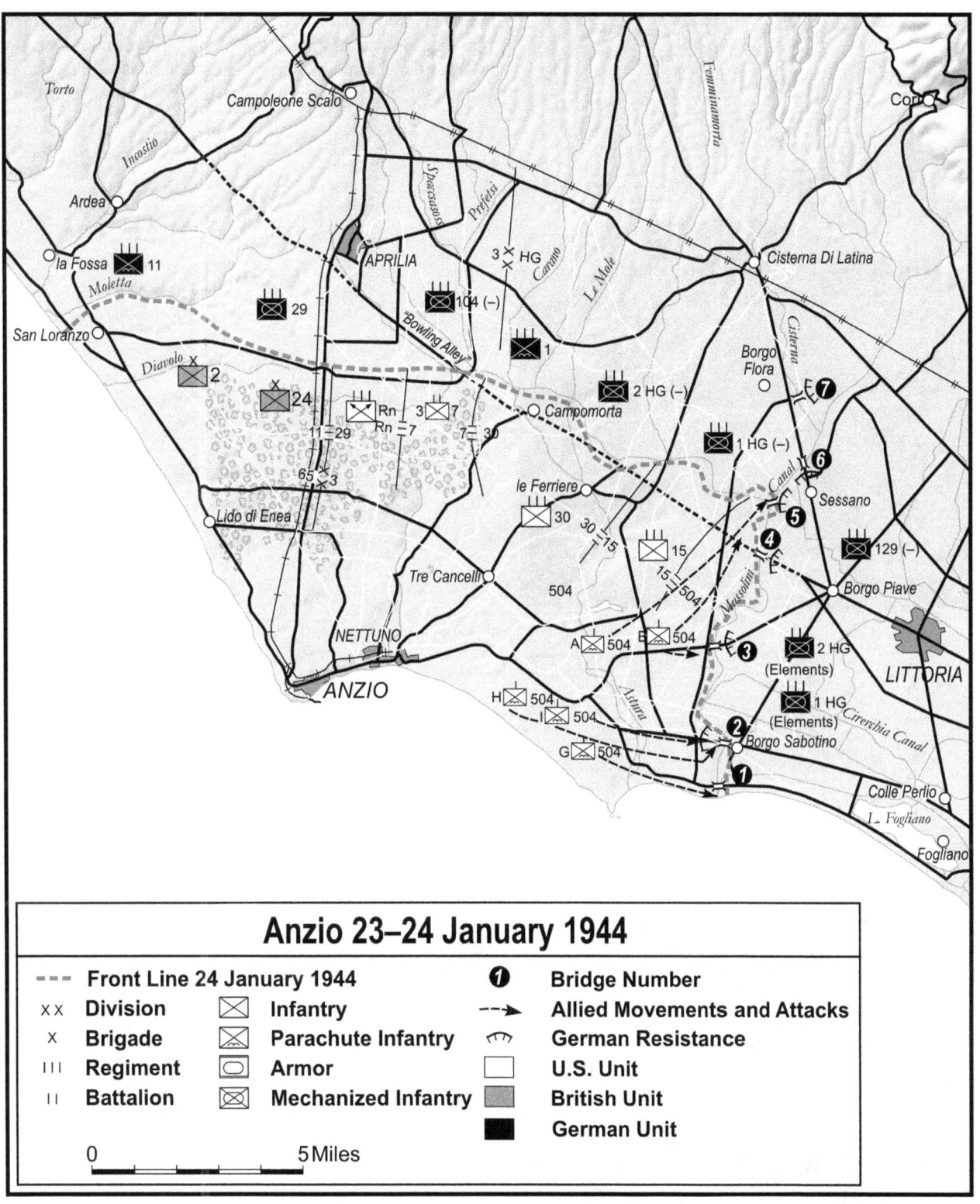

Three paratroopers observe enemy positions and movement from their outpost along the top of the western embankment of the Mussolini Canal. The team's armament includes a Browning Automatic Rifle. *Photograph courtesy of William S. Mandle.*

Two paratroopers (left) lie just below the top of the eastern embankment and observe the enemy in the distance, while a third trooper (far left) holds a radio hand set and is likely reporting the information to headquarters. A fourth trooper is at the bottom right of the photo. *Photograph courtesy of William S. Mandle.*

A paratrooper advances past a farm building during an attack across the flat ground east of the Mussolini Canal. *United States Army Signal Corps photograph, courtesy of William S. Mandle.*

At 13:25 the artillery fired their initial preparations and the battalion moved out at 13:30. It had gone but a short distance when it seemed to run into its own artillery fire. Lieutenant [Robert E.] Fern called Lieutenant [Chester A.] Garrison to get the artillery to lift the fires. This was to no avail as the fire was of enemy origin. He had sensed the reason for the artillery and fired into our own concentration, then lifted his fires so that it looked like our own artillery was firing upon us. As a result, Lieutenant Fern had our fires placed upon the objective and to be fired on call. This cut the effectiveness of the artillery and the attack as a whole. It left the men 1,500 yards of open flat ground to cross before reaching the objective, and had used up the better part of an hour to accomplish. D Company moved out on a dead run towards the north side of the town and had nearly the whole company across the road running north from Borgo Piave when 20mm flak guns opened up on them from the town and from the north. This pinned the company down, so E Company swung to the right and pushed on into the town. The enemy then counterattacked from the north and east of the town, cutting D Company off from the rest of the battalion and into two parts, and isolating E Company in the town. Five tanks and eight half-tracks mounting 20mm guns were used by the enemy, and our troops had no antitank protection at all. Our three tanks were rendered ineffective by the banks of the canal and a desire not to get on top of the banks of the canal for fear of high velocity [enemy antitank] fire. Major [Melvin S.] Blitch ordered F Company to pick up some antitank weapons and get D Company out of their situation. It was getting dark by the time F Company could bring any pressure to bear on the situation, as all the antitank weapons were left with the regimental supply in the rear and had to be brought forward. E Company was having a bad time in town. They had been hit hard twice by three medium tanks and two flak-wagons, plus about two companies of infantry. Lieutenant [Hanford A.] Files [Company E commander] at last withdrew to the west side of town and set up a perimeter defense on the three roads leading towards the canal. The town was being shelled by using the 536 radio to the CP and then relaying the directions through the normal channels. By these means the companies held out until 20:20, when they left an outpost of a platoon in position and F Company covered the area where D Company had been cut in two, as the remainder of the battalion withdrew. F Company withdrew at 02:00 to their old positions on the west side of the canal. D Company had only twenty-eight men left when they returned and their company commander [Captain William Roe] was still missing. But the missing men from the company continued to drift in all night long, until at 0845 the following day they had a total of forty men and officers. E Company held the outpost for the day with only an occasional exchange of artillery fire. They withdrew the evening of the 26th under cover of darkness. Captain Roe came in at 08:45 on the 26th with nine more men. He had gone all the way through Borgo Piave and had tried to hold the enemy from entering the town from Littoria and the northeast. He had no idea what had happened to his company when they had been hit, as he was with the point at the time. All he was concerned with was why no one had come to help him hold the enemy off. While our battalion had suffered heavily, the enemy had been hurt too. He had lost two dual-purpose 88mm guns, three flak-wagons, and one medium tank in the fight, and three other vehicles to mines left in the area. Three prisoners were taken and an estimated one hundred killed or wounded in the action. —Lieutenant William J. Sweet, Jr., Headquarters, 2nd Battalion, 504th Parachute Infantry

As the attack continues, two paratroopers observe a column of troopers advancing along a canal on their left. White smoke, probably from the explosions of white phosphorous shells fired by United States artillery, rises along the horizon at left. *United States Army Signal Corps photograph, courtesy of William S. Mandle.*

Troopers advance beyond the canal (left) while others (right center) move toward a group of farm buildings on the right. Black puffs of smoke (top right) indicate artillery air bursts. *United States Army Signal Corps photograph, courtesy of William S. Mandle.*

Troopers with the 504th Parachute Infantry advance across the table top flat ground of the Anzio beachhead. This photo is likely of the area east of the Mussolini Canal. *Photograph courtesy of William S. Mandle.*

Ambulance drivers and medics with the 504th Parachute Infantry load troopers wounded during the attack for evacuation to the field hospital near the beach. *United States Army Signal Corps photograph, courtesy of William S. Mandle.*

A medic has just finished applying a bandage to the head of a wounded trooper during the intense fighting around the Mussolini Canal. *United States Army Signal Corps film still image.*

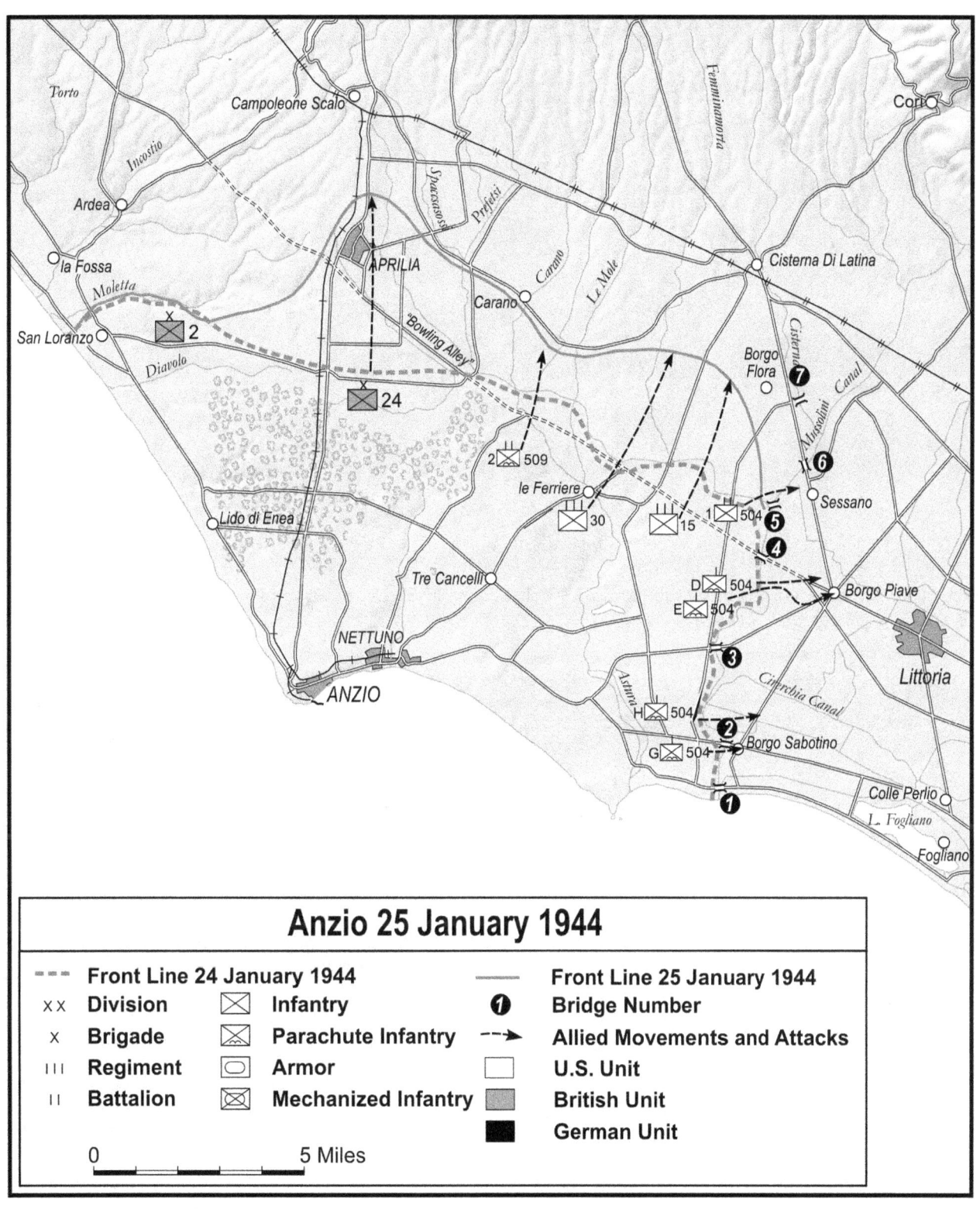

THE BATTLE FOR THE MUSSOLINI CANAL 23–30 JANUARY 1944

The 504th Parachute Infantry crosses the Mussolini Canal during an attack on January 26, 1944. *United States Army Signal Corps photograph, National Archives.*

These paratroopers are afforded limited cover and concealment behind a house, shielding them from view of German artillery observers positioned on the hills surrounding the tabletop flat terrain along the Mussolini Canal. *Photograph courtesy of William S. Mandle.*

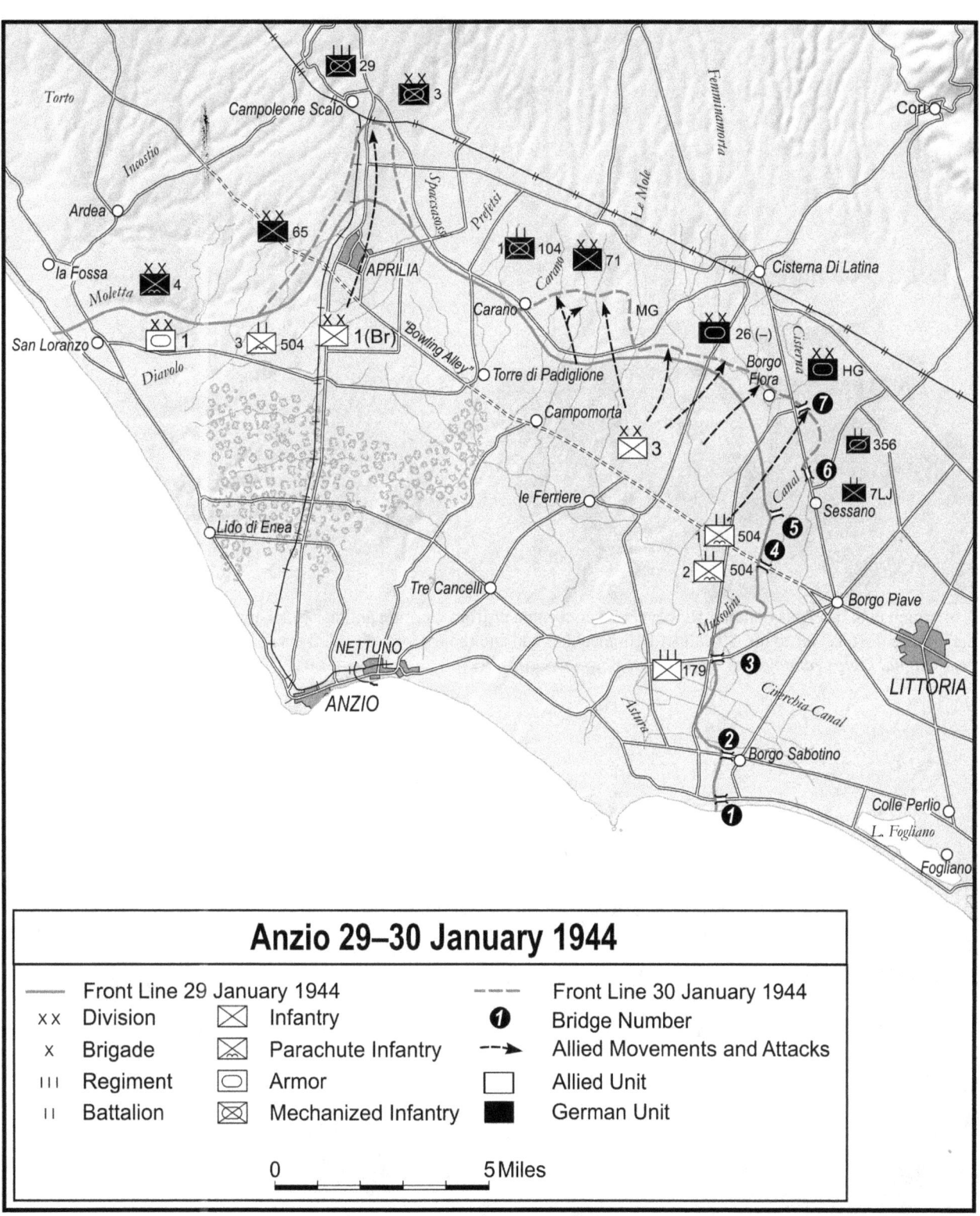

A Sherman tank uses this building for cover and concealment from German antitank guns and artillery as the trooper on the right opens the receiver to his .30 caliber light machine gun and the trooper to his left eats part of his K-ration. *United States Army Signal Corps photograph, courtesy of William S. Mandle.*

Troopers in a ditch observe a tank destroyer (left center) and a light tank (center) assigned to support an attack by elements of the 504th Parachute Infantry. *Photograph courtesy of William S. Mandle.*

Tanks and tank destroyers were extremely vulnerable to German antitank gun fire from the hills beyond the flat ground of the beachhead. *Photograph courtesy of William S. Mandle.*

Small arms fire, mortar fire, and artillery fire became intense. Groups of enemy which had been bypassed during the night advance in the maze of irrigation canals began to fire into the rear of the assault companies, who by this time were fighting for the north-south road into Sessano. A dual 20mm cannon some two hundred yards south of the battalion headquarters group laid direct fire into the group and upon the supporting tanks, the lead tank of which was engaging a machine gun to the east. Lieutenant Colonel [Warren R.] Williams, realizing that this fire was not only pinning down the battalion CP group, but causing heavy casualties in Company B, unhesitatingly climbed aboard a second tank which was button up, while 20mm shells bounced off alongside him. He attracted the attention of the tank crew and accurately directed the tank's fire, which knocked out the dual gun. In the meantime, a heavy firefight was in progress about two hundred yards to the east of Company C positions and Company A was fighting for the row of houses along the road. Lieutenant Colonel Williams led a composite force of tanks and infantry up the road and moved in upon the enemy from the north, toward Bridge [Number 6]. During this time, from four to five machine guns in the houses were spraying the roads and fields. In addition, SP [self-propelled] artillery and mortars were pounding the route of advance on the road. 20mm guns from the south of the [Mussolini] Canal were also putting grazing fire into the area. Despite this fire from two directions, Colonel Williams led the tanks on foot and directed the fire of both tanks and infantry from a completely exposed position. Company A then reported that it was engaged in an extremely heavy action with numerous local counterattacks, which were mounting in intensity. Company C was now also engaged in a firefight. Intense artillery fire was interdicting the area. Lieutenant Colonel Williams immediately committed Company B, his reserve company, which he personally led toward Bridge [Number 6 across the Mussolini Canal]. After a fierce assault upon the houses from which the enemy was engaging Company A, his force broke through to the bridge. Company A was to secure the canal bank and blown bridge. He then contacted his tank force and swung toward Bridge [Number 7] and the houses nearby, which were being hotly contested. Deploying the armor against the houses along with a portion of Company B, Lieutenant Colonel Williams started for Bridge [Number 7] on foot, alone. The fight around the houses and bridge increased in intensity. Enemy artillery fell with increasing rapidity. The assaulting troops were taking casualties and were hard pressed. With utter disregard for his personal safety, Lieutenant Colonel Williams joined this group and with his command radio was able to obtain additional supporting artillery fire and was able to direct the deployment of reinforcements at the most critical juncture in the battle.—Colonel Reuben H. Tucker, III, Headquarters, 504th Parachute Infantry

One of the 504th Parachute Infantry command groups advances along a dike during an attack by the regiment in the area of the Mussolini Canal. An officer (third from left) is using an SCR-536 radio, known as a walkie-talkie, while the trooper at left talks using the handset of the radio carried on his back. A sergeant (fourth from left) carries a Thompson submachine gun, while the trooper (fifth from left) is carrying two M1 rifles, with the second probably belonging to the officer using the SCR-536 radio. *Photograph courtesy of William S. Mandle.*

The going was slow as nearly every house was defended and the enemy small arms fire from the canal banks kept the troops down low in their advance. A system was worked out whereby the troops would advance until fired on from a house or strongpoint, then the tanks would move up, blast the defenders out, to be taken by our troops. The further the advance continued the more fire was received from the right flank. At last, E Company had to be committed to clear the dyke along the Mussolini Canal, [east] of the 1st Battalion. F Company took up the lead, using the same tactics, and advanced fairly well until they hit a strongpoint. Here the enemy did not break from the tank fire and the tanks were unable to advance or flank the position. The company had to flank, and reduce it from the east and rear. While F Company was doing this, the rest of the battalion was left strung out in a column along the road, and we got our first taste of the Germans' Nebelwerfer, or 'Screaming Meemies'. The entire column was shelled for about ten minutes by this fire and then hit by 88mm or antiaircraft fire. Several men from D and Headquarters Companies became casualties and the column was spread into the fields. E Company forced the Germans across Bridge Number 7 and experienced the same thing as the 1st Battalion. The Germans blew the bridge as soon as they had withdrawn across it. F Company reduced the [strongpoint] position and took twenty-five prisoners, then moved along the road to Fso di Cisterna. Here the Germans blew Bridge Number 8. Now it was apparent that the enemy had decided to deny us any crossings for armor in the area, so a race started for Bridge Number 9. Before D Company could get well under way, with the tanks, the Germans blew that one, leaving us with no armor crossings of the Mussolini Canal or of Fso di Cisterna. —Lieutenant William J. Sweet, Jr., Headquarters, 2nd Battalion, 504th Parachute Infantry

A tank destroyer supporting an attack by the 504th Parachute Infantry sits atop one of the dikes of the Mussolini Canal. A German 88mm dual purpose antiaircraft/antitank gun has been destroyed (right) during the attack. *Photograph courtesy of William S. Mandle.*

Troopers pose by the knocked out 88mm gun shown in the photo above. The trooper in the center with a Thompson submachine gun shows off one of the gun's shells. The Albano hills seen in the background were occupied by German troops and used for observation of the beachhead area. *Photograph courtesy of William S. Mandle.*

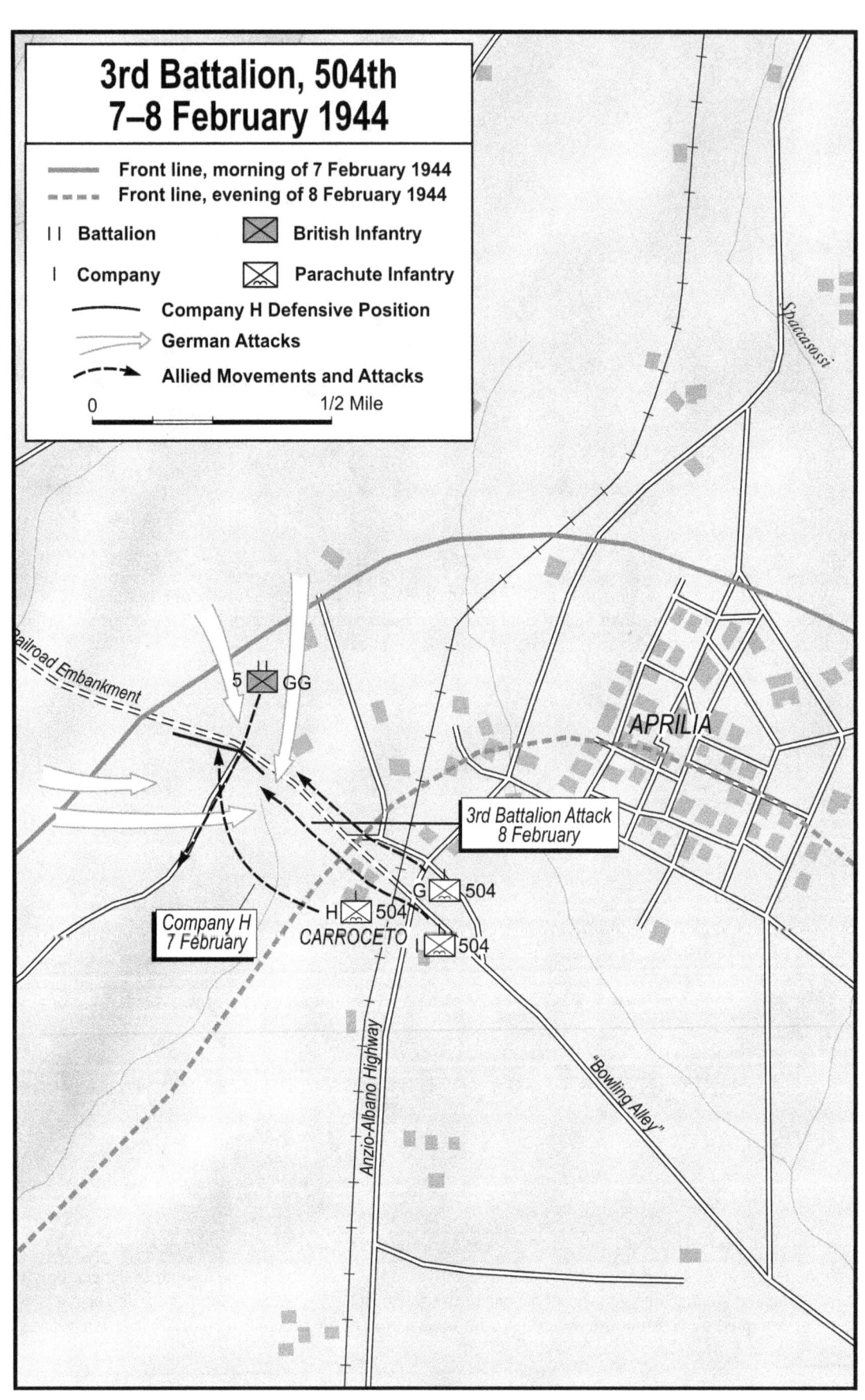

THE BATTLE FOR CARROCETO AND APRILIA
3–8 FEBRUARY 1944

This is an aerial photograph of Aprilia which was known as "The Factory" and was in the British area of operations to the north. It and the town of Carroceto to the south were the scenes of heavy fighting during a full scale assault by nine battalions of German infantry supported by a battalion of tanks, which commenced on February 3, 1944. The 3rd Battalion, 504th Parachute was attached to the British army during that assault and stopped the German breakthrough. The battalion would later be awarded a Presidential Unit Citation for outstanding performance during the period of February 3–15, 1944. *United States Army Signal Corps photograph, National Archives.*

This view of the overpass (known as the "Flyover") looks northwesterly and was where the 3rd Battalion, 504th Parachute Infantry was positioned when a massive German attack struck a salient held by British troops to the north. The highway and railroad to the village of Carroceto and the area of "The Factory" at Aprilia extend from left to right (south to north) underneath the overpass. *United States Army Signal Corps photograph, National Archives.*

On February 4, 1944, my company was given the mission to straddle the Albano road north of Carroceto to help support the withdrawal of British troops. Soon after getting my company in position, British troops started passing through our lines going to the rear. They completed their withdrawal as darkness set in. Within an hour, a strong German force attacked our position, but we responded with devastating fire, to include artillery fire, which disrupted their attack causing them to stop and withdraw. I was sure they would try again, so I had my platoon leaders locate the British units on our flanks. I was rather disgusted to learn that they were several hundred yards behind us on an old railroad embankment. I then moved my company back to the same embankment in order to have contact on my flanks with the British. —Lieutenant Edward J. Sims, Company H, 504th Parachute Infantry

A German self-propelled gun sits in the ruins of Carroceto after German troops overran the British soldiers holding the town. A knocked out Sherman tank (center) and a German half-track each sit next to the walls of buildings to provide protection against incoming artillery. The 3rd Battalion, 504th stopped the massive German assault along a railroad embankment to the south of Carroceto. *Photograph courtesy of the Imperial War Museum.*

STALEMATE
8 FEBRUARY – 23 MARCH 1944

German dead lie in one of the many ditches which crisscrossed the Anzio battlefield. They were killed while attempting to infiltrate during the night of February 27, 1944. While ditches offered concealment for movement across the flat ground, they could become death traps if an enemy machine gun covered the ditch. Night reconnaissance and combat patrols were very dangerous, but were conducted by both sides to gain information through the capture and interrogation of prisoners as well as to kill enemy troops primarily to spread fear among the opposition. The 504th Parachute Infantry was particularly feared by the German army for its prowess at conducting such patrols. A diary found on a dead German officer was translated and it read: *American parachutists—devils in baggy pants—are less than one hundred meters from my outpost line. I can't sleep at night. They pop up from nowhere, and we never know when or how they will strike next. Seems like the black-hearted devils are everywhere.* The 504th troopers became known as devils in baggy pants as a result. *United States Army Signal Corps photograph, National Archives.*

It was during Anzio that I saw more dead bodies in a brief period of time than in all my other combat experience. One of our judge advocate (lawyer) officers was assigned as GRO (grave registration officer) for a part of that campaign, and I was assigned as his aide. It was our job to pick up dead bodies, both American and German, and transport them back to the beachhead cemetery at Nettuno. We had a jeep with a utility trailer with which to do our work, so there was not much dignity in those soldiers' last ride. Except for the levees on both sides of the canal, the terrain in our sector was very flat and under German observation. For this reason, when there were bodies to be picked up near the canal, we would ease up under cover of darkness with the jeep engine barely above idle, recover the bodies, and ease back out, hoping not to attract any German artillery fire. One night, we had driven almost to the bank of the canal and loaded three German bodies into our trailer. When we started to drive off, I looked in my rearview mirror and saw one of the German soldiers rise out of the trailer. Drawing my forty-five, I got out of my jeep in a hurry, but once we stopped there was no further movement. It turned out that, unnoticed by us in our haste and in the darkness, this man had somehow become entangled in a down telephone wire, one end of which was still attached to the pole. When we moved out, this wire had drawn him partly out of the trailer. It gave us quite a start until we determined the cause, because we were quite certain that soldier was dead when we loaded him into the trailer. —Private First Class Darrell G. Harris, Headquarters Company, 504th Parachute Infantry

The German army shelled the Anzio beachhead with two Krupp K-5E 280mm railroad guns the Germans named *Robert* and *Leopold*. The Allied soldiers nicknamed them Anzio Annie and the Anzio Express. The guns were captured in June of 1944. *United States Air Force photograph, www.fold3.com.*

They transported us to some docks and loaded us on to landing barges, and out to a British hospital ship. The loading had not been completed when "Anzio Annie" sent a round to the right of the bow; the next one to the left [of it]. The procedure was repeated at the stern and the ship was bracketed. There was a shudder as the ship got underway, leaving barges full of wounded sitting in the water. —Private Francis W. McLane, Company I, 504th Parachute Infantry

Wounded troops were evacuated by landing craft such as this LCT (Landing Craft Tank) from the Anzio beachhead and then by ship to Naples. *United States Army Signal Corps photograph, National Archives.*

LCT-152 gets underway with a large group of wounded soldiers who will be transported to a hospital ship offshore, out of range of German artillery. *United States Army Signal Corps photograph, National Archives.*

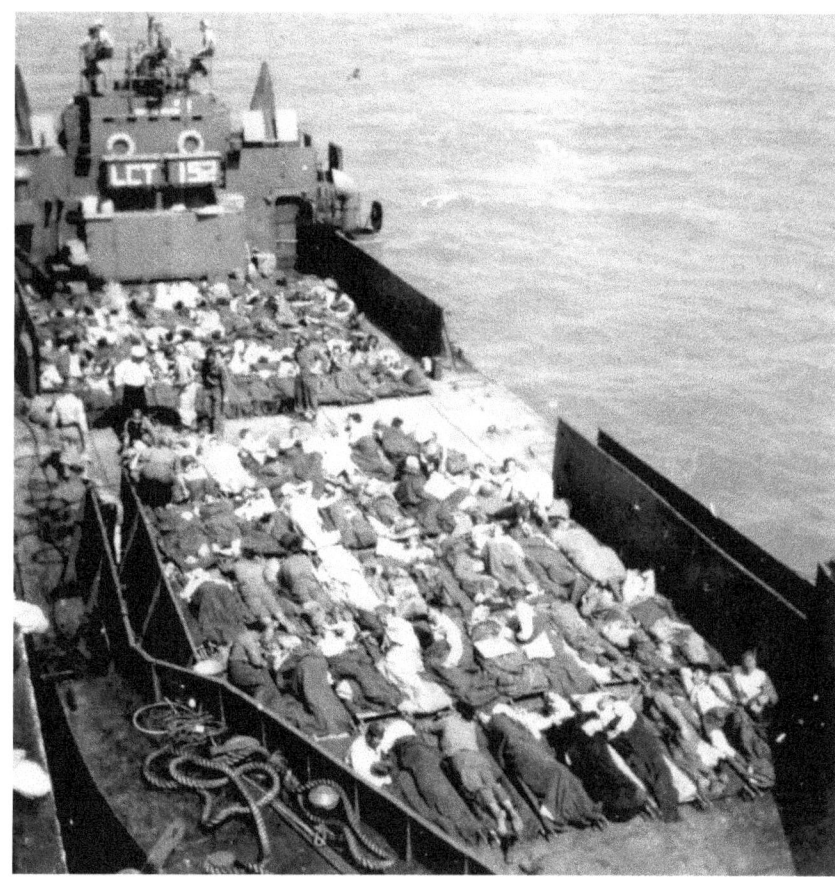

Stretchers are hoisted from the deck of LCT-152 up the side of the hospital ship, where attendants will carry these patients to a triage area for evaluation. Despite the huge red crosses painted on the hospital ships, enemy aircraft targeted these defenseless ships. *United States Army Signal Corps photograph, National Archives.*

The troopers of the 504th Regimental Combat Team assemble on the beach on March 23, 1944 for departure to Naples. *United States Army Signal Corps photograph, National Archives.*

Lieutenant General Mark Clark, commanding officer of the Fifth Army, decorated the guidons of the 3rd Battalion, 504th Parachute Infantry with a Distinguished Unit Citation streamer for outstanding performance at Carroceto during the Anzio campaign. Clark reviewed the regiment during a ceremony conducted at the regiment's bivouac at Bagnoli, on the outskirts of Naples. The buildings in the background were a German intelligence headquarters complex and had been painted with a camouflage pattern. *United States Army Signal Corps photograph, courtesy of William S. Mandle.*

SELECTED BIBLIOGRAPHY

PUBLISHED SOURCES

Baugh, James Emory, *From Skies of Blue*, iUniverse, 2003.

Bell, Elmo, and The University of Southern Mississippi Center for Oral History and Cultural Heritage, *An Oral History with Brigadier General Elmo Edwin Bell: A Saga of a Survivor,* The University of Southern Mississippi, 2003.

Bos, Jan, *Circle and the Fields of Little America*, 376th Parachute Field Artillery Battalion Association, 1992.

Bradley, Omar N., and Blair, Clay, *A General's Life*, Simon and Schuster, 1983.

Burriss, T. Moffatt, *Strike And Hold*, Brassey's, 2000.

Carter, Ross S., *Those Devils In Baggy Pants*, Buccaneer Books, Inc., 1976.

Covais, Joseph S., *Battery!: C. Lenton Sartain and the Airborne GIs of the 319th Glider Field Artillery*, Andy Red Enterprises, 2010.

Fifth Army Historical Section, *Fifth Army at the Winter Line (15 November 1943-15 January 1944)*, United States Army Center of Military History, 1990.

Fifth Army Historical Section, *From the Volturno to the Winter Line (6 October-15 November 1943)*, United States Army Center of Military History, 1990.

Fifth Army Historical Section, *Salerno: American Operations From the Beaches to the Volturno (9 September-6 October 1943)*, United States Army Center of Military History, 1990.

Gavin, James M., *On To Berlin*, Viking Press, 1978.

Harris, Darrell G., *Casablanca to VE Day*, Dorrance Publishing, 1995.

Lebenson, Len, *Surrounded By Heroes*, Casemate, 2007.

Megellas, James, *All The Way To Berlin*, Ballantine Publishing Group, 2003.

Nordyke, Phil, *All American All The Way, The Combat History of the 82nd Airborne Division in World War II*, Zenith Press, 2006.

Nordyke, Phil, *Four Stars of Valor, The Combat History of the 505th Parachute Infantry Regiment in World War II*, Zenith Press, 2005.

Nordyke, Phil, *More Than Courage, The Combat History of the 504th Parachute Infantry Regiment in World War II*, Zenith Press, 2008.

Pierce, Wayne W., *Let's Go!: The Story of the Men Who Served in the 325th Glider Infantry Regiment*, privately published, 1997.

Ridgway, Matthew B., and Martin, Harold H., *Soldier: The Memoirs of Matthew B. Ridgway*, Greenwood Press, 1956.

Taylor, Maxwell D., *Swords and Plowshares*, W. W. Norton, 1972.

The Devils In Baggy Pants, Combat Record of the 504th Parachute Infantry Regiment April 1943 – July 1945, compiled by Lieutenant William D. Mandle and Pfc. David H. Whittier, Draeger Freres, Paris, 1945.

Turnbull, Peter, *I Maintain the Right: The 307th Airborne Engineer Battalion in WWII*, Author House, 2005.

Van Lunteren, Frank W., *Brothers in Arms*, privately published, 2006.

UNPUBLISHED DIARIES, LETTERS, MEMOIRS AND WRITTEN ACCOUNTS

Adrianson, Donald L., diary, Robert W. Gillette.

Alexander, Mark J., "Italy – 1943," Mark J. Alexander.

Anderson, Howard C., written account, Howard C. Anderson

Bailey, Douglas M., dairy, Douglas M. Bailey.

Beach, Norbert P., "Army Life As Remembered By Norbert P. Beach," Norbert P. Beach.

Blank, William L., memoirs, 82nd Airborne Division War Memorial Museum.

Bommer, Jack L., questionnaire, Cornelius Ryan Archive, Alden Library, Ohio University.

Bowman, David V., "Memoirs of a Machine Gunner," David V. Bowman

Coleman, Charles A., written account, Charles A. Coleman.

Dunfee, William T., "Parachute Infantry Training – Fort Benning, Georgia – July 1942," William T. Dunfee.

Dunfee, William T., "Sicily Invasion – Operation Husky – July 9–10, 1943," William T. Dunfee.

Dunlop, Lawrence H., written account, Alex Kicovic.

Fielder, Robert A., written account, Robert A. Fielder.

Gault, Joe, "Company F 325th Glider Infantry," Joe Gault.

Gilbert, Glendon C., "Service in the 325th Glider Infantry," Wayne W. Pierce.

Hanna, Roy M., written account, 82nd Airborne Division War Memorial Museum.

Hart, Raymond F., written account, Alex Kicovic.

Hays, William R. Jr., "A Paratrooper in WWII," William R. Hays, Jr. family.

Helmer, James, "Story of the 82nd Airborne Division and the 325th Glider Infantry Regiment," Kathy Stepzinski.

Jorgensen, Starlyn R., "456th Parachute Field Artillery History," Starlyn R. Jorgensen.

Kent, Thomas W., "My Military History: March 1942 – September 1945," Thomas W. Kent.

Knight, Milton V., response to questionnaire, Alex Kicovic.

McIlvoy, Dr. Daniel B., memoirs, Mrs. Annie McIlvoy Zaya.

McLane, Francis W., "Francis W. McLane a.k.a. "Mac" World War II, Journal," Francis W. McLane.

Miale, Frank M., written account, Frank M. Miale.

Nagel, Arnold G., written account, Alex Kikovic.

Norris, Patrick F., written account, Wayne W. Pierce.

O'Loughlin, Dennis G., "Fierce Individualists," 1977, Frank P. Woosley.

Pahler, Regis J., "Devils in Baggy Pants" column, *The Static Line*, Lou Hauptfleisch.

Pippin, Ross, "A Paratrooper's Story:—My World War II Experiences as told to Gary Shaffer," Ross Pippin and Gary Shaffer.

Porcella, Tomaso W., written account, Tom W. Porcella.

"Prop Blast," February 1943, compiled and edited by Steven J. Mrozek, 82nd Airborne Division Historical Society, 1986.

Randall, Fredrick W., written account, courtesy of Wheatley T. Christensen.

Reid, Pat, "Chow," 82nd Airborne Division War Memorial Museum.

Sampson, Otis L., "Time Out For Combat," unpublished memoir, Otis L. Sampson.

Sims, Edward J., "Army Service Experience Questionnaire," United States Army Military History Institute.

The Clay Blair Papers, United States Army Heritage and Education Center.

The James M. Gavin Papers, United States Army Heritage and Education Center.

Thomas, David E., letter to Alfred W. Ireland, September 6, 1997, 82nd Airborne War Memorial Museum.

Vandervoort, Benjamin H., "Drop Zone Europe," United States Army Heritage and Education Center.

Wigle, Cloid, written account, Cloid Wigle.

Woosley, Frank P., memoirs, Frank P. Woosley.

Zinn, Bennie, "Travels of Bennie Zinn, World War II, 1940–1945," Bennie Zinn, Jr.

INTERVIEWS WITH AUTHOR

Hunter M. "Bill" Bishop, Jr.,
Reneau G. Breard
Floyd N. Dixon
W. A. Jones,
Howard C. Goodson
Leo M. Hart
Russell D. McConnell
Louis E. Orvin, Jr.

RESPONSES TO AUTHOR'S QUESTIONNAIRES

Berge Avadanian
Joseph I. O'Jibway
Harvill W. Lazenby

Markus Rupaner
Irvin W. Seelye
Bernard P. Wenneman

ORAL HISTORY TRANSCRIPTS

Jones, James E., Eisenhower Center, University of New Orleans.
Miller, Charles H., Eisenhower Center, University of New Orleans.

MILITARY REPORTS, JOURNALS AND MONOGRAPHS

"82nd Airborne Division In Sicily And Italy," 82nd Airborne Division War Memorial Museum.

82nd Airborne Division, "World War II Casualties, Decorations, Citations," 82nd Airborne Division War Memorial Museum.

Headquarters, Third Battalion 504th Parachute Infantry, APO 469, U.S. Army, "The Anzio Beachhead, Italy."

Kellogg, Lieutenant William G., "Report of the 2nd and 3rd Sticks, 1st Platoon, Company C, 307 Engineer on Avellino Jump," National Archives.

Komosa, Captain Adam A., "Airborne Operation, 504th Parachute Infantry Regimental Combat Team (82nd Airborne Division), Sicily, 9 July–19 August, 1943, Personal Experience of a Regimental Headquarters Company Commander," Advanced Infantry Officers Course, Infantry School, 1946–1947, Donovan Research Library, Fort Benning, Georgia.

Lekson, Major John S., "The Operations of the 1st Battalion, 504th Parachute Infantry (82nd Airborne Division) in the Capture of Altavilla, Italy, 13 September – 19 September, 1943, (Naples-Foggia Campaign), (Personal Experience of a Battalion Operations Officer)," Infantry School, 1947-1948, Donovan Research Library, Fort Benning, Georgia.

Piper, Major Robert M., "The Operation of the 505 Parachute Infantry Regimental Combat Team (82nd Airborne Division) in the Airborne Landings on Sicily, 9-11 July 1943 (Sicilian Campaign) (Personal Experience of Assistant Regimental Adjutant)," the Donovan Research Library, Fort Benning, Georgia.

"Report of the 504th Parachute Infantry Combat Team in Operation Avalanche," 82nd Airborne Division War Memorial Museum.

Sayre, Major M. Edwin, "The Operations of Company A 505th Parachute Infantry (82nd Airborne Division) Airborne Landings In Sicily 9–24 July 1943 (Sicily Campaign) (Personal Experience of a Company Commander)," Infantry School, 1947, the Donovan Research Library, Fort Benning, Georgia.

Sweet, Captain William J. Jr., "Operations of the 2nd Battalion, 504th Parachute Infantry Regiment (82nd Airborne Division) on the Anzio Beachhead, 22 January – 23 March 1944, (Anzio Campaign), (Personal Experience of a Battalion Operations Officer and Company Commander)," Infantry School, 1947-1948, Donovan Research Library, Fort Benning, Georgia.

Tucker, Colonel Reuben H., III, Recommendation for Award, Lieutenant Colonel Warren R. Williams, Jr., June 18, 1945, Mike Bigalke.

"Unit Journal of the 2nd Battalion, 504th Parachute Infantry, 82nd Airborne Division," 82nd Airborne Division War Memorial Museum.

INDEX

Acate River, Sicily, 151
Adams, Lieutenant Colonel Emory S. "Hank", Jr., 284
Adams, Private First Class James J., 227
Adrianson, Private First Class Donald L., 128, 139, 145
Agerola, Italy, 250
Agerola–Gragnano tunnel, 231, 250
Agropoli, Italy, 228
Alabama Area, 62, 67, 68
Albanella River, Italy, 224
Albano, Italy, 317, 320
Alexander, Major Mark J., 204
Alexandria, Louisiana, 16, 19
Algiers, Algeria, 127
Altavilla, Italy, 234, 239, 277
Amalfi, Italy, 231, 232, 249, 250
Anderson, Private Howard C., 43
Ansonia, Connecticut, 277
Anzio, Italy, 297–325
Anzio Annie, 322, 323
Anzio Express, 322
Apennine Mountains, Italy, 274, 275
Aprilia, Italy, The Factory, 319
Arnone, Italy, 271
Atlas Mountains, 118
Avadanian, Private Berge, 82, 90, 144
Avola, Sicily, 153, 154, 155
Bagdolio, Marshal Pietro, 199
Bagnoli, Italy, 325
Bailey, Private First Class Douglas M., 134
Battles, Staff Sergeant Leonard D., 121
Baugh, Lieutenant James E., 19, 72, 78, 79, 81, 254
Bay of Salerno, 228, 231
Beach, Private Norbert P., 67, 69
Beaver, First Class Lawrence S., 76
Bell, Corporal Elmo E., 42, 155
Berkut, Lieutenant Michael, 21
Bermel, Lieutenant Colonel Peter E., 38
Berteau, Lieutenant Thomas F., 279, 280
Bertsch, Lieutenant Colonel William H., 36
Biazzo Ridge, Sicily, 159, 160, 162, 163, 164, 165, 166, 167, 168, 169
Billingslea, Lieutenant Colonel Charles, 227
Biscari, Sicily, 157, 163
Bishop, Sergeant Bertram J. "Jack", 253
Bishop, Sergeant Hunter M. "Bill", Jr., 160, 162
Bizerte, Tunisia, 246
Blank, Sergeant William L., 68, 90, 91, 262
Blitch, Major Melvin S., 307
Bommer, Private Jack L., 291
Borgo Piave, Italy, 307, 308

Boswell, Technician Fourth Grade Henry D. "Duke", 162
Bowman, Private David V., 49, 89, 90, 91, 134
Boyd, Captain Frank D., 74
Boyd, Lieutenant Colonel Richard K., 127, 188, 206
Bradley, Major General Omar N., 15, 16, 22, 23, 25, 27, 30, 104, 106, 125
Breard, Lieutenant Reneau G., 82, 228
British Military Units
    British Army Units
        Eighth Army, 274
Brooklyn, New York, 202
Browning, John M., 23
Burriss, Lieutenant T. Moffatt, 64, 86, 128, 145, 146, 183
Camp Beauregard, Louisiana, 19
Camp Billy Mitchell, Alabama, see Alabama Area, 62
Camp Claiborne, Louisiana, 15–39, 71
Camp Don B. Passage, French Morocco, 83–86
Camp Edwards, Massachusetts, 77–79
Camp Kunkle, French Morocco, 88, 109
Camp Mackall, North Carolina, 74
Camp Marnia, French Morocco, 88, 89, 90, 94
Canne River, Sicily, 185
Carroceto, Italy, 319, 320, 321, 325
Carter, Corporal Ross S., 176, 178, 194, 283, 291
Casablanca, French Morocco, 80, 81, 83–87
Castillo, Sergeant Tony, 168
Castellammare de Golfo, Sicily, 203
Castellammare di Stabia, Italy, 231, 250, 253, 254
Castelvetrano, Sicily, 199, 277, 278, 279
Cerro, Italy, 274
Chattahoochee River, 67, 68
Chiunzi Pass, Italy, 231, 232, 249, 282
Clark, Lieutenant General Mark W., 98, 100, 104, 105, 106, 116, 224, 227, 245, 249, 255, 257, 258, 262, 269, 279, 280, 325
Private First Class William L. Clay, 227
Cole, Private F. S., 202
Coleman, Lieutenant Charles A., 75, 76, 87
Colli, Italy, 274
Columbus, Georgia, 67, 68
Comiso airfield, Sicily, 209, 210, 226
Condon, Lieutenant Robert D., 171, 179
Connelly, Captain Matthew J., 168
Cook, Major Julian A., 181
Crawford, Lieutenant Colonel Joseph, 169, 279, 280
Crosbie, Sergeant James F., 246
Crossman, Lieutenant Raymond M., 62
Cutler, Colonel Stuart, 39

Darby, Colonel William O., 249
DeCoursy, Private First Class John W., 227
Denison, Texas, 140
Distinguished Service Cross, 76, 277, 278, 279
Dixon, Lieutenant Floyd N., 232
Dobrychlop, Private First Class Valentine, 227
Donnelly, Captain Paul D., 175
Drysdale, William B., 145
Duncan, Captain Charles W., 234
Dunlop, Private First Class Lawrence H., 194
Dunn, Brigadier General Ray A., 210
Dunn, Colonel Theodore L., 60
Dunfee, Sergeant William T., 42, 44, 53, 55, 57, 93, 107, 109, 126, 128, 134, 138, 145, 151, 197
Easton, Private Rockwell R. "Rocky", 291
Eaton, Colonel Ralph P., 127, 206
Eden, Sir Anthony, British Secretary of State for War, 77
Eisenhower, General Dwight D., 104, 116, 117, 278
El Alem, Tunisia, 118
Elliott, Private Eugene R., 227
Emmanuel, King Victor, III, 199
Enfidaville, Tunisia, 119, 128, 134, 139, 145
Engebritzen, Sergeant Floyd V., 290
England, 272
Faby, Captain Albert, 140
Faith, Captain Don C., Jr., 127, 188
Farmer, Staff Sergeant Frank G., 127, 186, 249
Fassett, Private First Class Reed S., 270
Fern, Lieutenant Robert E., 307
Fez, French Morocco, 87
Fielder, Lieutenant Robert A., 161
Files, Lieutenant Hanford A., 307
Florence, South Carolina, 73
Foisie, Sergeant Jack, correspondent, *Stars and Stripes*, 139, 140
Follmer, Captain Willard R., 145, 151
Fornelli, Italy, 274
Fort Benning, Georgia, 16, 40–69, Parachute School at 40, 41, 77
Fort Bragg, North Carolina, 37, 38, 70–82
Fort Fisher, North Carolina, 71, 76
Fort Keesler, Mississippi, 77
Fort Maxwell, Alabama, 77
Fort Worth, Texas, 136
Fowler, Corporal John, 202
French Morocco, 83–119, 214
Fso di Cisterna, Italy, 316
Gallo, Italy, 274
Garibaldi, Giuseppe, 258
Garibaldi Square, Naples, Italy, 255, 256, 257
Garrison, Lieutenant Chester A., 228, 235, 284, 291, 307
Gary, Indiana, 202
Gault, Lieutenant Joe B., 37, 73

Gavin, Colonel James M., 60, 67, 77, 90, 95, 97, 106, 126, 137, 138, 139, 141, 157, 158, 159, 160, 163, 164, 168, 185, 187, 189, 204, 250, 255
Gela, Sicily, 128, 141, 146, 149, 157, 159, 168, 173, 179, 181, 185, 201, 207, 208, 246
Gerle, Lieutenant Peter, 282
German Military Units
    Fallschirm-Panzer Division 1 Hermann Göring, 160, 163
    Kampfgruppe Links, 160
    Panzer Grenadier Regiment 1, 160
    Kompanie 2, Schwere Panzer Abteilung 504, 160
Gibellina, Sicily, 207
Gilbert, Private First Class Glendon C., 104
Goodson, Private Howard C., 52, 107
Gorham, Lieutenant Colonel Arthur F., 169
Gould, Lieutenant Edwin F., 279, 280
Gragnano, Italy, 231, 250
Granado, Corporal John, 282
Gruenther, Major General Alfred M., 104
Gustav Line, Italy, 283
Guttry, Corporal Carlos B., 227
Hagan, Major William J., III, 159, 163
Hanna, Lieutenant Roy M., 146
Harmon, Staff Sergeant Tom, 282
Harris, Private First Class Darrell G., 321–322
Harris, Private Kenneth L., 162
Harrison, Captain Willard E., 116, 179
Hart, Private Leo M., 57
Hart, Sergeant Raymond F., 128
Hayes, Lieutenant William H., 43, 47, 49, 53, 55, 56
Helmer, Lieutenant James B., 73
Hensley, Private Dickie L., 274
Hewett, Admiral Henry K., 127
Highway 6, Italy, 283
Hill 424, Italy, 239, 240, 241, 277
Hill 950, Italy, 281, 284, 289, 290, 291
Hill 1017, Italy, 274
Hill 1205, Italy, 281, 283, 284, 286, 287, 288, 289, 291, 294
Hirsch, Private First Class Joe, 234
Huth, Technician Fifth Grade Jerome V., 210
Hutton, Lieutenant Robert S., 232, 302
Irvin, Lieutenant James M., 183
Isernia, Italy, 274
Jones, Private James Elmo, 78
Jones, Private W. A., 43
Kairouan, Tunisia, 118, 119, 121, 122, 124, 125, 134, 212, 214, 246
Karlson, Sergeant Claus H., 175
Keerans, Brigadier General Charles L. "Bull", Jr., 79, 137, 198
Kellogg, Lieutenant William W., 278, 279, 280
Keyes, Major General Geoffrey, 185
Kivisto, Private First Class Walter, 112, 113
Kogut, Staff Sergeant Michael "Mike", 282

Komosa, Captain Adam A., 89, 104, 121, 141, 175, 178
Kouns, Lieutenant Colonel Charles W., 144
Krause, Major Edward C. "Cannonball", 145, 157, 159, 163, 166, 197, 204
Kroos, Captain Arthur G., Jr., 187, 188
La Cosa Creek, Italy, 234
Lake Biviere, Sicily, 146, 151
Lane, Private Thomas, 136
Laurinburg–Maxton Army Airfield, North Carolina, 71, 73
LaRiviere, Lieutenant Richard G. "Rivers", 282
Larsen, Private Robert, 241
Lazenby, Sergeant Harvill W., 183
Lebenson, Technician Fourth Grade Leonard, 22, 73, 78, 82, 127, 152, 188, 249
Lee, Major General William C., 36
Legacie, Private James H., 194
Lekson, Lieutenant John S., 226, 228, 234, 239
Les Angades Aerodrome, French Morocco, 88, 109
Letino, Italy 274
Lewis, Colonel Harry L., 25, 82, 95, 222
Licata, Sicily, 141, 222, 223, 224, 226, 241, 242, 243, 245
Linosa, Sicily, 145
Littoria, Italy, 308
Long, Private James D., 162
Lowery, Technician Fourth Grade Robert W., 227
Ludlam, Sergeant Gerald L., 162
Lynch, Lieutenant Colonel George E., 127, 206
Macchia, Italy, 274
Maggazolo River, Sicily, 185
Maiori, Italy, 231, 232, 246, 249, 282
Maliborski, Private Valentine, 282
Malta, 145, 146
March, Lieutenant Colonel Francis A., 37
Marsala, Sicily, 190, 194, 199, 207
Marshall, General George C., Army Chief of Staff, 77
May, Lieutenant Robert L., 163
McCarthy, Private First Class Thomas J., 227
McCauley, Colonel Jerome B., 138
McConnell, Private Russell D., 90, 140, 160, 168
McIlvoy, Captain Daniel B., Jr., 168
McLane, Private Francis W., 290, 322
McNair, Lieutenant General Leslie, 36
Megellas, Lieutenant James, 53, 282, 303
Menfi, Sicily, 189
Mexia, Texas, 274
Miale, Sergeant Frank M., 168
Miley, Brigadier General William M., 25
Miller, Private Charles H., 57
Montallegro, Sicily, 185
Monte Cassino, Italy, 283
Monte (Mount) Summacro, Italy, Hill 1205, 283, 284, 294
Montello, Italy, 279
Morang, First Sergeant Frank L., 189

Mount Croce, Italy, 281
Mount San Angelo, Italy, 245
Mount Soprano, Italy, 234
Mount Vesuvius, Italy 252, 254
Musa, Private James, 282
Mussolini Canal, Italy, 303–317
Nagel, Private Arnold G. "Dutch", 150
Naples, Italy, 249–270, 272, central post office explosion, 267–268, 282, 299, 325
Neptune, Major Robert H., 79, 82, 86, 181
Nettuno, Italy, 321
Nogues, General Auguste, 100, 104, 105, 106
Normandy, France, 272
Norris, Sergeant Patrick F., 87, 90, 93
Northern Ireland, 272
Norton, Major John "Jack", 255
Noto, Sicily, 183
O'Jibway, Staff Sergeant Joseph I., 140
O'Laughlin, Private Dennis G., 69, 141
O'Mohundro, Lieutenant Colonel Wiley, 234
Objective Y, Sicily, 149, 150, 169
Operation Avalanche, 208, 223
Operation Giant, 212
Operation Horrified, 118
Operation Husky, 90, 127
Operation Shingle, 299
Orgaz, Lieutenant General Luis, 100, 104, 106
Orvin, Private Louis E., Jr., 44
Oujda, French Morocco, 87, 88, 89, 90, 94, 100, 104, 109, 113, 116, 118, 119, 126, 127
Paestum, Italy, 209, 225, 226, 227, 228, 233, 234, 241, 243, 244, 245
Pahler, Sergeant Regis J., 226
Palermo, Sicily, 199, 202, 203, 222, 246
Palmer, Major Robert S., 38
Parks, Major General Floyd, 31
Pass, Private Wesley, 37
Paternapoli, Italy, 279
Patton, Lieutenant General George S., Jr., 100, 104, 106, 125, 127, 186, 199
Phenix City, Alabama, 60, 68
Piano Lupo, Sicily, 169
Pierce, Lieutenant Wayne W., 73, 118
Piper, Lieutenant Robert M., 139
Pippin, Private Ross, 67
Pittsburgh, Pennsylvania, 202
Platani River, Sicily, 185
Plaza Plebisceto, Naples, Italy, 258
Pompei, Italy, 254, 255
Ponte Olivo airfield, Sicily, 141, 208, 209
Pope Army Airfield, North Carolina, 73, 77
Porcella, Private Tomaso W., 55
Pozzuoli, Italy, 299
Prata, Italy, 274
Prechowski, Private First Class Ervin L., 253
Presidential Unit Citation, 231, 319, 325

Punta Socca, Sicily, 179
Rabat, French Morocco, 87
Randall, Sergeant Frederick W., 168
Realmonte, Sicily, 185
Reber, Private First Class Larry, 170
Reid, Private Richard E. "Pat", 107, 162
Ribera, Sicily, 185, 186, 187, 188, 189
Rice, Private Daun Z., 202
Ridgway, Major General Matthew B., 15, 16, 25, 27, 30, 31, 32, 34, 36, 37, 77, 89, 90, 98, 100, 105, 106, 107, 116, 117, 121, 125, 127, 144, 152, 185, 186, 187, 188, 189, 198, 199, 210, 224, 227, 249, 257, 262, 269
Rochetta, Italy, 274
Roe, Captain William, 308
Rolak, Lieutenant Bruno J., 227
Rome, Georgia, 140
Rome, Italy, 211, 212
Roosevelt, President Franklin D., 277, 278, 279
Rupaner, Private Markus, 140
Salerno, Italy, 208, 209, 222, 224, 225, 226, 227, 228, 229–249, 282
Ryan, Technician Fourth Grade Edward R., 232
Salm River, Belgium, 76
Sampiere, Sicily, 141
Sampson, Sergeant Otis L., 61, 68, 69, 126, 140, 145
San Pietro, Italy, 283, 286, 292, 293
Sarno Plain, Italy, 252
Savinski, Verona, 234
Sayre, Captain Edwin M., 144, 145, 148, 169
Schellhammer, Lieutenant Colonel Frederick M., 206
Sciacca, Sicily, 185, 190, 199
Seelye, Private Irvin W. "Turk", 140
Sele River, Italy, 235, 246
Serrano, General Francisco Delgado, 105
Sessano, Italy, 315
Shirley, Emmitt C., 204
Sicily, 90, 108, 121, 126, 127, 128, 134, 137, 138, 139, 140, 141, 143, 144, 146, 147–228, 246, 282
Sims, Lieutenant Edward J., 182, 190, 231, 274, 320
Slivitz, Private Albert E., 24
Solomon, Sergeant Elfren, 175
Sorrento, Italy, 231
Sorrento Peninsula, Italy, 231, 249, 250
Sousse, Tunisia, 123, 124
Spaatz, General Carl A., 104
Spanish Morocco, 87, 100, 104, 105, 106
Speth, Private Dennis T., 176
Starling, Private Ellis A., 253
Spotswood, Master Sergeant James E., 127
Suer, Captain Alexander P. Pete, 168
Sweet, Lieutenant William J., Jr., 308, 316
Swenson, Lieutenant Colonel John H. "Swede", 82
Swingler, Lieutenant Harold H. "Swede", 164, 165, 166
Swope, Private Herman, 246
Szopo, Corporal Michael, 76

Taylor, Brigadier General Maxwell D, 15, 25, 117, 125, 172, 185, 187, 198, 199
Taylor, Sergeant Stokes M., 76
Termini-Imerese, Sicily, 246
Thomas, Technician Fifth Grade Claude W., 234
Thomas, Major David E., 60
Thompson, Jack "Beaver", *Chicago Tribune*, 138, 158, 204
Thompson, Private Raymond H. "Tommy", 68
Thornton, Master Sergeant Alvin, 244
Trapani, Sicily, 196, 197, 198, 199, 201, 203, 204, 206
Tripoli, Libya, 183
Tucker, Colonel Reuben H., III, 60, 90, 95, 172, 180, 181, 185, 224, 226, 234, 277, 279, 280, 315
Tunis, Tunisia, 179
Tunisia, 118, 121–146, 175, 201
Tyrrhenian Sea, 228
United States Military Units
  United States Army Units
    Army Ground Forces, 36
    EGB 448, 80, 82
    Provisional Armored Corps, 185
    Signal Corps, 189, 223
    3131st Signal Service Company, 189
    1st Infantry Division, 90, 141, 169, 175
    16th Infantry Regiment, 169, 279
    26th Infantry Regiment, 169
    1st Ranger Battalion, 283
    1st Special Service Force, 283
    2nd Armored Division, 199
    3rd Auxiliary Surgical Group, 234
    2nd Battalion, 509th Parachute Infantry Regiment, 119, 214–221
    II Corps, 106, 125, 141
    3rd Infantry Division, 141, 185
    3rd Ranger Battalion, 283, 284
    4th Ranger Battalion, 283
    Fifth Army, 98, 100, 104, 106, 224, 245, 262, 274, 277, 279, 283, 325, Airborne Training Center, 88, 109
    VI Corps, 224, 226, 234, 239
    Seventh Army, 100, 104, 106, 127, Force 343, 141
    9th Infantry Division, 185
    39th Regimental Combat Team, 185
    12th Army Group, 25
    XVIII Airborne Corps, 25
    13th Airborne Division, 71
    17th Airborne Division, 25
    27th Armored Field Artillery Regiment, 279
    36th Infantry Division, 16, 233, 234, 235, 239, 283, 284, 293
    141st Infantry Regiment, 235
    143rd Infantry Regiment, 235, 283, 293
    45th Infantry Division, 90, 141, 157, 159, 163, 168

80th Airborne Antiaircraft (Antitank) Battalion, 71, 72, 75, 76, 78, 79, 80, 81, 87, 231, 232, 246, 247, 254
82nd Infantry Division, 15, 16, 17, 22, 23, 24, 25, 26, 30, 31, 34, 36, 37
82nd Airborne Division, 31, 36, 37, 60, 71, 78, 81, 82, 88, 89, 104, 106, 107, 119, 121, 125, 127, 141, 144, 152, 172, 180, 185, 186, 187, 188, 192, 193, 194, 198, 199, 204, 207, 213, 214, 224, 227, 231, 241, 242, 243, 244, 245, 246, 247, 249, 250, 259, 261, 269, 272, 279
82nd Airborne Reconnaissance Platoon, 226
82nd Armored Field Artillery Battalion, 185
83rd Chemical Mortar Battalion, 185
101st Airborne Division, 25, 36, 37
101st Military Police Battalion, 279
307th Airborne Engineer Battalion, 145, 157, 168, 175, 185, 224, 227, 231, 246, 247, 251, 278, 279, 285
307th Airborne Medical Company, 246, 247, 248
307th Engineer Battalion, 38
319th Field Artillery Battalion, 36
319th Glider Field Artillery Battalion, 71, 81, 109–112, 231, 232
320th Field Artillery Battalion, 37
320th Glider Field Artillery Battalion, 71, 112–115, 246, 247
325th Glider Infantry Regiment, 38, 71, 72, 73, 75, 78, 81, 82, 83, 87, 89, 90, 93, 94, 95, 104, 118, 201, 222, 245, 246
325th Infantry Regiment, 16–21, 25, 37
325th Regimental Combat Team, 118, 119
326th Glider Infantry Regiment, 60, 71
326th Infantry Regiment, 20, 27, 28, 35, 37, 39
327th Infantry Regiment, 37
328th Infantry Regiment, 23
376th Parachute Field Artillery Battalion, 37, 71, 74, 78, 79, 80, 81, 82, 86, 94, 121, 170, 171, 175, 181, 232, 246, 247, 270, 273, 274, 289, 300, 302
401st Glider Infantry Regiment, 36
456th Parachute Field Artillery Battalion, 62, 71, 108, 134, 145, 232
504th Parachute Infantry Battalion, 60, 67
504th Parachute Infantry Regiment, 60, 62, 64, 67, 68, 71, 80, 86, 89, 95, 104, 108, 116, 122, 123, 126, 128, 136, 141, 143, 144, 145, 146, 171, 172, 174, 175, 176, 178, 179, 181, 182, 183, 185, 189, 190, 194, 196, 198, 199, 202, 203, 224, 225, 226, 227, 228, 231, 234, 235, 239, 240, 241, 246, 253, 274, 275, 277, 279, 281, 282, 283, 284, 285, 286, 287, 289, 290, 291, 292, 293, 294, 295, 300, 301, 302, 303, 304, 309, 310, 312, 314, 315, 317, 319, 320, 321, 323, 325
504th Regimental Combat Team, 119, 171, 172, 175, 181, 185, 192, 201, 272, 299, 324
505th Parachute Infantry Regiment, 60, 61, 62, 67, 68, 69, 71, 77, 78, 80, 82, 89, 90, 91, 92, 93, 94, 95, 97, 98, 99, 100, 101, 103, 106, 108, 109, 121, 124, 126, 128, 129, 134, 138, 139, 140, 141, 143, 144, 145, 148, 150, 151, 153, 154, 155, 157, 158, 159, 160, 161, 162, 163, 164, 165, 166, 168, 169, 183, 189, 197, 198, 199, 201, 204, 210, 246, 250, 255, 256, 257, 259, 260, 262, 271
505th Regimental Combat Team, 90, 119, 138, 141, 149, 170, 187, 201
509th Parachute Infantry Battalion, 214
813th Tank Destroyer Battalion, 231
United States Army Air Corps Units
Northwest African Air Force, 104
Northwest African Troop Carrier Command, 224, 225
51st Troop Carrier Wing, 210
52nd Troop Carrier Wing, 134, 208, 211, 212, 225, 227
316th Troop Carrier Group, 138
802nd Medical Air Evacuation Transport Squadron, 234
United States Navy Units
LCT-152, 323, 324
USAT *George Washington*, 80, 81, 82, 83
USAT *Monterey*, 80, 83
USAT *Santa Rosa*, 81, 82, 83
USS *Monrovia*, 127, 152
USS *Texas*, 82
Western Naval Task Force, 127
Ussery, Private Henry D., Jr., 78, 81, 82, 94, 171
Valle Agricola, Italy, 274
Vandervoort, Major Benjamin H., 61, 96, 97
Venafro, Italy, 281, 282, 283, 291, 292, 295
Vittoria, Sicily, 157
Volturno River, Italy, 271, 273, 275, 282
Warthman, Private Lawrence C., 51, 53, 55
Wenneman, Sergeant Bernard P., 232
Weschler, Lieutenant Ben L., 157, 159
Wienecke, Lieutenant Colonel Robert H., 206
Wigle, Private First Class Cloid B., 161
Williams, Lieutenant Colonel Warren R., 226, 315
Wood, Captain George B., 168
Woosley, Lieutenant Frank P., 67
Wright, Private First Class Earl H., 162
York, Sergeant Alvin C., 23
Zinn, Major Bennie A., 16, 37, 78, 82, 83, 89, 93, 94, 118